toward a HOPEFUL FUTURE

Collective
conversation

www.uccresources.com
artist Spencer Burke ✓
only New Century Hymnal ✓
[D]mergents

"This book is thoughtful and well-researched; it contains practical ways for typical churches to move into a faithful and effective ministry with a new generation."

— Martha Grace Reese, president, **GraceNet, Inc.**,
and author of the *Unbinding the Gospel Series*

"Phil Snider and Emily Bowen have given careful and critical attention to the church at the margins and have a clear and hopeful idea of what these communities offer the established church and vice versa. This book is far overdue."

— Nadia Bolz-Weber, founding pastor,
House for All Sinners and Saints, Denver, Colorado,
and author of *Salvation on the Small Screen?*
24 Hours of Christian Television

"At the end of his 1913 edition of *The Quest of the Historical Jesus*, Albert Schweitzer compared 'conservative and liberal' forms of Christianity to 'two thin streams that wind alongside each other between the boulders and pebbles of a great river bed.' But, 'when the waters rise and overflow the rock, they meet of their own accord.' But when and how will that happen? 'When desire and hope for the kingdom of God,' he said, 'and fellowship with the spirit of Jesus govern them as an elementary and mighty force.' One hundred years later, at the start of a new century, this present book, *Toward a Hopeful Future*, proves that contemporary streams of 'emergent' and 'progressive' Christianity are turning Schweitzer's hope into a reality."

— John Dominic Crossan, Emeritus Professor of Religious Studies,
DePaul University, and author of *God and Empire*

"Phil Snider and Emily Bowen sort through the cacophony of information that clamors around emergent movements, and write a clear and compelling symphony."

— Carol Howard Merritt, pastor, Western Presbyterian Church,
Washington, D.C., and author of *Tribal Church*

toward a HOPEFUL FUTURE

Why the Emergent Church Is Good News for Mainline Congregations

PHIL SNIDER & EMILY BOWEN

THE
PILGRIM
PRESS
Cleveland

To our friends at Brentwood Christian Church (from both of us)
To Mom, Dad, Sara, and Adam (from Emily)
To Amanda, Eli, Sam, and Lily Grace (from Phil)

The Pilgrim Press
700 Prospect Avenue
Cleveland, Ohio 44115-1100
thepilgrimpress.com

10 11 12 13 14 15   5 4 3

Cataloging-in-Publication Data is available from
the Library of Congress
ISBN-13: 978-0-8298-1847-5

CONTENTS

Part Two
EMERGENT ETHOS

Part Three
EMERGING WORSHIP

ACKNOWLEDGMENTS

Our friends at Brentwood Christian Church have been supportive to us throughout the process of writing this book, and we are so very thankful for the vision, encouragement, and understanding they have extended to us time and again. This book is a product of their faithfulness much more than it is of ours. We extend a special thanks to Nathaniel Carroll, Bob Bledsoe, Nate Bledsoe, Susan Bowen, Camielle Famous, Kaylee Smithey, Stephanie Stockstill, and Kourtney Wilson. Without your musical gifts, the Awakening never would have gotten off the ground.

We are also grateful for those who helped in the formulation of this project by generously sharing their wisdom and support in a myriad of different ways: Mark and Shannee Steinmeier, Nadia Bolz-Weber, Rita Nakashima Brock, Peter Rollins, Rich Kirchherr, Ross Lockhart, Carol Howard Merritt, Alex Ruth, Kim Bechtel, Stephanie Spellers, Brandon Gilvin, John Schmalzbauer, Jared Perkins, Tom and Michelle Billionis, Brian and Grace McLaren, Joey and Micki Pulleyking, Chad and Amber Mattingly, Phyllis Bixler, Jon Bormann, Greg Turner, Doug Pagitt, Matt and Hilary Gallion, and Peter Browning.

We also owe an enormous debt of gratitude to our families: Emily would especially like to thank her parents, Maurice and Susan, and her siblings, Sara and Adam. Phil would like to thank his parents, Terry and Ann, as well as Jamie and Terri Holstein, Amy Hampton, Cara Jones, and each of their respective families. In addition, Phil wishes to especially thank his wife, Amanda, and their three children: Eli, Sam, and Lily Grace.

Finally, we express our gratitude to everyone at Pilgrim Press for turning this project into a reality. We extend a special thanks to Joan Blake, John Eagleson, Kim Martin Sadler, and Timothy Staveteig for their assistance along the way.

toward a
HOPEFUL
FUTURE

INTRODUCTION

Progressive Christianity is that part of the established institution presently in place that's going to remain in the center or circle around the emerging church. — Diana Butler Bass[1]

The biggest change on the religious front is that young Evangelicals are leaving their roots. Can we put aside our elitism? Can we reach out to them? If we can, this could be a time of tremendous growth and renewal for our congregations.
— Carol Howard Merritt[2]

As the tidal wave of books and resources on the emerging church continues to flood the shelves of local bookstores — as well as on websites and blogs across the Internet — one of the great ironies is that the all but forgotten mainline Protestant traditions are once again on the sidelines of the conversation. Even though their theological legacies offer wonderful opportunities of connecting with emergents who are longing for more progressive approaches to the Christian faith, all too many mainliners feel lost in a sea of unfamiliar language and practice.

When you add to this the growing number of postmodern communities that are exploring new styles of emerging worship that are difficult to categorize (especially for those unfamiliar with the language and culture widely associated with postmodernism), a growing number of mainline congregations are beginning to let out a collective "uh-oh!" Many of these established churches already feel at least a generation behind, and now they are scrambling to catch up with the growing number of emergents who wish to connect with communities of faith in fresh ways that simply don't fit existing mainline models. Many wonder if their own church might end up, shall we say, "left behind?" Not in a "scare the socks off you apocalyptic rapture" kind of way, but in the more serious "does our church have any chance of being relevant in the postmodern culture" kind of way.

It would be easy for us to cite statistic after statistic pointing to the diminishing number of young adults actively attending church — especially within mainline Protestant congregations — but our primary focus isn't on stating what many reading this book already know and feel.[3] Instead, we would like to be voices of hope that point to the ways in which possibilities for progressive mainline congregations to connect with emerging generations are far more fertile now than they've been in decades. This isn't because progressives need to develop a different theological identity that is somehow more attractive to emergents — in other words, becoming something they are not — but instead it is about digging deeply within the rich traditions that have already shaped their identity in formative ways. If congregations have the eyes to see, they will observe several surprising connections springing up among progressive mainline traditions and emergent church movements. Emergents, like progressives, long for open and inclusive approaches to the Christian faith. Emergents are less interested in having all the answers than in living the questions. Emergents wish to participate in communities of faith that take the Bible seriously, but not always literally. Emergents believe that following Jesus isn't just about getting to heaven when they die, but is about partnering with God to bring heaven to earth in the here and now.

Jim Wallis has persuasively argued that the Religious Right's monolithic dominance of all things spiritual and religious in the United States is quickly coming to a close, and the deep shifts taking place in evangelical culture are due in large part to the emphasis that young evangelicals are placing on issues of justice, diversity, hospitality, and peace. The result is an utter transformation of the ways in which these young Christians — popularly referred to as emergents — approach the Bible, faith, ethics, worship, and the very witness and mission of the church. There is a new generation, Wallis says, "who are no longer captive to the Religious Right."[4] As emerging pastor and bestselling author Dan Kimball (Vintage Faith Church, Santa Cruz, California) observes, participants in the emerging church

> . . . wonder if what they were taught about evangelism is really the right way to think about, and practice, sharing the gospel of Jesus. They are wondering if being a Christian and being "saved" is more than just saying a prayer to get to heaven. They are asking why the church doesn't talk more often about the Kingdom of God and why most Christians don't take interest in social justice.[5]

By taking into consideration the broad streams of emerging and emergent thought that have paved the way for the advent of emergence Christianity, this book is intended to function on at least two levels. First, it offers an introduction to the emergent conversation by highlighting the remarkable theological similarities that are shared among progressives and emergents. This analysis offers mainline progressives an opportunity to become more conversant with the emergent church in general and emerging worship in particular. At the same time, it offers those already part of the emergent conversation the kind of mainline perspective that is usually lacking in most of the literature on the emerging church. We believe that the emergent conversation — which includes a nice dash of postmodernism — is good news for progressive communities of faith, and this is the argument that we pursue throughout the course of this book.

Second, we hope to offer opportunities for mainline progressives to consider the ways in which they might offer hospitality to emergents, especially in and through the practice of emerging worship.

We are highly committed to the transforming power of ritual, and emergents are hungering for music and liturgy from a progressive perspective and often don't know where to find it. While the growing popularity of emerging forms of worship within evangelical circles has been explored in significant detail,[6] few progressives have been part of the conversation, and even fewer resources and reflections are available for progressive communities of faith that are exploring such possibilities. We hope to help bridge this gap.

We contend that the unexpected advent of emergence Christianity — as well as the emerging forms of worship that go with it — are gifts to progressive mainline congregations with the courage to engage. We don't contend that the emergent conversation is the salvation of the church, but we do believe that it consists of a diverse number of participants who are wrestling with what approaches to faith might look like within the postmodern, post–Christendom, post–Religious Right context that is shaping North American expressions of Christianity. The word "emergent" just happens to be the en vogue term that is trying to name these dynamics — especially among young evangelicals — but its fluidity can hardly be restricted to a singular movement, and many of the concerns it brings to the table are shared among a wide range of Christians, mainline and otherwise. Contrary to popular opinion, the emergent conversation goes much deeper than twenty- or thirty-something Christians who own Macbooks, have a blog, and wear trendy suburban clothes (with trendy glasses to match, of course).[7]

Frederick Buechner once wrote that the place where God calls you to is the place where your deep gladness and the world's deep hunger meet. To be sure, there is a deep gladness among progressives who value justice, diversity, and peace, and there is a deep hunger among emergents longing to connect with communities of faith that express these deep commitments. Such a combination leads to one of the greatest challenges — and possibilities — facing mainliners today.

On generational diversity

While we are mindful of the missing generations in the pews of many mainline congregations, it is important to state at the outset that what is taking place within emergent culture is far more complex than simple generational preferences and concerns. Therefore, we are hesitant to draw sharp boundaries that separate the "young" from the "old." Emergent culture — particularly the theological ethos that goes with it — speaks beyond any one or two generations. And within the context of ritual, our experiences have indicated that emerging worship from a progressive perspective connects with a broad cross-section of generations. Throughout this book, we approach emergent thought by privileging cultural shifts more than generational ones.[8]

At certain points along the way, however, it becomes necessary to distinguish between generations. When doing so, we fall back on sociologist Robert Wuthnow's categories by defining young adults as twenty-, thirty-, and early forty-somethings who have, in his words, come "after the Baby Boomers." When talking about young adults, we use the phrases "postmodern generations" (or postmoderns for short) and "emerging generations" interchangeably.[9]

On religious diversity

For the purposes of this book, we define progressives as those whose ethics are grounded in social justice, peace, hospitality, and diversity, and whose faith is shaped by the theological schools of thought and approaches to the Bible that are generally reflected in mainline Protestant seminaries. While this conveys the mainline Protestant perspective from which we write, we also recognize that we are painting with broad brush strokes. After all, there is no monolithic definition of progressive theology, and we would be foolish to consider every strand of mainline thought as one and the same. For instance, the phrase "progressive theology" is often used to encompass liberation and feminist theology as well as some schools of postliberal and process thought, just to name a few examples.

The ways that words and phrases function are much more important than the definitions we try to give them, and while we are hesitant to paint with such large brush strokes, we do view the phrase "progressive theology" as that which — for the present time at least — best captures the theological streams of thought rooted in mainline traditions and embraced by the emergent conversation. We will say more about this later, but right now we offer this disclaimer in order to state that efforts which try to speak in a monolithic fashion diminish the very diversity of thought that progressives and emergents value so much.

Even more importantly, we also wish to state that mainline Protestants hardly have a monopoly on a progressive approach to faith. Indeed, how can one think about social justice movements without recalling inspirational Catholic leaders like Dorothy Day and Oscar Romero or evangelicals like Jim Wallis and Tony Campolo? Emergents, like progressives, are drawn to expressions of faith that, at their very best, build bridges and cross divides of race, culture, class, and gender to be part of God's faithful witness in the world — not witnesses of singularity and particularity, but of diversity and plurality. We care deeply about the future of the mainline church and anticipate most of you reading this do the same, but at the same time we strongly affirm that the Holy is beyond our own tradition (or any other).

We also recognize the problems associated with the term "mainline." In terms of function, it points to historic Protestant liberal denominations such as the Presbyterian Church U.S.A., United Methodist Church, Disciples of Christ, the United Church of Christ, and the Episcopal Church. These denominations are, of course, no longer mainline — especially in terms of cultural influence. Some have quipped that it is more accurate to call the established mainline denominations sideline denominations, and in many ways they are correct. For the purposes of this book, we've retained usage of the term "mainline," hoping that readers will recognize that we are pointing to a specific historical movement that continues to live on today, despite the fact that it is no longer at the center of the culture (which we don't necessarily view as a bad thing).

Context and convictions

The reflections, perspectives, and resources in this book have emerged from a specific worshiping community in Springfield, Missouri: "The Awakening" at Brentwood Christian Church — the place where "progressive theology meets progressive worship." The Awakening's style of worship grew out of a very intentional theology of welcome and justice, and it sought to address the hunger for progressive religious thought and practice in a very fundamentalist part of the Bible Belt. From its inception, the Awakening's purpose has been to be an oasis for those longing to connect with a progressive religious community through liturgy that matches — rather than detracts from — its theology, as well as to be a place of healing for those of all ages who have been spiritually hurt or alienated by the church and are looking for a more open and inclusive approach to the Sacred.

Little did we know that when we started this worship service we would have the opportunity to worship with so many young evangelicals who are now popularly referred to as emergents. Springfield is home to several universities and colleges, including four with roots in fundamentalist or evangelical denominations. To our great surprise and delight, several students from these schools found a home at the Awakening, and we began to learn about emergent culture firsthand. We started to notice the wonderful ways that progressive communities can offer hope and healing to those who don't wish to discard their faith but rather are looking for different ways to approach it. And in the process, we also started to learn just how much the emergent conversation can teach us. This book is an outgrowth of experiences that began personally and locally, and the process of writing it has helped us locate the ways in which what has been happening in our congregation is reflected in the broader landscape of North American Christianity.

The reflections and resources offered in this volume have been cultivated within a community of faith that values hospitality, diversity, peace, justice, wonder, and mystery. Some people call them progressive; others call them postmodern. We like to call them Christian. While these reflections and resources may appear new, they are deeply grounded in Christian traditions that span centuries. Such perspectives have resonated with progressives and emergents who are longing for fresh encounters with the Holy that lead to "justice rolling down like waters, and righteousness like an ever-flowing stream" (Amos 5:24). We hope they will help you as you seek to be faithful to the Sacred in your midst.

Working definitions

In the two-plus years since we started this book, conversations on the emerging church have shifted from the periphery of North American church culture to the point of occupying a significant — if not substantial — place within it. Very few ecclesial structures have remained wholly unaffected by the emergent conversation, so much so that the popular vernacular being used to describe the emerging church is shifting as well. Instead of tirelessly trying to define what constitutes

"The Emerging Church," participants are becoming much more interested in describing its effect. In other words, the emphasis isn't placed nearly as much on questions like "What is the Emerging Church?" as it is on questions like "What kind of emergence is taking place?" There is a recognition that emergence Christianity isn't a separate movement unto itself, but is part of a larger religious shift affecting North American Christianity as a whole.

In light of these dynamics, we view phrases like "the emergent church" or "the emergent conversation" as synonymous with phrases like "emergence Christianity," "the church emerging," or "the Great Emergence."[10] This language isn't intended to be confusing, but rather reflects the popular vernacular that is currently in use. It is also a more accurate description of a movement that necessarily transcends categories and labels and is better understood as a verb (activity) than a noun (entity).

While each of the following definitions will be fleshed out in detail throughout this book, here is a brief glossary to help orient readers who are perhaps new to conversations on postmodernism and the emergent movement or are seeking further clarification of what we generally mean by these terms.

Emerging generations: Twenty-, thirty-, and early forty-something young adults. Synonymous with "postmodern generations."

Emerging Worship: Organic approaches to worship grounded in the context and theological convictions of specific communities of faith. These approaches carry special appeal to emerging generations and are very popular among "emergents." Emerging forms of worship tend to be participatory, multisensory, and interested in a return to ancient practices and symbols, all the while remaining open to postmodern expressions of faith and life.

Emergents: Comprised mostly of evangelicals (or postevangelicals) who are seeking a more open, inclusive, and socially aware approach to Christianity than what has recently been the norm in most North American evangelical circles. Many (but not all) emergents are from "emerging generations."

Mainline Protestants: Denominations such as the Presbyterian Church U.S.A., United Methodist Church, United Church of Christ, Christian Church (Disciples of Christ), the Episcopal Church, and the Evangelical Lutheran Church in America.

Postmodern generations: Twenty-, thirty-, and early forty-something young adults. Also called "postmoderns" for short. Synonymous with "emerging generations."

Postmodernism: A prominent philosophical movement that challenges all claims to Absolute Truth. In postmodern theory, there are "no facts, only interpretations" (paraphrased Nietzsche). Postmodern philosophy should not be confused with "postmoderns," which points to a specific age group (twenty-, thirty-, and early forty-somethings).

Progressives: Broadly speaking, those whose ethics are grounded in social justice, peace, hospitality, and diversity, and whose faith is shaped by the theological schools of thought and approaches to the Bible that are generally reflected in mainline Protestant seminaries.

One other note: Throughout this book, we share several different stories. Unless full names and precise locations are mentioned, the names of people and congregations (as well as a few details) have been changed in order to maintain anonymity. Some of the stories shared are Phil's and some are Emily's, but we've told them in first person for the sake of smoother reading. We have included in the book extensive resources for your use. For additional resources, go to *www.uccresources.com*.

Part One

EMERGENT
BACKGROUND

Chapter One

BECOMING CONVERSANT
WITH THE EMERGENT CHURCH

The irony of twenty-first-century ministry is that the church will find its relevance not in reflecting the culture around it, but in transcending it, offering something that extends back thousands of years.
— Christian and Amy Piatt[1]

For churches that haven't even adapted well to boomers, terms like "emergent" have barely hit the radar screen.
— Martha Grace-Reese[2]

BOXING MATCHES ON THE MAGNIFICENT MILE

As I sat in the beautiful gothic sanctuary of Chicago's Fourth Presbyterian Church, located in the heart of the world-famous Magnificent Mile, I was surrounded by majestic arches, intricate sculptures, and breathtaking rose windows. While I prepared for worship in the midst of this cathedral-like setting, I was surprised to hear ambient music quietly pulsating through the speakers. Moments later, when a video showed a scrawny, muddied twenty-something going toe to toe in a boxing match against a huge oak tree (a match the oak tree most assuredly won), the puzzled look on my face as well as the other mainline pastors around me was classic. I couldn't help but come up

13

with my own version of a popular commercial: "Registration fee for Chicago's Festival of Homiletics? $235. Nightly stay at the Westin Hotel on Michigan Avenue? $150. Look on mainline Protestant pastors' faces when experiencing emerging worship for the first time? Priceless."

The year was 2005, and hundreds of pastors from the United States and Canada had gathered for a five-day preaching conference. In addition to hearing incredible sermons by the likes of Fred Craddock, Anna Carter Florence, and Otis Moss III, many of us were given the opportunity to experience worship led by noted emergent artist Spencer Burke (ROCKHarbor, Costa Mesa, California). Conversations on the emerging church were quickly becoming all the rage, but many of us were skeptical that this was just another gimmick intended to lure twenty- and thirty-somethings into the church.

It turns out that the two-minute boxing match we witnessed on screen was a prayer of confession, but if it wasn't for the bulletin we received upon entering the sanctuary, few of us would've known it. It's not that we didn't know what a prayer of confession was; in fact, when the liturgy called for one the evening before, we read our part in bold like we had a thousand times before. We just didn't expect a prayer of confession to be a video in the form of a frustrated individual punching a huge oak tree over and over, only to fall flat time and again out of exhaustion and fatigue.

Some of us got together for dinner later in the day, and the unease associated with the experience quickly became apparent. One pastor thought the service made a mockery of the liturgy. Some played the familiar card of dismissing it as merely entertainment. Others thought it was too trendy. Evident in each of the critiques leveled that evening was the fundamental assumption that the worship service — and the emergent church in general — lacked significant connections to the depths of the Christian tradition.

To be sure, I didn't fully understand all that went on that day. But it slowly dawned on me that the liturgy itself had actually followed a very traditional pattern that went back centuries: Gathering, Word, Table, Dismissal. The incorporation of ancient prayers and rituals into the liturgy further immersed us in the kind of Mystery many of us entrenched in modernity had long forgotten.

When I recalled the pastors' accusation of the service being merely entertainment, I couldn't get the image of the oak tree confession out of my mind. After all, from a vocational standpoint, I couldn't think of anything that more aptly illustrated the frustration felt by so many mainline pastors and congregations. No matter how many times we've tried connecting with younger generations, each failed effort makes us feel more and more exhausted, and we just don't know if we can get up again. Talk about needing an assurance of grace.

On an individual level, the oak tree confession led me to reflect on the many ways I have tried to pull myself up by my own bootstraps, thinking I can overcome great obstacles by my efforts alone, forgetting about the relationships that sustain and support me, that are so integral to who I am. I recalled how the young man was boxing the oak tree in the middle of a forest, all alone. All alone. I couldn't think of a better image to capture the unbridled individualism that permeates our broken culture and lives. Kyrie Eleison. Lord have mercy, indeed.

The oak tree confession on the Magnificent Mile had more intentionality than what first met the eye. It functioned on several levels at once, offering much more depth than I originally thought. Though I never had it explained to me, I began sensing its deep implications within my own vocational, personal, and communal life.

I was around the age of thirty when I went to the conference in Chicago, so one might think that, given my age, I would have had a much larger grasp of the emergent church at the time. Though I had graduated from a progressive mainline seminary just three years before, the emerging church had never been a topic of conversation while I was there. While I had been vaguely aware of emerging trends that were taking place across North America, I must confess that I regarded them as little more than passing evangelical fads.

However, my experiences in Chicago — coupled with several other opportunities and conversations — piqued my curiosity and motivated me to learn as much as I could about emerging worship, particularly the implications that it potentially offered my own community of faith. I soon discovered that in order to understand the dynamics of emerging worship, it would be necessary to first gain a much broader understanding of the emergent conversation from which it evolved. Upon returning from Chicago, I immersed myself in emergent books, worship resources, blogs, and video posts, and I participated in as many conferences on the emergent church as possible. My doctoral research focused on postmodern expressions of faith, and that allowed the further opportunity of formally identifying the dynamics at work in emergent expressions of Christianity. During this journey, I've been grateful for conversations not only with well-known emergent theorists but also with many emergent leaders who may not be household names, but are passionate about trying to make all of this happen on the ground. Some of them are part of emergent collectives that meet in places like homes, pubs, warehouses, bookstores, and coffee shops, others meet in established congregations, and still yet others aren't sure what kind of faith community — if any — they are connected to. I'm amazed at the number of people both inside and outside the walls of "church" who are intrigued by the emergent conversation, and I love the way that emergents intentionally welcome diverse voices around the table. It didn't take long for my eyes to be opened to the striking similarities that emergents and progressives share with one another.

With that said, our primary contact with emergents has taken place in and through the unexpected connections that our congregation has made via the implementation of an emerging worship service (the Awakening) which has deeply resonated with both emergents and progressives alike. The Awakening attracts those who grew up with a wide variety of church backgrounds (among them Catholics, Evangelicals, mainline Protestants, Quakers, Mennonites, and Unitarians), as well as those with little or no church background at all. A wide range of seekers who aren't sure what to make of God, religion, faith, and so on, often find themselves participating at the Awakening. Perhaps these folks believed in God at one time in their life, and perhaps they still do, but the name of God is connected with so much baggage that they wonder what kind of value, if any, it can hold for them. Part of the reason the Awakening attracts so many seekers is because it was started as an intentional effort to reach out to those in the Bible Belt who had felt hurt and alienated by the church, and didn't know if they could ever step foot in church again. Many of those most hurt had come from fundamentalist backgrounds, and they had rejected the beliefs of their childhood.

It turns out that several young evangelicals started worshiping at the Awakening, and this is a demographic we continue to attract. Like many of those we hoped to connect with, these participants aren't giving up on their faith, but they are looking for different ways of approaching it. The evangelicalism they've inherited isn't necessarily one they want to see define the rest of their lives. We suspect that they are attracted to the Awakening not because we've manufactured some sort of postevangelical approach to Christianity (though to them it may feel that way[3]), but simply because we've unapologetically dug into the depths of progressive mainline traditions, whether emergents are aware of it or not. When mainliners quip (as they tiresomely do) that those sitting on the pews would cringe if they ever heard about the kinds of theologies that are taught in mainline seminaries, they clearly don't have emergents in mind. The theological approach held dear by emergents draws them, like progressives, to communities that value justice and diversity, compassion and peace, the mind and the heart. They just aren't sure if these communities exist, at least within the context of established congregations. This book is, more than anything, a result of the unexpected emergences we've experienced on the ground: experiences that have led us to believe that emergents and progressives offer great gifts to one another.

FEELING LONELY AND LEFT OUT

Trey, a good friend of mine, works at a nearby bookstore. There are few people that I enjoy talking with more, especially when the topic of conversation is about theology and church. Trey is in his late thirties, grew up in church, and has struggled finding a place to connect. He has a passion for social justice, yet he shares a love-hate relationship with the church. Both of us share an interest in the emergent church, and he regularly lets me know when new books are coming out on emerging conversations that he thinks I might like. More times than not, he's absolutely right.

I started to notice a curious dynamic taking place each time Trey called to let me know about another great emergent book about to hit the market. For some odd reason, his recommendations made me feel partly frustrated, and I struggled understanding why. After all, I loved the books he recommended. I (Phil) am a former evangelical, and much of what is being said in emergent circles expresses similar concerns that I had while in the evangelical world. Indeed, many of the things written by authors like Brian McLaren identify the very reasons that I decided to shift from an evangelical movement to a more progressive one. I love the advent of the emergent church, and I couldn't figure out why the very things that I viewed as so much good news were at the same time causing me so much frustration.

But on a cold, blustery, midwinter morning, as I walked out of the bookstore and toward my car, a realization hit me like a ton of bricks. It turns out that I was increasingly frustrated because emergents were articulating their perspectives in and through progressive voices (especially mainline Protestant ones), yet the mainline churches that I love so much weren't anywhere near the conversation. Some of the most vibrant, passionate, and important conversations on the future of the church were taking place, but North American mainline churches — which have increasingly lost their relevance since the 1950s — were once again relegated to the sidelines.

My frustrations had nothing to do with the perspectives and critiques that emergent conversations offered the church, for they were perspectives and critiques that I thought needed to be heard. Instead, the emergent church made me feel lonely and left out — not only for myself, but on behalf of my church, my denomination, and the mainline movement in general.

When Sharon Watkins (the general minister and president of my denomination, the Disciples of Christ) was asked by President Barack Obama to preach at the National Prayer Service on the morning following his inauguration, those within my denomination were elated. I posted a *New York Times* article announcing the event to my Facebook profile, and the article stated that one of the primary reasons she was selected was because "she delivers a message of unity and inclusivity and tolerance and hope."[4] Several of my Facebook friends — many of whom grew up in the Bible Belt but haven't stepped foot in church for years — said they'd love to go to a church that articulated such a perspective, if only they could find one. How I wish they knew about progressive mainline traditions![5]

The United Church of Christ, our sister denomination, has a running list of "firsts" on its website that identifies the faithful leadership they have offered in their proud history. In 1700, for instance, they were responsible for the first anti-slavery pamphlet distributed by a

church in the United States; in 1785 Lemuel Haynes became the first
African American person ordained by a Protestant denomination; in
1853 Antoinette Brown became the first woman since New Testament times ordained as a Christian minister. These "firsts" continue
to this day, with the most recent one on the list being the 1995 publi-
cation of *The New Century Hymnal* — the first hymnal released by a
Christian church that honors in equal measure both male and female
images of God.[6]

The enduring legacies of progressive traditions such as these are
vast, and numerous examples could easily be drawn from a wide
variety of mainline denominations. Over the past few years — along
with significant support from progressive leaders within Catholic and
interfaith traditions — progressive mainliners have consistently advo-
cated for accessible healthcare, comprehensive immigration reform, a
living wage, and alternatives to war, even when it has been unpopular
to do so.[7]

Like my reactions to Trey's book suggestions, conversations on the
emergent church can make mainliners feel increasingly frustrated and
alone. Not only have progressive communities of faith already felt
isolated and misrepresented by the dominant religious voices of the
last few decades that have consistently articulated a brand of Christianity hardly congruent with a progressive approach to faith, but
now, as emergents clamor to start up or connect with communities
of faith that value social justice, inclusivity, and peace, they all too
often don't think to look at mainline congregations that have already
been putting these values into practice for years.

Of course, mainliners such as myself can spend all kinds of time
bemoaning the current state of affairs (something we are quite good
at doing), yet all the while the future lies before us, full of possibility and hope. Perhaps mainliners would do well to learn a lesson
or two from the emergent conversation. After all, emergents are not
interested in being territorial or in having the corner on progressive

approaches to faith; rather, they are passionate about collaborat-ing with a wide variety of Christians who are committed to making God's realm a reality on earth, whether or not folks self-identify as "emergent" or not.

The emergent church is not new

In the quest to understand the emerging and emergent movement, one of the first mistakes mainliners make is the assumption that the emergent church lacks connections to historic Christian traditions that have come before. Like my colleagues around the dinner table in Chicago, mainliners often dismiss the emergent movement as just a surface-level gimmick evangelical churches employ to make church more entertaining for younger generations.

To be sure, words like "emerging" and "emergent" can be mislead-ing, and a trip to the local bookstore doesn't necessarily help things out. With bestselling emergent titles such as *The New Christians: Dispatches from the Emergent Frontier* (by Tony Jones), *The Secret Message of Jesus: Uncovering the Truth that Could Change Every-thing* (by Brian McLaren), and *The Lost Message of Jesus* (by Steve Chalke and Allen Mann), words like "new," "secret," and "lost" can reinforce the idea that a whole new paradigm has just been discovered or conceived. But a closer look shows that what is billed as "new" and "secret" in emergent books like these is quite similar to what has been articulated throughout the centuries by a myriad of Christian voices, mainline and otherwise.

Peter Rollins (Ikon, Belfast, Ireland) likens the emergent turn to a story G. K. Chesterton once considered writing about an English yachtsman who miscalculated his journey and returned to England with the belief that he had discovered a new land. Chesterton reflects on this idea:

There will probably be a general impression that the man who landed (armed to the teeth and talking by signs) to plant a British flag on that barbaric temple which turned out to be the Pavilion at Brighton, felt rather like a fool. I am not here concerned to deny that he looked like a fool. But if you imagine that he felt like a fool, or at any rate that the sense of folly was his sole or his dominant emotion, then you have not studied with sufficient delicacy the rich romantic nature of the hero of this tale.[8]

Rollins is an academic drawn to the emergent conversation not because he thinks it is breaking new theological ground, but because it is through this diverse network that he has "been lucky enough to encounter others on a similar quest."[9] In his words, "the energy and vitality that exists within the emerging conversation is exhilarating, and at times it seems as if those involved are charting a new direction for Christianity. Yet time and again familiar-sounding place names gently remind us that this discovery is at the same time a re-discovery."[10]

Likewise, even though Jones's book is titled *The New Christians*, he continually reminds readers that one of the best things about emergents is that they, like progressives, "are in conversation with two thousand years of Christian theology and four thousand years of Jewish theology before that."[11] Throughout his book, readers can sense Jones's passionate engagement with theological traditions that have inspired, influenced, and challenged him. He is quite interested in the very progressive concern of retrieving the "deep theological tradition of wrestling with the intellectual and spiritual difficulties inherent in the Christian faith."[12]

Brian McLaren is the most influential emergent writer on the contemporary scene, and he too is astutely aware of the conversation he is having with a broad range of theological traditions. To cite one example from *The Secret Message of Jesus,* McLaren gives voice to the emergent movement's passion for social justice, and he wonders why evangelicals have struggled with understanding the social implications of Jesus' message for so long. In a chapter entitled "Why Didn't We Get It Sooner?" McLaren writes: "The understanding of Jesus' secret message is certainly not original. I'm sure I never would have had the courage to question my conventional interpretations of Jesus' teachings if it weren't for a number of Biblical scholars and theologians whose writings tapped into my own suppressed disquiet."[13] The biblical scholars and theologians McLaren names along the way are many of the same ones who have long influenced mainline Protestants, including but not limited to: Walter Brueggemann, Stanley Hauerwas, Walter Wink, and Sharon Welch.

When one takes a look at the biblical and theological underpinnings incorporated into one of McLaren's more recent volumes, *Everything Must Change: Jesus, Global Crises and a Revolution of Hope*, one sees that the book is deeply grounded in the body of work represented by progressive intellectuals such as Richard Horsley, John Dominic Crossan, and Chris Hedges, each of whom have either significantly influenced mainline thought or have been significantly influenced by it. In *Everything Must Change,* McLaren offers a major critique of empire. He emphasizes the dynamics of systemic sin by explicitly turning to the thought of both Walter Rauschenbusch and John Wesley, encouraging people of faith to consider a "social gospel" (Rauschenbusch) concerned with "social holiness" (Wesley).[14]

The emergent turn is not new, nor do emergent leaders claim it to be. Emergents are interested in connecting to the depths of Christian traditions both past and present, and they increasingly express their faith in ways that are remarkably similar to mainline progressive voices. If one was to ask, "Is the emergent church progressive or evangelical," the answer would be yes. "Is it Catholic or Orthodox?" The answer is yes. "Is it ancient or postmodern?" The answer is yes. As Simon Hall (Revive, Leeds, U.K.) comments, "My main aim for the (emerging) community is not to be 'post' anything but to be 'and' everything. We are evangelical *and* charismatic *and* liberal *and* orthodox *and* contemplative *and* into social justice *and* into alternative worship."[15]

Across the ocean and into the past

North American expressions of the emerging church trace their origins to alternative worship movements that emerged in the United Kingdom in the late 1980s and early 1990s.[16] Most of the alternative worship gatherings in the U.K. grew out of established church traditions (both evangelical and mainline, and sometimes a combination of both), and participants sought to reimagine worship by combining ancient practices and rituals with postmodern expressions of faith. At the same time that contemporary worship movements across the United States were removing as much religious imagery as possible from their auditoriums (formerly known as sanctuaries), alternative worship gatherings in the U.K. (as well as in Australia and New Zealand) were doing all they could to recover traditional items like icons, candles, and labyrinths. When music was used, it wasn't uncommon for the lyrics to be in Latin or Greek. As a natural expression of the urban club culture out of which alternative worship in the U.K. grew, ancient creeds were often mixed with electronic forms of club music. While contemporary worship in the United States was busy making the sacred secular, alternative expressions were making the secular sacred, thereby striving to dismantle the boundaries between the two. Worship experiences tended to be creative, participatory, artistic, multisensory, image driven, nonhierarchical, content rich, and deeply connected to historic Christian traditions.

It didn't take long for the hunger to connect with Christian traditions both past and present to be felt on our side of the Atlantic as well, and soon alternative worship gatherings from the U.K. began to catch on in North American evangelical circles (stateside expressions of alternative worship are known as "emerging worship"). When one takes into consideration the ecclesial context in which young evangelicals were reared, it's not surprising that emerging forms of worship have generated so much interest and enthusiasm. After all, young evangelicals from North America came of age in evangelical congregations that had replaced sanctuaries with auditoriums and chancels with stages. Connections with historic traditions of faith had been all but excised, and the Mystery of the Wholly Other had been traded in for seven steps for successful living. Sally Morgenthaler, who offers an extensive background working with evangelical communities trying to refashion worship within a postmodern context, says that "when it comes to irony, worship in late twentieth-century evangelicalism takes the prize. Just as the world was re-enchanting the universe . . . user-friendly Christianity was practicing religious reductionism: shrinking the divine to the size of a three-point outline and four songs in the key of perpetually happy."[17] Briefly put, emergents from evangelical contexts started to echo the same kinds of concerns regarding contemporary worship as identified by Presbyterian scholar Thomas Long:

When the chancel is a stage . . . and the music is performed by musicians gripping hand-held mikes, and the interspersing of talk and music and skit moves with the rapid and seamless pacing of *Saturday Night Live* then the referent here is unmistakable, too. This is not a retelling of the biblical narrative; it's the recapitulation of prime time. Even if the music is stimulating, the prayers uplifting, the messages inspiring, and the experience heartwarming, the underlying structure of the service is still basically telling the wrong story, the story that will not finally take one to Christian depth but only to "see you next week, same time, same station."[18]

As a result, emerging congregations on both sides of the Atlantic started to draw on a wealth of resources from historic Christian traditions, not the least of which include progressive mainline ones. This can easily be seen at Kansas City's thriving Jacob's Well church, one of the largest emergent gatherings in North America. At Jacob's Well, over a thousand participants gather weekly in a large, renovated Presbyterian building that was originally built in the 1930s. When Jason Byassee visited Jacob's Well a couple of years ago in order to write an article for the *Christian Century,* he noticed that a quote from mainline theologian Stanley Hauerwas was emblazoned on a recreation room wall and that the invocation for worship was written by progressive scholar Walter Brueggemann (who, by the way, is quickly becoming a household name in emergent circles). Byassee says that while participants within emergent communities such as Jacob's Well are usually "sons and daughters of evangelicals or fundamentalists, they take their cues from mainline theologians."[19] The worship service at Jacob's Well serves as "a rebuke to those churches that, in imitation of cutting-edge 1970s evangelicalism, deliberately strip themselves of historical symbols, creeds and practices in an effort to grow." As it turns out, Jacob's Well attracts emerging generations precisely by moving in the opposite direction.[20]

According to D. H. Williams, professor of patristics at Baylor University, "Evangelicalism is coming to a point where the early church has become the newest staple of its diet."[21] In a recent feature on the shifts taking place within evangelical culture, *Washington Post* writer Jacqueline Salmon notes the ways that young evangelicals "have grown disillusioned with the contemporary, shopping-center feel of the megachurches embraced by baby boomers, with their casually dressed ministers and rock-band praise music."[22] Many emerging collectives are beginning to observe seasons of the church year such as Lent, and several others are adopting use of either Catholic or mainline lectionaries for daily readings and weekly worship.

The move toward an "ancient-future"[23] approach to Christianity is certainly reflected in mainline expressions of emerging worship. On the West Coast, Seattle is home to Church of the Apostles, an Episcopalian and Evangelical Lutheran collective that is one of the most influential emerging churches in the United States. Like most emergent communities, Church of the Apostles is much smaller than Jacob's Well. However, one of the striking characteristics of emerging communities both large and small, evangelical and mainline, is the deep desire to embrace the depths of religious traditions. Church of the Apostles describes its worship service as neither traditional nor contemporary, but ancient-future. This approach to liturgy "speaks across generations and draws equally upon ancient (hymns, chant, candles, communion) and techno-modern (alt. rock, art, ambient, projection, video) sources."[24] With an emphasis on communal proclamations of prayer and praise for the *Mysterium Tremendum,* Church of the Apostles offers a beautiful assortment of music that draws on an eclectic range of traditions, including but not limited to Celtic, Roman Catholic, Jewish, Orthodox, Evangelical Lutheran, and Anglican-Episcopal. The last thing that liturgy and music from Church of the Apostles should be confused with is contemporary.[25]

Though alternative and emerging forms of worship are markedly different from their contemporary counterparts, one of the myths emergents consistently try to dissolve is the idea that they represent some sort of gimmick or that they are trying to do something altogether new. In the midst of all the hype surrounding the emerging church, Laura (Sanctus1, Manchester, U.K.) offers some much needed perspective: "Everybody wants to know what emerging church is.... Everybody wants it to be the future, the hope, the new big thing.... But we're only doing what Christians have done for two thousand years.... It might look sexy and new and fantastic and brilliant and everyone's excited, but it's kind of real and it's kind of what church is about."[26]

DEFINING THE EMERGING CHURCH — OR NOT

Even though the emerging conversation has created a major buzz in evangelical circles, progressive mainliners are just now beginning to pay attention to the possibilities (and critiques) that it offers. Perhaps the best way to define the emerging church is by recognizing the impossibility of doing so, for there is no such thing as one form of "The Emergent Church" anymore than there is one form of democracy. Perhaps the most common characteristic among emergent expressions of church in North America is that they take on the flavor and feel of their own context.

A variety of factors has led to the rapid development of the emergent church. These include, most notably, the cultivation of alternative and emerging forms of worship, the influence of postmodern culture, ongoing frustrations with hierarchical, inhibitive, and self-aggrandizing church structures, and a general reaction (especially among evangelicals) against the exclusive brands of Christianity that have dominated North American Protestantism over the latter half of the twentieth century.

While we highlight several of the most influential voices in the emergent conversation, it is important to note that the leaders we mention don't share a set of uniform beliefs or practices. As professor (and emerging scholar) Scot McKnight observes, emergent culture "can't be simply defined; it can't be simply categorized. And it's causing no end of frustration for people who would like to have tidier boxes."[27]

Tony Jones served as the national coordinator for Emergent Village from 2005 to 2008, and he has been part of the conversations on the emerging church ever since its inception in the United States. Emergent Village is the most visible network of emergents, and they maintain a relatively loose definition of Emergent by simply describing themselves as "a growing, generative friendship among missional Christians seeking to love our world in the Spirit of Jesus Christ."[28] According to Jones, the spectrum of emergent beliefs is so diverse that it's impossible to make sweeping judgments about them,[29] and this holds true to the kind of "open source" approach to church, theology, and worship that emergents tend to value. As McKnight comments, emergents are "less certain of theological ideas and this appeals to a generation that is given to dialogue and to discussion and to conversation."[30]

McKnight describes emerging churches as prophetic (oriented toward social justice), postmodern (holding that access to truth is limited and, to a certain degree, constructed), praxis-oriented (with a missional focus in which orthopraxy is just as important as orthodoxy, if not more so), post-evangelical (drawn to narrative forms of theology more than systematic ones and resistant to the exclusive ethos of evangelical culture), and political (engaged politically and attempting to offer an alternative to the Religious Right).[31]

For some people, the emergent movement represents "nothing more than a new style and approach to worship ('couches, candles, and coffee'). To others it signals an appreciation for postmodernism. To yet others it means a return to a more ancient, primitive, and pristine form of Christianity."[32] In the most comprehensive analysis of the emerging church currently available (both scholarly and practically), professors Eddie Gibbs and Ryan Bolger summarize their research by offering the following definition:

> Emerging churches are communities that practice the way of Jesus within postmodern cultures. This definition encompasses nine practices. Emerging churches (1) identify with the life of Jesus, (2) transform the secular realm, and (3) live highly communal lives. Because of these three activities, they (4) welcome the stranger, (5) serve with generosity, (6) participate as producers, (7) create as created beings, (8) lead as a body, and (9) take part in spiritual activities.[33]

Again, it's important to keep in mind that the very attempt to define emergent approaches to faith and church runs counter to the ethos of the movement. Diana Butler Bass has noted that a major characteristic among emergents is the desire to move beyond labels entirely, and given the contextual nature of emergent culture, this isn't a surprise. "You can be a really serious Christian and break through all kinds of boundaries and not have to fit with any particular label," she says. "A lot of people find that very refreshing."[34] In an intentional effort to avoid labels altogether, one emerging worship gathering at a mainline church in Texas (The Search, University Christian Church, Fort Worth) describes their service as "alternative worship, emergent worship, postmodern worship . . . blah, blah, blah,"[35] which we think is quite a nice way to put it, though we recognize that this attempt at avoiding labels serves as a label in and of itself. Maurice Broaddus doesn't like the label "emergent" because it gives people too many "preconceived ideas of what you are and what you're supposedly about."[36] Likewise, because the emerging church is so "diverse and fragmented," many both within and outside the emergent movement prefer not to think of it as a movement at all, but rather as a conversation among a wide variety of Christians.[37] As one person within the emergent conversation reflects on her experiences:

Four years ago, I became a part of a local Emergent cohort, an exceptional group of people who not only gave me a space to sort through so many of the questions that have characterized my life, but who embraced me in all my diversity, *without having to define me.* I have been in churches of all stripes, organizations, bands, and multiple intimate relationships, but I never found on anywhere near this scale the profound acceptance I have among these people whom I see only once a month, for the most part. It has been literally life-changing.[38]

Emergents are often referred to as "evangelical expatriates" who have a fairly good idea where they came from; they just aren't sure where they are going.[39] Some emergents seek to transform evangelical culture from within, while others seek to establish new communities of faith altogether. Occasionally — like the emergents drawn to the Awakening — they discover progressive communities of faith that deeply resonate with their newfound approaches to Christianity. Often they drop out of intentional Christian communities altogether.

Therefore, when we talk about emergents, we're not pointing to a singular movement that shares a set of uniform beliefs and practices. Instead, we're speaking of various patterns and characteristics that have been observed in relationship to the shifting postmodern culture of Christianity in North America, especially in and among evangelicals who are drawn to more open and inclusive approaches to Christian faith that value justice and peace. The emerging conversation can hardly be restricted to a monolithic whole, nor should it be.

Given this context, it's not surprising that most emergents are interested in knocking down the walls that have historically separated fundamentalist/evangelical Christians from other faith traditions. As a result, when it comes to cultivating their faith, emergents tend to draw on a vast range of Christian expressions. One of the primary reasons they are attracted to progressive communities of faith (when they know about them) is because progressives place a significant emphasis on ecumenical expressions of faith that emphasize conversation, diversity, and respect. Many within the emergent conversation like to practice what Emergent Village refers to as a "deep ecclesiology" that is committed to honoring the church in all its forms: Orthodox, Roman Catholic, Protestant, Pentecostal, and Anabaptist. Rather than "favoring some forms of the church and critiquing or rejecting others," emergents think that "every form of the church has both weaknesses and strengths, both liabilities and potential." Similarly, emergents tend to "believe the rampant injustice and sin in our world requires the sincere, collaborative, and whole-hearted response of all Christians in all denominations, from the most historic and hierarchical, through the mid-range of local and congregational churches, to the most spontaneous and informal expressions."[40]

I am incredibly grateful for my immersion into emerging forms of worship that first took place at Fourth Presbyterian Church in Chicago. In the time since — as I've encountered emergent collectives across North America — I've been refreshed and encouraged by their engagement with ancient and postmodern expressions of faith that are deeply rooted in the kinds of progressive traditions held dear by many mainliners. Though these approaches have often been confused with fads or gimmicks, they actually point to something much deeper taking place across the landscape of Christianity in North America, especially in and among evangelicals who are looking for more progressive ways of cultivating their faith. Though the underpinnings of the emergent conversation started with critiques of worship, it quickly became clear that the theology behind such critiques pointed to a much deeper shift taking place in evangelicalism across the board, especially in response to a growing discontent with the Religious Right.

In the next chapter, we will continue paying attention to these dynamics by trying to tackle the ever-so-difficult task of highlighting the diverse communities that represent the emerging and emergent church.

Chapter Two

DIFFERENT TYPES OF
THE EMERGENT CHURCH

The current religious landscape is cluttered with various expressions of faith that claim to rethink Christianity at the dawn of a new cultural epoch. However such groups often accomplish little more than the repackaging and redistribution of faith as we currently understand it. A repackaging that involves flashing lights, video projectors and "culturally sensitive" leaders who can talk about the latest mediocre pop sensation.

—Peter Rollins[1]

Most emergents are children of the twentieth-century church. Like most Americans, they grew up going to Sunday school and church camp.... But somewhere along the way, they lost faith in the church, if not faith in God. That is, while many of their peers disengaged from faith altogether, the emergents found the problem to be the way the gospel had been presented to them, the way it had been lived out, and the way that churches had been structured to promulgate that message. —Tony Jones[2]

Trevor's story

Not long ago, my friend Trevor told me about the enthusiasm he initially felt upon hearing about a new emerging worship service in his community. When you take into consideration his strict fundamentalist background, it's a wonder that he even thinks about attending church at all. The Christianity he was reared in left little, if any, room for questions. Several years ago, when he had gone back to visit his rural hometown during one of his college breaks, he had the opportunity to ask his childhood pastor some questions about the Bible that had been bothering him. He had taken an introduction to religion course the previous semester, and it prompted him to think about his own faith in ways he had never considered before. The conversation went over even worse than Trevor had anticipated. In essence, Trevor was told that questioning like that could put him in danger of the fires of hell. The pastor told him he "needed to get right with God" so he could go back the next semester and "share God's true Word" with his classmates, so that they wouldn't be led astray by the "liberal professors" whose goal is to "sow seeds of doubt in the lives of students."

His pastor's harsh response further confirmed what Trevor had already been thinking and feeling for some time about his religious upbringing, and he now points to that conversation as a defining moment in his life in which he became determined to let go of the fundamentalism of his past. For several years now, Trevor has hoped to find a faith community where he can wrestle with the questions that continue to be at the forefront of his life and faith. He's struggled to find such a place but was mildly optimistic when a friend sent him a link to a website for a new emerging church that met for worship on Thursday nights. The venue was a restored downtown pub remodeled into a coffee house that doubled as an art studio. The worship gathering offered the promise that everyone, no matter who they were or where they came from, would be welcomed.

When Thursday rolled around, he decided to check out the coffee house/art studio/emerging church his friend told him about, and things got off to a good start. The setting was low-key and informal, which Trevor liked. Most of the people there were in their twenties or thirties, which made Trevor (who is twenty-nine) quite comfortable. Those he met were friendly; certainly no one was rude. The smooth, ambient music offered a nice feel for casual conversation. The coffee was good, and, better yet, it was free.

After Trevor had been there for nearly twenty minutes, the background music faded and a couple of musicians walked onto the stage with their acoustic guitars. After singing "I Still Haven't Found What I'm Looking For," they invited participants to join them in the song "40" (both of these are old-school U2 songs). Following the music, the lead pastor read the parable of the prodigal son from *The Message* version of the Bible and then invited anyone who wanted to share their reflections on the passage to feel free to do so. As Trevor heard people share deeply from their hearts, he began to wonder if, after looking for a place to worship for nearly two years, he had finally found what he had been looking for. When the pastor took a seat on a stool up on the stage, Trevor anxiously anticipated what he had to say.

Just as quickly as Trevor's hopes were raised, they came crashing down. After the pastor walked the listeners through several of the prodigal son's struggles, he softened his voice and started talking about the way everyone has the opportunity to "come back home" to Jesus today, if only they will leave the "far country" behind. Red flags started going up in Trevor's mind, and the oft-repeated litany of those who needed to come home included, among others, those "struggling in homosexual relationships" and those who "haven't accepted Jesus into their hearts as their personal Lord and Savior." The pastor said those who wanted to "come back home" didn't have to come forward during an altar call or anything like that, but they could simply speak to him after the service or get ahold of him later in the week.

Trevor, whose best friend is Jewish and whose brother is gay, immediately felt the walls going up. In telling this story, he started to vent about several frustrations he feels with the church and why he often wants to throw in the towel altogether. Trevor's story is just one of thousands representative of emergents who don't wish to abandon their faith, but are looking for different ways of cultivating it. They don't want to go back to the fundamentalism or evangelicalism of their past, and are therefore open to different expressions of church. They are looking for safe, thoughtful, and engaging ways to develop their faith, yet are growing tired of trendy church movements and worship services that pretend to offer a different approach but in the end merely co-opt a fashionable style that conveys the same narrow message they are trying to get away from.

It turns out that Trevor didn't go back to church for another six months. While one of his friends from work kept inviting him to the Awakening, he figured it was just another bait-and-switch gimmick that tried to serve up the same message in different garb. When he finally did visit, he remained extremely cautious, and rightly so. It took several months of "checking things out" before he had the courage to let down his guard, and it wasn't until he started going out to lunch on Sundays with participants from the Awakening that he finally felt like he belonged.

Trevor's story points to one of the most pressing concerns taking place within emerging and emergent conversations: Is the emerging church representative of a "deep shift" in approaches to theology and faith, as Brian McLaren and others (including ourselves) have argued? Or are emerging approaches simply about changing the style and form of doing worship and church while maintaining the same message, as in the case of Trevor's emerging church experience? In other words, can a deep shift be underway given the kind of experiences that people like Trevor have had?

FOUR LANES ON
THE EMERGING/EMERGENT HIGHWAY

While writing this book, I bumped into one of my friends at a local coffee house. He asked what the book was about, and after I gave him a brief description he then asked another question that helps shed light on some of the concerns raised by Trevor's experience. He asked, quite precisely, "Is your book about those in the 'emerging' conversation or those in the 'emergent' conversation?" I immediately knew he was well versed in emerging/emergent literature. While the two terms sound ridiculously similar, each functions with different nuances that demand our attention.

In order for readers to best understand the contexts in which the unexpected convergences taking place among progressives and emergents are located, it's necessary to make some significant linguistic distinctions that may seem minor on the surface level, but actually make a profound difference in the argument we are making. To help in this process, we will draw on an image developed by emerging pastor and author Mark Driscoll (Mars Hill Church, Seattle), an image to which we will refer throughout the course of this book. In this typology, Driscoll names "Four Lanes on the Emerging Highway" and then describes the general ethos and characteristics of each lane.[3] His categorizations of emerging church culture articulate the distinctions that we believe are critical for understanding the context of emerging and emergent movements in North America.

The first lane named by Driscoll is comprised of "Emerging Evangelicals." This group represents those who maintain most of the doctrines traditionally associated with evangelicalism. For instance,

"Emerging Evangelicals" hold fast to the beliefs that the Bible is God's inerrant and infallible word, that Jesus died for our sins, that there is a literal heaven and hell. What makes this group emerging, Driscoll says, is that they're interested in making Christianity and the church "more relevant and applicable for people who otherwise have no interest." As a result, this group is primarily focused on reconsidering such things as worship styles and ecclesial structures. While most "Emerging Evangelical" gatherings aren't quite as conservative as the one Trevor encountered, this lane represents the general approach of the emerging church that he visited. For emerging drivers in lane one, the message itself doesn't change, but the means by which it is presented does.[4]

The second lane described by Driscoll are "House Church Evangelicals." For the most part, this group maintains the same theological tenets as the "Emerging Evangelicals" from lane one, but they are primarily interested in getting rid of the buildings, paid staff members (clergy and otherwise), bureaucracy, and other trappings they associate with institutional churches. They aren't interested in changing their theological beliefs, but they would like to stop doing "big church" as it has been done and instead meet in places like houses and coffee shops. The most significant shift represented by lane two "House Church Evangelicals" is their increased emphasis on social justice. "New Monastics" tend to drive in lane two (if they own cars, that is!).[5]

Driscoll next identifies the third lane, which he calls "Emerging Reformers." He and his church are represented in this lane. "Emerging Reformers" maintain most of the same theological beliefs as those in lanes one and two, but they add a particular emphasis on the desire to return to their interpretations of the reformed teachings of towering figures like John Calvin, Martin Luther, and Jonathan Edwards. Some of the more recent heroes appreciated by participants in lane three are, according to Driscoll, figures like Billy Graham, J. I.

Packer, Francis Schaeffer, John Piper, and D. A. Carson. Given the fact that every one of the leaders mentioned by Driscoll happens to be a Eurocentric white male, it's not surprising to learn that "Emerging Reformers" don't allow women as pastors. Driscoll justifies this through the proof-texting of deutero-Pauline texts from First Timothy and Titus (yet in his attempt to be biblical, he somehow finds a way to leave out Galatians and Romans, where women are given mutual standing within the early Christian communities).

By contrast, Driscoll differentiates the first three lanes of the emerging church from the fourth lane, which he refers to as "Emergent Liberals." In terms of reimagining worship and ecclesiology for a postmodern world, this group shares many of the same motivations as those in the first three lanes. What differentiates them from the others, however, is their approach to theology and faith. In Driscoll's words, "Emergent Liberals" are "calling into question too many Christian doctrines that really shouldn't be questioned," including such things as popular atonement theologies, the exclusiveness of Christ, the sinfulness of homosexuality, and literal notions of hell. This group is representative of several thinkers who associate themselves with the aforementioned Emergent Village, and Driscoll includes Brian McLaren, Doug Pagitt (Solomon's Porch, Minneapolis), and Rob Bell (Mars Hill, Grand Rapids) in this group. Like many other evangelicals, Driscoll has a "serious concern for the content of their instruction." He believes "Emergent Liberals" from lane four make the mistake of questioning doctrines that have been around for a very long time, and they have "totally gotten off the highway and are lost out in the woods."[6] One gets the impression that Driscoll believes "Emergent Liberals" are driving on the highway to hell.

Though not everyone within the emerging/emergent conversation follows Driscoll's classifications, there is an increasing emphasis among participants in the great emergence to distinguish between the terms "emerging" and "emergent." For the purposes of this book, it's vitally important to notice that Driscoll identifies the first three lanes as groups who are part of the "emerging" movement, but identifies the fourth lane as the "emergent" movement. This is a subtle, yet important, distinction. When we speak about the deep resonance that is shared among emergent and progressive approaches to faith, close readers of this book will notice that we are primarily referring to the more precise "emergent" categorization ("Emergent Liberals" from lane four), for those from the first three lanes of the emerging movement don't necessarily find progressive approaches to faith as refreshing as do those from lane four, and they often find them downright suspect.

For instance, a friend of mine pastors a mainline church on the West Coast. A couple of years ago, they started an emerging worship service that was extremely appealing to several college students from a nearby evangelical campus. The students loved the participatory aspect of the gathering, and the service was causing quite a buzz at the university. For a while, three to five college students visited each week simply because they wanted to check things out. Much of this changed, however, when the students learned that the pastor was affirming of gay men and lesbian women, saying that she believed they should be as full a part of the church as anyone else. While a handful of students found the pastor's affirmation liberating and encouraging—and therefore a reason to stay—most of the students felt this was simply too much to handle.

In this example, the students who quit attending this church were like the "Emerging Evangelicals" in lane one. They were interested in rethinking worship styles and church structures, but not their beliefs. By contrast, those who stayed had more in common with "Emergent Liberals" from lane four, for they represent those who have experienced progressive approaches to Christian faith as drinks of cold water in a parched land.

These categorizations are not, of course, as nice and tidy as we would like them to be. Though they are helpful, we also recognize the limitations of constructed categories like these, for there is certainly a great deal of overlap and fluidity that runs between them, and one is hard pressed to find any kind of typology that neatly locates everyone in one particular box or another. Thank goodness!

For example, thinkers like Rob Bell and Shane Claiborne (The Simple Way, Philadelphia) — two of the best-known emergents — are especially difficult to pin down, and this is one of their finest virtues. In Bell's bestselling book *Velvet Elvis,* much of his approach to interpreting Christian scripture is informed by progressive scholar Marcus Borg, and these appropriations of scripture are highly criticized by Driscoll.[7] Yet at the same time, Bell's *Velvet Elvis* also encourages readers to "read everything by John Piper,"[8] who is one of Driscoll's favorite authors. While Claiborne shares many of the same critiques of institutional church culture named by the "House Church Evangelicals" from lane two, it's important to point out that his critiques are rooted in the "Emergent Liberal" approach to theology typified by emergents from lane four.

It's a mistake to think that these typologies can contain each and every person within the emerging/emergent conversation, and certainly the categories are not mutually exclusive. We use them, however, because they help frame the conversation we are trying to have in this book. They are able to orient readers to the various streams of thought within emerging culture, and, more than anything, help readers understand that when we speak of the emergent church being good news for progressive communities of faith, and, conversely, of progressive communities of faith being good news for emergents, we are generally referring to the kinds of "Emergent Liberals" described in lane four. As such, we are intentionally using the term "emergent" as opposed to "emerging," and most of the collectives we cite tend to reflect emergent perspectives more than emerging ones.[9] With that said, however, it's also important to note that the phrase "emerging worship" still points to expressions of worship shared among both emerging and emergent communities of faith, from all four lanes of the emerging and emergent highway. (We really wish the terminology wasn't so confusing, but in order to accurately represent what we are doing, it's vital to make these distinctions.)

It's not surprising that a growing number of theorists have noticed the theological connections between emergents and progressives.[10] While the majority of emerging Christians are more at home with the theology generally shared among those in the first three lanes, it's not necessarily accurate to think that those from lanes one through three are always turned off by the kinds of progressive approaches valued by "Emergent Liberals" from lane four. Indeed, even some of the staunchest critics of the emerging church recognize some of the helpful diagnoses emergents offer:

> We too are wary of marketing gimmicks, how-to sermons, watered-down megachurches, and the effects of modernism. We fully recognize that the Bible has been abused and no one understands it exhaustively. We agree that there is more to Christianity than doctrinal orthodoxy. We welcome the emergent critique of reductionistic methods of "becoming Christian" (sign a card, raise your hand, say a prayer, etc.). We are glad for the emergent correction reminding us that heaven is not a cloud up above for disembodied souls in the sky, but the re-creation of the entire cosmos. We further agree that we ought to be concerned about bringing heaven to earth, not just getting ourselves to heaven. In short, we affirm a number of the emergent diagnoses. It's their prescribed remedies that trouble us most.[11]

It's usually the case that several driving in the first three lanes are quietly asking a lot of similar questions, and once they become familiar with possible alternatives like the ones available in lane four, they often consider putting on the blinker and changing lanes. While they concur with most of the emergent diagnoses, they aren't necessarily comfortable with the remedies prescribed within traditional evangelical contexts either. One of my friends from college used to drive in lane one, but he recently told me how tired he was of doing so many "hermeneutical gymnastics and theological acrobatics" that he came close to abandoning Christianity altogether. After reading the first few pages of McLaren's *A Generous Orthodoxy*, however, he said he felt like he was walking into a whole new world, like Lucy walking through the wardrobe and into Narnia. This friend is a youth pastor in a quite conservative evangelical church, and I learned of this story when he called me on the phone to ask what it would take for him to have his ordination recognized by the Disciples of Christ. He no longer knew where he fit.

My friend's experiences were also shared by Trevor, for in revisiting Trevor's story, we find a second layer at work that helps point to the fragile predicament in which evangelicals from any of the four lanes of the emerging/emergent highway sometimes find themselves. While some evangelicals within emerging settings may be interested in a different approach to faith than the one in which they've been reared and to which they are accustomed, they're often afraid that their only two options are (1) continuing the "hermeneutical acrobatics and theological gymnastics" of which my friend spoke or (2) abandoning Christianity as a whole. For instance, when Trevor first started questioning his understanding of the Bible as God's literal, infallible, inerrant Word, he felt like he was sawing off the very limb of the tree that was holding him up.

When those from any of the four lanes named by Driscoll begin the process of reconsidering their approach to Christianity, they're often afraid that if they question one thing — especially their approach to interpreting the Bible — then everything else comes crashing down. What is helpful for them to realize is that there is a deep place within Christian tradition that leaves room for the very approaches to faith that are beckoning them. Emergent writers like Brian McLaren are helping them recognize that such questions and reconsiderations don't necessarily saw off the limb that holds them up, for their very concerns are deeply rooted in Christian traditions both past and present.

THE BRIAN MCLAREN EFFECT

When one considers the impact of Brian McLaren's influence in the emergent conversation, one is reminded of what Episcopalian bishop John Shelby Spong has called "The Church Alumni/ae Association." This group includes thousands of people who were familiar with the church and its teachings as children, but became alienated and dissatisfied for various reasons. Some of them have left the church because they felt they had to believe, as Mark Twain put it, "twelve unbelievable things before breakfast." This list includes having to believe in "creationism" while rejecting evolution, or having to believe that every passage in the Bible has to be taken literally with no questions asked. If bumper stickers like "The Bible says it, I believe it, that settles it" or "In case of rapture this car will be unmanned" reflect the breadth and scope of Christianity, then they don't want any part of it. Nor do emergents.

In 2005, *Time* magazine recognized McLaren as one of America's twenty-five Most Influential Evangelicals. His books continue to fly off the shelves of local bookstores, and he has become one of the most sought after speakers in the country. Phyllis Tickle summarizes the influence of McLaren:

> In the same way that Martin Luther became the symbolic leader
> and spokesman for the Great Reformation, so too has Brian

McLaren become the symbolic leader and spokesman for the Great Emergence. His 2005 volume, *A Generous Orthodoxy...* is both an analog to Luther's ninety-five theses and also a clearly stated overview of many of the parts of post-Constantinian Christian theology that are now undergoing reconsideration.[12]

Just a few years before publishing the landmark book *A New Kind of Christian* in 2001, McLaren had gone through a faith crisis of his own. At one point along the way, he thought to himself, "one year from now...I will be out of the ministry. One year from now I'm not sure I will attend church anywhere."[13]

A New Kind of Christian (and both of its sequels[14]) documents the relationship between "Dan," a middle-aged evangelical pastor, and "Neo," a former Presbyterian minister turned science teacher. Through his conversations with Neo, Dan begins to rethink his evangelical assumptions. It ought not go unnoticed that Neo is now an Episcopalian layperson — a mainliner, in other words. Some of the issues reconsidered include the relationship between religion and science, the meaning of salvation, scriptural authority, literal interpretations of hell, and respectful approaches to religious pluralism.

After *A New Kind of Christian* hit the market, thousands and thousands of evangelicals felt that someone had finally named what they had been thinking for a long time but were either afraid to say or unable to fully articulate. All of a sudden they didn't feel nearly as alone, and to this day one of the appreciative refrains McLaren regularly receives in his email inbox runs along the lines of "I thought I was the only one who believed these things!"[15] As one blogger summarizes, "McLaren illustrates nicely the way people who are apparently nodding their heads and following along in mainstream evangelical churches may quietly be questioning it all, and how they may not know how to bring up their questions for fear of looking foolish or less faithful."[16]

Our friend Trevor represents one of many emergents who have found a home within a progressive community of faith, and we believe that many others in communities across North America are longing to make such connections. To be sure, not all of them are going to be drawn to an established community of faith, whether progressive or not. Many have been so burned by churches that they don't want to be around anything that reeks of church (and congregations need to respect their wishes). Yet at the same time, the reality is that many of them are hungering for communities of faith that can help them reconstruct their faith in meaningful and important ways. In these situations, the theological approaches within progressive communities of faith can be great gifts to emergents like Trevor, if only they have the opportunity to know about them. In some ways, the question becomes whether or not established mainline congregations are able to be hospitable to those longing to make such connections.

Chapter Three

LISTENING TO ECCLESIOLOGIES OF THE EMERGENT CHURCH

Often the most destructive element in the development of a community arises from the very statement that one is attempting to build a community. — Peter Rollins[1]

I think that people will be more attracted to the Spirit than to anything you could ever do to "hook" them.

— a friend of Tony Jones[2]

GOING ORGANIC

One of the hallmarks of emergent collectives is the way in which they simply happened, *unexpectedly*, in a wide variety of contexts. They weren't fancy, they weren't trying to be sexy, and they are hardly formulaic. Emergent leaders are adamant in trying to dispel the myth that declares it possible to buy some model and implement it in any given context. Instead, what is happening in emergent circles involves the kind of creativity and indigenous nature that is sensitive to one's given context, whether that context be an established congregation, a house church, or one of many other expressions of emergent communities. This is especially seen from the perspective of worship.

49

When Gibbs and Bolger describe several characteristics of alternative gatherings in the U.K. — their sensitivity to postmodernism, their celebration of the Eucharist, their utilization of popular culture, their lack of paid leaders, their appreciation of the visual arts — they're quick to point out that the most important contribution of alternative gatherings "is their method of making worship for themselves in ways that are native to their own culture."[3]

Kim Bechtel (St. Luke United Methodist Church, Bois D'Arc, Missouri), who also never heard the word "emergent" in her mainline seminary, is the pastor of the fastest growing United Methodist congregation in the state of Missouri. Since she arrived two years ago, worship attendance at St. Luke United Methodist has nearly doubled. Eighty percent of their new members are under the age of forty, many of whom haven't set foot in church since they were kids. St. Luke United Methodist embodies many of the characteristics that emergents tend to value: an ancient-future approach to worship (Kim has extensive experience cultivating emerging worship in a variety of settings), a missional focus and an inclusive approach to faith and spiritual formation that is grounded in conversation and dialogue. Part of the beauty of this story is that while this congregation has brought in several new young members, the established members have also experienced transformation and renewal in their own lives as well as in the life of the congregation. Worship at St. Luke United Methodist is multigenerational ("if all ages can't be together," Kim says, "what's up with that?"), multisensory, and deeply grounded in progressive mainline traditions.

Because of the vitality and growth that has taken place at St. Luke United Methodist, Kim is often asked to speak at denominational workshops and get-togethers, especially in her district and conference. At these events, outsiders invariably want to know what her congregation did so that they can experience the same kind of transformation. Time and again, she reminds them that what happened in her church can't translate over to another congregation in some formulaic way, but that each congregation needs to figure out what works best in their respective contexts. "Find your niche," she simply advises. Emergent isn't manufactured; emergent happens. *J A*

Don't market the emergent church

As reflected in Kim's conversations with other church leaders, one of the more misguided assumptions that established congregations make is that it's possible to simply understand the general characteristics of emergent culture (or of a particular demographic for that matter) and then manufacture programs that will strategically appeal to them. However, such attempts have much more to do with manipulative forms of church marketing than with authentic expressions of faith, and that is precisely what many emergents have rejected, for good reason.

Much of the "church growth" literature over the last several years has advised congregations to discern trends and patterns of a particular demographic in order to develop a marketing strategy that brings the desired demographic within the walls of the church. We must emphatically state that we do not advocate this approach. We certainly want to help progressives connect with emergents, but not by advocating some sort of extreme faith makeover. Instead, we wish to point to the convergence that we've observed in relationship to emergent church culture and progressive faith traditions — a convergence that is spontaneous, organic, and *unexpected*. The shared characteristics among progressives and emergents help each connect with the other via authentic expressions of faith, as opposed to contrived attempts of marketing. In other words, they are beyond manufacture.

Please don't misunderstand us. When we say that the emergent church resists marketing, we're not saying that communities of faith ought not tell others about the activities, ministries, and events that they offer. Not at all. We encourage congregations to network with others through options like Facebook and Twitter, to put flyers and postcards at coffee houses and bookstores and universities and just about anywhere else possible. If you have the chance to talk about what you're doing on the radio, take that opportunity. If a local newspaper wants to do a story on your church, all the better. You might even consider writing a book about it! By all means, use creativity and let people know what is going on in your church. The last thing you can expect is for folks to just magically find your congregation.

When we say that the emergent church resists marketing, we mean that congregations don't need to feel like they have to become cool and emergent and hip and happening and all that goes with such a persona, if there even is such a thing (we really don't think there is). We mean that emergents are not drawn to fancy worship services as much as they are to an in-depth engagement with faith. We mean that emergents reject congregations that are more interested in being successful than in being faithful.

From this perspective, progressive congregations should pay primary attention to the ways in which they might grow more deeply within their own theological traditions in all aspects of their ecclesial life (not just worship), for these are traditions of inclusivity and justice, compassion and peace, hope and promise — the very kind that emergents are crying out for most. Contrary to prevailing assumptions (mainline and otherwise), emergents are hungering for depth and authenticity much more than flashing lights and state of the art PowerPoint presentations.

For far too long, mainline progressives wishing to connect with emerging generations have felt the need to become something they are not. I'm reminded of a story I once heard about one of the Dalai Lama's visits to the United States, in which he gave a speech in New York City's Central Park. One of the individuals most moved by his words was a young Christian woman. She was delighted to have the opportunity to personally express her appreciation to him, and in the process of telling him how much she loved his speech, she also said that she would like to convert to Buddhism and asked him what steps to take next. The Dalai Lama asked her what religion she belonged to, and she told him she was a Christian. Then he smiled and said, "There is no need to convert, you only need to grow more deeply within your own faith." As is often the case, the path to transformation is found not in conversion, but in deepening one's roots.

In Diana Butler Bass's magnificent book *Christianity for the Rest of Us,* she takes readers on a journey through several mainline Protestant congregations that are connecting with those from all different kinds of backgrounds, including those who grew up in the church, left the church, and spent much of their lives suspicious of the church. In each of the congregations that she profiles, the path to revitalization, transformation, and connection hasn't come by running from the depths of progressive mainline traditions, but rather by embracing them. To cite just one of many examples, she describes the transformation of Trinity Episcopal Church (Santa Barbara, California) by saying:

> They did not abandon the classic traditions of Protestant liberalism; rather, Trinity linked its progressive vision to a new sense of spirituality and a renewed appreciation for Christian tradition. Walks for the homeless and walking the Labyrinth. Living wage and a way of living the Benedictine rule. Attention to inclusive language and deep attentiveness to the Bible. Social justice and spirituality joined in an open community of practice. People said they came because they were hungry for exactly what Trinity offered. They wanted a different kind of Christianity than that of their childhoods, but still wanted to connect with the Christian tradition. They wanted the Bible, prayer, and worship. They

NSCC –
Be our own selves!
best

wanted open, nonjudgmental, and intellectually generous community. They wanted to serve and change the world. And they wanted it all to make sense in a way that transformed their lives.[4]

Strikingly, Bass states that the congregations she studied "embraced no evangelistic strategy, no programmatic style of church growth. Rather, they were their own best selves." One Lutheran pastor told her that mainline renewal isn't rocket science: "You preach the gospel, offer hospitality, and pay attention to worship and people's spiritual lives. Frankly, you take Christianity seriously as a way of life."[5]

MEGACHURCH OR MEGASUBVERSION?

With all of the enthusiasm and excitement that has surrounded the emerging church in recent years, one of the great ironies is that most emergent collectives are relatively small in size. Whether these collectives gather in established congregations, bars, houses, in a new monastic community, or in some other location (there is a seemingly endless variety of venues), very few have more than a hundred participants. Within our own context, for instance, the Awakening has about 150–175 active participants, but if 80 of them show up on any given Sunday it feels like a big crowd.

With all due respect to established mainline congregations, the point of connecting with emergents is not to increase the members in an established church so it will look good in the denominational yearbook. If your primary motivation is to connect with emergents in order to increase your church budget, add numbers to your membership rolls, or find young faces to serve on lifeless committees, then you've picked up the wrong book, and you needn't read any further. The emphasis of the emergent conversation is not in numbers, which of course goes hand in hand with its utter rejection of megachurch culture and the individual brands of consumerism that go with it.

Emergents love the parable of the mustard seed, especially from an ecclesial perspective. This parable is usually interpreted as the smallest and weakest of things becoming the biggest and most dominant of things. Certainly this has been the most popular interpretation throughout the Constantinian era of Christendom, in which Christianity has been the dominant form of faith, life, and culture in the Western world. But this parable is undergoing reconsideration in a post-Christendom era, especially within emergent contexts.

Emergents are following the lead of progressive scholars like Brandon Scott, who persuasively argue that a more helpful interpretation of the parable of the mustard seed isn't nearly as much about small and weak things becoming big and dominant things but instead is more concerned with small and weak things *subverting* big and dominant things. From this perspective, the reign of God is compared to a small mustard seed that *subverts*, rather than overthrows, the dominant structures of the Roman empire. This newfound interpretation reflects the import of the parable in the pre-Constantinian world in which it was first cast.

Early Christians embodied alternative communities that subverted the domination system of the Roman empire. They weren't necessarily big (like the towering cedars of Lebanon), but they were subversive (like the mustard weed, growing among the ordered vegetation of the garden). Emergents would much rather be part of a megasubversion than a megachurch, for they are more interested in critiquing the status quo than reflecting it. One is reminded of the still haunting words from Martin Luther King Jr.'s "Letter from Birmingham City Jail." There was a time when, Dr. King wrote,

> the church was not merely a thermometer that recorded the ideas and principles of popular opinion; it was a thermostat

that transformed the mores of society. Whenever the early Christians entered a town the power structure got disturbed and immediately sought to convict them for being "disturbers of the peace" and "outside agitators." But they went on with the conviction that they were "a colony of heaven," and had to obey God rather than man. They were small in number but big in commitment. They were too God-intoxicated to be "astronomically intimidated." They brought an end to such ancient evils as infanticide and gladiatorial contest. Things are different now. The contemporary church is often a weak, ineffectual voice with an uncertain sound. It is so often the archsupporter of the status quo. Far from being disturbed by the presence of the church, the power structure of the average community is consoled by the church's silent and often vocal sanction of things as they are. But the judgment of God is upon the church as never before. If the church of today does not recapture the sacrificial spirit of the early church, it will lose its authentic ring, forfeit the loyalty of millions, and be dismissed as an irrelevant social club with no meaning for the twentieth century. I am meeting young people every day whose disappointment with the church has risen to outright disgust.[6]

Like the European-American pastors to which Dr. King's letter was originally addressed, church leaders across the landscape of North American churches (both conservative and liberal) have been more committed to placating potential *consumers* (that is, actual and potential church members) than in proclaiming the subversive edge of the gospel. Emergents are increasingly irritated at the ways in which modern churches have imbibed the mores of society more than they have transformed them, and their disappointment with the church has risen to outright disgust. If you didn't know when Dr. King penned these prophetic words, you might get the feeling that the young people he's describing are the emergents of today.

Elephant in the emergent room

Unfortunately, the emergent interest in subverting rather than reflecting the status quo points to a major elephant in the emergent room that demands our attention. This elephant points to the ways that the emergent conversation has primarily, though not exclusively, emerged within relatively affluent Eurocentric white expressions of evangelical culture in North America, and more times than not male voices have dominated the conversation. "If the emerging church exists as a real and identifiable movement," Kevin DeYoung and Ted Kluck write, "then its spirit is surely captured in authors like Brian McLaren, Doug Pagitt, Peter Rollins, Spencer Burke, David Tomlinson, Leonard Sweet, Rob Bell, and Tony Jones."[7] In other words, Eurocentric white males. While it might be said that representative voices within the emergent movement are diverse in thought, this is certainly not the case in terms of gender or race.

However, as with progressives, this is one of the primary issues that emergents have found most dissatisfying in their own church backgrounds and something they would like to see the emergent church help remedy. Some theorists have argued that emergent communities embody the diversity that is glaringly lacking in emergent literature, though such arguments usually relate more to gender than to race. As Gibbs and Bolger (yet two more Eurocentric white males) observe:

> Some may judge the movement to be deficient multiculturally. At this point in time, the detractors may be right. Part of the reason this particular culture predominates is that many of the pioneering emerging churches arose out of the evangelical charismatic subculture, which has these same characteristics. We must say, however, that in our interviews we were deeply impressed by what we found in regard to the social and cultural practices

of emerging churches. Virtually all these communities support women at all levels of ministry, prioritize the urban over the suburban, speak out politically for justice, serve the poor, and practice fair trade.[8]

Peter Rollins is perhaps the most original thinker among emergent theorists, and he consistently draws on the work of Slavoj Žižek in order to call attention to the ways in which Christians remain captive to the very systems they seek to transform. He often talks about the way Christians can participate in weekly "outreach projects" — like building a house for Habitat for Humanity — and then fool themselves into thinking that their authentic selves are manifested in their particular behavior on that particular day of the week. But in reality, all they've done is taken part in a symbolic gesture one day of the week that — by making them feel good about themselves — hides the fact that their behavior is still the same the other six days of the week. Rollins highlights these tendencies because they are deeply connected to the kind of systemic violence/injustice in which the privileges of a few depend upon the oppression of the many. These systems are perpetuated by symbolic gestures made by privileged classes that in the end only serve to further solidify their own hold on power.

Rollins illustrates this idea by examining the life of comic book hero Bruce Wayne. By day Wayne is a wealthy industrialist; by night he is Batman. Following in the footsteps of his father, Wayne is obsessed with eliminating crime on the streets of Gotham City. Though his father tried to do this by being a philanthropist, Wayne (as Batman) decided to use his wealth to start his own vigilante war on terror. What neither father nor son realize, however, is that the subjective crime they try to remedy on the streets is actually a direct manifestation of the objective crime that their industrial company perpetrates on a daily basis. One could even go so far as to say that it is the very philanthropic work of [Wayne's] Father and the crime-fighting of Wayne that actually provide the valve that allows them both to continue in their objective violence. What better way to feel good about yourself than volunteering at a local charity in the evenings (like his Father) or beating up on street criminals in the evenings (like Wayne). Such acts (like a prayer meeting, worship service or bible study) can recharge the batteries and make us feel like our true identity is pure and good, when in reality it simply takes away the guilt that would otherwise make it difficult for us to embrace our true (social) self who is expressed in the activities we engage in for the rest of the week. The philosophy here is exposed as "do something so that nothing really changes."[9]

United Methodist scholar Justo Gonzales adds a different perspective on this subject by stating that the guilt felt by privileged classes does not change the oppressive systems of this world inasmuch as it further perpetuates them. This plays out by privileged classes regularly hearing about the ways in which God calls them to be part of the change God wishes to enact in this world, and the basic message is that such change can come about if they are willing to partner with God in making it happen. This can lead privileged people to feel quite guilty about themselves because they know that their so-called "quality of life" is far too dependent on the way the system is currently set up, and they aren't sure they want to transform it. Therefore, as they continually hear about the dreams of God for this world, their guilt isn't assuaged, but rather intensified. However, Gonzales says, it is precisely by continuing to feel guilty about such matters that those from privileged classes are able to maintain their hold on power, for such guilt subtly makes them believe that they are still the ones with the power to change things if they so desired. Therefore, in a quite tragic way, such guilt further solidifies the place of privileged people within the power structures of society because it implies that they are still the ones holding the power.[10]

Because emergent conversations — like many others in the history of Christendom — have been generated by a disproportionate number of participants from privileged classes, emergents and progressives alike must consider whether their rhetoric serves as a tool of transformation or merely as a symbolic gesture that only serves to strengthen the power structures that be. Does the emphasis that emergents and progressives place on mutuality and social justice become incarnated on the ground through embodied practice, or does it function only as a rhetorical means of making privileged Christians feel good about themselves so that oppressive systems remain fundamentally unchanged? Just how telling is the white elephant in the emergent room?

While questions such as these remain open, some of the good news here is that emergents at least appear sensitive to these critiques and wish to move in new directions. In 2009, for instance, some of the best-known European-American emergents promoted "Christianity 21," a long overdue emergent conversation that featured twenty-one *female* voices addressing the future of Christianity. Representatives were young and old, gay and straight, African-American and European-American, evangelical and progressive, emergent and mainline. A few years earlier, European-American emergent leaders led by Tony Jones, Brian McLaren, Dan Kimball, and Doug Pagitt responded to these criticisms by highlighting the importance of Latin American, African, Asian, and First Nations voices within the emergent conversation. This is also the reason that McLaren is much more interested in postcolonial approaches to Christian faith than postmodern ones.[11]

Additionally, even though most emergent church literature has been written by (straight) white males, it should be noted that emergent movements on the ground and in the blogosphere are becoming much more diverse in scope. It should also be noted that three of the most influential emergent leaders (each with roots in mainline traditions) are women: Karen Ward (Church of the Apostles, Seattle), Stephanie Spellers (The Crossing, Boston), and Nadia Bolz-Weber (A House for All Sinners and Saints, Denver). Ward and Spellers also represent two of the most prominent African-American voices in the emergent conversation.

The (white) elephants that continue to lurk in emergent and progressive rooms mustn't be far from our minds. Is it possible for emergents and progressives to embody expressions of Christianity that aren't just egalitarian in rhetoric, but also in practice? Such a question can't be answered in a book, but can be answered only on the ground.

SOME PRESSING QUESTIONS

When Doug Pagitt talks about the emergent church, he sometimes incorporates a quadrilateral that highlights some of the very real tensions that exist when established congregations wish to connect with emergents (see the following page).[12] This quadrilateral is based on Pagitt's suggestion that culture has four components to each of which he assigns a body part: head, heart, gut, and hands. The top two quadrants in Pagitt's quadrilateral are labeled "head" and "heart," while the bottom two quadrants are labeled "gut" and "hand." From an ecclesial perspective, the top two quadrants are related to theological ideas (thinking and values), and the bottom two quadrants are related to stylistic and structural objects (aesthetics and tools).

Pagitt uses this quadrilateral to contrast some of the most significant differences between the two groups traditionally understood as "evangelicals" (Evangelicals/Pentecostals) and "liberals" (Mainline/Denominational), especially in terms of their approaches to worship.

Ideas Level	**Head** Thinking	**Heart** Values	Evangelicals/ Pentecostals
Objects Level	**Gut** Aesthetics	**Hand** Tools	Mainline/ Denominational

As far as evangelical congregations are concerned, you can change objects all that you want (aesthetics, tools, structures, etc.), but as soon as you start messing with theological ideas (thinking, values, beliefs, etc.), then you risk major turmoil. In evangelical contexts such as these, it's possible to explore all kinds of different worship approaches, including emerging ones, as long as the theological message doesn't change. You can take out objects like pews and bring in some couches, you can throw away hymnals and put up some screens, you can say goodbye to the organist and bring in some guitarists. For the most part, aesthetics and structures remain open and fluid. Just don't mess with the theology.

Conversely, Pagitt says, the opposite is often true of mainline Protestant congregations. In these contexts, it's possible to explore various schools of theological ideas (thinking, values, beliefs, etc.), but as soon as you start messing with stylistic concerns (aesthetics, tools, structures, etc.), you begin to create major disruptions.

From the perspective of worship, our mainline friend and colleague Ross Lockhart (West Vancouver United Church, West Vancouver, British Columbia) summarizes this rather nicely: "We can tread on a lot of different theological ground in a sermon, but the minute you mess with the handbell choir they'll take you to the cross."[13]

One Presbyterian involved in the emergent conversation captures this tension:

> Many today have more questions than answers, and the church has not always done a good job of creating safe places for people to ask questions and share concerns. Whether one is part of a more conservative evangelical congregation that is not open to questioning certain doctrines or a mainline Protestant church that is not open to questioning certain traditions or the way things have always been done, churches today often do not present themselves as being open to critique and deconstruction.[14]

A few years ago, for instance, a Midwestern mainline congregation started an emerging worship gathering on Saturday nights that was intended to reach out to college students who had left the evangelicalism of their childhood behind, but weren't quite sure if they were ready to leave Christianity altogether. As it turns out, several participants were attracted to the gathering — some were college students, some were not. The participants from this gathering usually had at least two things in common: (1) they liked the emerging service's emphasis on justice and inclusivity; and (2) chances are they'd never darken the door of the church on a Sunday morning. Several of them had body piercings and tattoos, and virtually all of them were at least thirty years younger than those who sat on the pews of this church's established worship service. The reason they didn't go to the Sunday morning service wasn't because they didn't like the members of the church, and wasn't as if the members of the church had been rude to them. They just felt like fish out of water, like my dad at a Kanye West concert or like teenage grandkids competing in a shuffleboard tournament at their grandparents' retirement community.

The gathering wasn't all that big — maybe thirty or so people would show up each week — but it was certainly making a difference in the lives of those who participated. The established church — to its great credit — extended hospitality to this emerging community simply by giving them room to cultivate their faith in ways that weren't the norm, at least not within most evangelical and mainline establishments. This church allowed its young associate pastor (she was in her mid-twenties at the time) to have the freedom to create an alternative gathering that would resonate with "the walking wounded," meaning those who had been so hurt by Christianity that they were about ready to give up on faith entirely. Furthermore, the senior minister — to *his* great credit — didn't try to step in and interfere with the emerging worship service. He trusted the leadership of the associate minister.

Things went well, especially for the first few months. The participants at the emerging gathering continued to cultivate their faith and community life together, and the established members felt good about themselves for giving these participants a place to connect (and for providing a seminary-trained pastor to lead them). However, the (inevitable?) grumbling slowly started, and the hospitality that was initially shared by the congregation slowly turned into a source of resentment among several of the established members. Like most church conflicts, the turmoil started with a small incident that pointed to something much larger.

The emerging service had been meeting for about nine months, but on one Sunday morning, just a few minutes before the established worship service started, a member of the church's worship committee noticed that candle wax had been spilled on the chancel carpet. She assumed it had to come from the alternative gathering the night before. It was barely noticeable, but it hadn't been cleaned to her satisfaction. Needless to say, this member was not pleased. Immediately after the service, she tried to find the senior minister so she could voice her complaints: "I thought they cleaned up after their service!" she fumed. "How are we expected to keep *our* sanctuary nice if *they* don't care about it?" The senior minister tried to explain all of the work that went into setting things up and taking things down for an emerging worship gathering. He tried to assure her that they'd done their best and just missed a spot, and he further reminded her that this group didn't have any of the custodial support that the established service receives.

But, as you might expect, the explanation didn't help. As time went by, the resentment continued to build. Even though most of those from the emerging gathering had no idea such resentment existed at all (and most members from the established service were perfectly happy with the newer participants), a handful of the most power-ful members in the church kept fanning the flames of bitterness. Comments started to fester:

"Have the new people started paying their way yet? We do have bills, you know."

"Why do they want to use our building but don't want to come to Sunday School? They don't seem to care about us."

"When are they going to start attending the 'real' worship service? At some point they need to mature."

It didn't take long for the senior pastor to be asked by the board to step in and take over the alternative gathering. Both the senior pastor and the associate pastor sensed this was a mistake, but they gave in because the conflict caused more stress than either of them wanted to deal with. Soon afterward, the associate minister got in touch with her denominational judicatories and inquired concerning the possibilities of planting an emerging church.

In this example, the theological ethos of the alternative worship gathering was never a point of contention (thinking and values). Instead, the aggravated members of this church were frustrated with matters of style (structure and aesthetics). Even though the emerging worship gathering hardly interfered with the established worship service and programs (aside from a little candle wax on the floor every now and then), and even though the newer participants were building strong bonds of community with one another, some members of the establishment were bitter that the new participants weren't assimilating to church culture in ways they deemed necessary (never mind the fact that several who attend the established service didn't, as the parishioners put it, serve on committees, go to Sunday School, or "pay their way" either!).

While this situation caused significant conflict and disappointment for the church as a whole, the deeper tragedy was that participants who had connected through the alternative gathering once again felt marginalized by the church establishment. Only this time — unlike their experiences in evangelical culture — it wasn't because of theological concerns.

Time and again, it seems, the efforts established congregations make to preserve aesthetics and structures lead to significant levels of disillusionment among emergents who are already on the verge of giving up on church entirely. This is one of the primary reasons that emergents who don't give up on the faith tend to start their own collectives from scratch.

While writing this book, I met Michael and Christy, a young couple who embody several of the characteristics shared by emergents driving in lane four. They told me about the elation they initially felt upon discovering a relatively small mainline congregation in the heart of the Bible Belt that shared their passion for justice, inclusivity, and peace. Though Michael and Christy were from the Bible Belt, both of them had long since abandoned the fundamentalism of their childhood. Like many other emergents, they hadn't set foot in church for several years. They found out about this particular congregation through a newspaper article that announced a vigil the church was putting together in memory of those who had been victims of hate crimes (in honor of the anniversary of Matthew Shepard's death). The vigil sounded important to them, so they decided to go, and their experiences there led them to attend the church's worship service the next Sunday. To their surprise, they found a worship service that deeply resonated with their own theological convictions.

It didn't take long for both of them to become active in the church. They helped with a community food garden and volunteered for the church's afterschool tutoring program. The congregation was so excited about the passion Michael and Christy brought to their church that they asked them if they'd like to head up the outreach committee. It seemed like a win/win situation for everyone — until they went to their first board meeting. (At this point in the story, most mainline leaders probably have some idea of what comes next.) *NSCC*

To put it mildly, the board meeting lacked vision. The first twenty minutes were spent trying to figure out why the Advent decorations were put back in the wrong place, which was followed by the grave concern of why some dry erase markers were missing from one of the Sunday School rooms. Then, it morphed into a glorified property committee meeting that focused on what kind of lights to purchase for the new Christmas tree that had just been bought during the postholiday clearance sale. While all of this may sound too ridiculous to be true, all too many mainline pastors will tell you this is actually *yes* par for the course more times than we care to admit, and it's the kind of thing that would make us laugh if it didn't make us cry first.

It also left Michael and Christy feeling bewildered and disappointed. "At first," they said, "we just figured everyone was tired from all of the Christmas activities. We thought the next meeting would be a bit more visionary." But it wasn't. And when the third board meeting of the year was highly critical of the forty-something pastor's "untraditional" approach to confirmation classes, Michael and Christy felt like they couldn't get out of the room fast enough.

The pastor could sense Michael and Christy's unease with the board meetings, and she kept trying to assure both of them that the congregation needed their leadership. Their pastor was sincere, and she was absolutely right. The reality, however, was more than the pastor's words and presence could make up for. Michael and Christy regretted making the commitment to get so involved so quickly, and they looked forward to their year's term coming to an end. Why waste their time with such inane meetings?

Their attendance at worship slowly waned, and they soon asked for someone to take their place in the afterschool tutoring program. They still attend occasionally, but they're considering starting a house church of their own, and they even asked their pastor if she would like to be part of it. She said yes.

As these stories indicate, emergents often feel like they don't have a place within established church structures. On the one hand, they want to cultivate their faith in more open and inclusive ways (thinking and values), but this is rarely possible within most evangelical congregations. On the other hand, even though these approaches have a home in the theology of progressive mainline congregations, emergents are often turned off by a commitment to matters of style (aesthetics and structures) that are more concerned with preserving the church as an institution than in being the place where the Spirit speaks. Established congregations are rarely prepared to handle the changing dynamics that come with welcoming newcomers into the church, especially when newcomers have no desire to assimilate into an already established church culture. Established congregations may like the idea of connecting with emergents, but they often struggle with the tensions such connections create. It's no wonder that emergents often feel like nomads without a home, for they have been denied a place time and again by established congregations, both evangelical and mainline.

All of this leads to what is perhaps the most important question to ask in this book: Is there a place for emergents to engage progressive approaches to Christian faith within an established environment that isn't suffocated by commitments to institutionalism? Is this even possible within established congregations? If so, established congregations must consider new ways of being and understanding church. Karen Lebacqz's words are timely: "The church that genuinely welcomes the stranger does not simply let the stranger into a preformed routine, but accepts that the routine itself may be changed. We cannot cling to the past, or to the way things have always been done, because to do so is to deny the validity of the stranger's way of being."[15] Instead of being open only to theological streams of thought (thinking and values), churches must also be open to diverse structures and practices (aesthetics and tools).

HYPHENS HERE, HYPHENS THERE,
HYPHENS HYPHENS EVERYWHERE

Of course, we would be naïve to think that emergents are the only ones who feel like nomads. During a recent PBS interview focused on the emerging church, Diana Butler Bass remarked that mainliners are often "as dissatisfied with bureaucratic structures and denominational structures [as] emerging evangelicals are with traditional patterns of setting up evangelical congregations, so on both sides of this conversation they're reaching toward new kinds of structures."[16] These concerns are especially shared by mainline clergy members who love the progressive theological legacies of their respective denominations, but feel overwhelmed by the weight of their inhibitive structures.

To share a personal example, I (Phil) grew up in the Southern Baptist and Assemblies of God churches, but during college (like many of my friends from church) I started to question several of the beliefs that had been passed down to me. It may seem silly, but I couldn't imagine that people like Gandhi would forever burn in hell or, for that matter, anyone else who wasn't lucky enough to be born into a Christian culture. These concerns represent much of the proverbial banter that is hurled against Christianity, but nevertheless they were big issues to me at the time. These questions set off a chain reaction of other questions, and the next thing I knew I was no longer sitting in an Assemblies of God church but instead was on the pews of First and Calvary Presbyterian Church on the campus of Missouri State University, listening to Protestant liberal sermons that helped make sense of the disconnects that I was feeling in terms of my own faith journey. I had been angry at both God and the fundamentalism that was such a part of my upbringing, but I slowly found myself praying — joyfully, hopefully, quietly — in the balcony of this unfamiliar, yet beautiful, sanctuary. I had been introduced to the mainline church, and for that I will always be grateful.

By the time I entered seminary, I had been a member of the Disciples of Christ for only a little over two years, but I was intrigued by the way in which Disciples valued unity and celebrated diversity, as well as their passion for justice. Disciples didn't make me feel as if I had to do the kinds of "hermeneutical gymnastics and theological acrobatics" as described in chapter 2, and I hungered for the kind of progressive Christian vision articulated by several Disciples of Christ voices.

From a theological perspective, mainline Protestantism was a good fit. I just didn't realize all of the ecclesial struggles that mainliners were up against. The Presbyterian church I attended in college had a pretty strong generational mix of participants, and though the first Disciples of Christ church I attended was comprised of an older demographic, I was naive enough to assume it was just an anomaly.

Little did I know of the challenges I would later face as a young pastor called to help revitalize a graying congregation.

By contrast, Emily was born and raised in a progressive United Church of Christ congregation, and she continues to treasure such a heritage. Needless to say, both of us are drawn to the theological ethos of mainline Protestantism and deeply care about the mainline church. But like many emergents, we sometimes feel overwhelmed by inhibitive ecclesial structures at all levels of the church, both locally and denominationally. While this is rarely due to inept leadership on the part of the church's leaders, it is a reflection of the modern structure/system/institution that we have all inherited, clergy and laity alike. Though mainline ecclesial structures serve some useful and necessary purposes, they also breed way too much hierarchy, patriarchy, and hegemony, all of which are stronger than even the best efforts of our best leaders.

While there is a shared crisis among mainline clergy today, it's not limited to those of us who always seem to be the youngest ministers at virtually every denominational get-together.[17] To be sure, there are plenty of mainline clergy members content to ride things out until they collect their pensions, but most of the clergy to whom we speak still want to be part of transformational ministries that make a serious difference in the lives of others. Most of these pastors care deeply about the theological approaches of their respective denominations, and they are deeply touched by the times they've witnessed God's grace and love change lives. Yet at the same time, they've experienced ecclesial structures as debilitating and demoralizing, and they are left wondering if transformation within existing structures is even possible.[18]

Diana Butler Bass doesn't deny that the ecclesial structures within mainline Protestantism are in major trouble. "Some of its institutions, unresponsive to change, are probably beyond hope of recovery or repair." However, she is not without hope. As it turns out, the most wonderful dynamic responsible for transforming established churches is also the most wonderful gift that emerging churches offer progressives: namely, their organic nature. "Lively faith," she writes, "is not located in buildings, programs, organizations, and structures. Rather, spiritual vitality lives in human beings; it is located in the heart of God's people and the communities they form. At the edges of mainline institutional decay, some remarkable congregations are finding new ways of being faithful — ways that offer hope to those Americans who want to be Christian but are wary of the religion found in those suburban megachurches."[19]

Bass notes that Christian faith in and among mainline Protestant contexts is not experiencing a rebirth through maintaining or improving its inherited structures, but is instead rebirthing the best of its traditions.[20] Similar to the approach taken by emergents, transformation among mainline congregations is primarily rooted in an organic understanding of church that is deeply connected to the depths of Christian traditions, both past and present. As Tony Jones observes, "It's the institution of the church that's in its death throes, not the Christian faith itself."[21]

All this time we have been talking as if emergents and progressives are strict entities only unto themselves, but there's actually a great deal of permeability running in and among both movements. As the North American Christian landscape moves toward what Phyllis Tickle calls the emerging center, the old categories are starting to wear thin, and the distinctions maintained within modern institutionalism are giving way to a more fluid understanding of church that transcends rigid structures. Thus, emergents drawn to more progressive approaches to faith and progressives drawn to more emergent approaches to ecclesiology and worship aren't undergoing some sort of conversion experience from one to the other, but instead are beginning to model a different way of being church altogether.[22] We are entering into what Bass has called "a new conversation circle — a place not bounded by theological lines, but a place of institutional boundary crossing."[23]

This is much of the reason that a significant number of mainliners (clergy and otherwise) often find conversations within emergent culture more inspiring and visionary than many of the conversations taking place within their own denominations. Denominational conversations (at all levels of the church) are all too often concerned with preserving the very structures that are undergoing deconstruction, and instead of being open to reconstruction, these conversations seem more interested in salvaging modern institutions than in reimagining how God might transform them.

In response, several emergent denominational subgroups (some that are officially sponsored by their respective denominations and others that are not) represent a rapidly growing constituency within mainline culture, and they are especially predominant among emerging generations. With one foot in their respective denominational tradition and the other foot in the emergent conversation, members of these subsets are becoming known as "hyphenated Christians" (though most have dropped the hyphen). They include groups such as Presbymergents, Methomergents, Anglimergents, and Luthermergents, among others. [D]mergents (representing Disciples of Christ emergents) just made their way onto the scene, and emerging grassroots conversations are taking place among a wide network of participants within Anabaptist, Quaker, and United Church of Christ traditions, just to name a few. Our neighbors to the north launched the United Church of Canada's Emerging Spirit initiative in November 2006, and in 2009 the first Catholic emergent conference took place at Richard Rohr's Center for Action and Contemplation.

Phyllis Tickle compares the respective denominational traditions of hyphenateds to a house they inherited from their grandfather. From this perspective, hyphenateds feel a compelling need to honor the land upon which the house sits, but no need to retain its structural shape. While hyphenateds "may tear down the house, they will salvage some of the material out of which it was built and incorporate those honored bricks and columns, plinths and antique doors into the new thing they are building."[24] Hyphenateds love their traditions enough to make sure their inherited ecclesial structures don't snuff them out. As Eddie Gibbs and Ryan Bolger contend,

> Some outside the movement have said that those in emerging churches do not love the church or that they are full of negativity because of their propensity for dismantling church structures. This is to misread the movement entirely. What to some may appear to be pointless complaining is part of a larger process of dismantling ideas of church that simply are not viable in postmodern culture. Neither the gospel nor the culture demands these expressions of the faith. Emerging churches remove modern practices of Christianity, not the faith itself. Western Christianity has wed itself to a culture, the modern culture, which is now in decline. Many of us do not know what a postmodern or post-Christendom expression of faith looks like. Perhaps nobody does. But we need to give these leaders space to have this conversation, for this dismantling needs to occur if we are to see the gospel translated for and embodied in twenty-first-century Western culture.[25]

When we contextualize the emergent conversation within the broader scope of Christian history, we are again reminded that what is taking place is really nothing very new, but is actually quite similar to what Christians throughout the ages have been called to do. As the Protestant Reformers liked to say, we are "a reformed church always reforming." Or as the Catholic philosopher John Caputo might say, the deconstruction of the church is not intended to reduce our structures and practices to ruins, which is the popular distortion, but instead "is the ageless task imposed on the church and its way to the future, the way to be faithful to its once and future task, to express the uncontainable event from which the church is forged," which, "in the case of the church, is the kingdom that we call for, the kingdom that calls on us."[26]

Indeed, one of the great hallmarks of the Protestant movement is its living commitment to engage scripture, tradition, reason, and experience in ways that continually ask where and how God is active in the world. This challenges individuals and communities to remain open to where the Spirit is leading, especially when that lead takes one into uncharted waters. While the deconstruction of the church has sometimes led to the painful awareness of the tradition's own shortcomings (that is, its historic complicity in systems like racism, colonialism, homophobia, sexism), its continual openness to reform has paved the way for ever new faithful expressions grounded in restored integrity, hope, and vision.[27]

EMERGENT POSSIBILITIES

As emergents move into the twenty-first century, they will continue to find new ways of cultivating, articulating, and celebrating their faith, and the influence of progressive theology will play a significant — though not exclusive — role in this formation.[28]

Given the organic nature of emergent collectives as well as the organic way in which vital mainline congregations have undergone their own respective transformations, it's not surprising that most of the connections being made among emergents and progressives are taking place in localized, grassroots contexts. There are certainly situations in which the best thing established churches can do is simply get out of the way, but, thankfully, that isn't always the case. Progressives from mainline traditions are in a wonderful position to draw on a rich range of resources and gifts that enable emergents and progressives to encounter life-giving water.

Though the emergent conversation has been slow to catch on in the halls of the mainline establishment, denominational leaders are increasingly sensitive to the critiques and possibilities emergents bring to the table. More and more denominations are intentionally making room for these conversations to develop.[29] One of the best denominational responses to the emergent movement can be seen through "Fresh Expressions," a joint venture sponsored by the Church of England and the Methodist Church in the U.K., though (in the spirit of deep ecclesiology) not exclusive to them. With a sensitivity to the organic nature of the emerging church, Fresh Expressions has sought to nurture and support new communities of faith for the benefit of those who are not yet members of any church. These collectives meet in a wide assortment of venues, from art cafes to pubs to downtown cathedrals. Over the last four years, Fresh Expressions has gained significant momentum well beyond the U.K., and it increasingly serves as a model for North American denominational structures.

The United Methodist Church in the United States recently launched the "Methomergent Lab." Using the imagery of a laboratory is both intentional and insightful. As its website states: "A laboratory is meant to be a place of creativity, experimentation and innovation. This blog is meant to be a place for generative conversation among those who want to make a difference in the United Methodist Church."[30] Within this context, the United Methodist Church is trying to make room for the emergent conversation, but they aren't trying to colonize it. Established church structures would be wise to follow their lead.

When established mainliners try to understand emergent Christians, it's important to keep in mind that it's rarely possible to identify a set of "emergents" in the community that are looking for an "emergent church." To be sure, there are thousands of self-identified emergents who network with one another (in local collectives and via the Internet), but many who fall under the umbrella of emergent wouldn't even know what the word "emergent" refers to. Rather, they find themselves looking for something from their faith or church that they feel has long been missing. When they stumble upon emergent and progressive voices, they feel like they've finally found companions on the journey; they just don't always know where to turn next.

When it comes to cultivating communities of faith that offer hospitality to emergents and progressives, sometimes the best possibility is simply starting from scratch. While it may seem daunting at first, cultivating an emergent collective with this approach in mind can be helpful because it isn't bound to the institutional trappings we've named in this chapter. For instance, Hope Church (Boston), a joint venture between the Disciples of Christ and the United Church of Christ, has been able to draw on a wide variety of rich traditions in order to offer worship and community that is specifically committed to welcoming both longtime believers and those "visiting this crazy thing called 'church' for the first time." Instead of being bound to particular demands inherent in an existing institution, Hope Church has been able to infuse traditional rituals with their own flavor and feel, all with an intent to reach "people who are either trying church for the first time or the last time."[31]

It's not that new church starts aren't without their own set of problems. However, there is something invigorating about creating a collective unbound by structures that, quite frankly, don't always matter to postmodern generations. Peter Rollins has taken this to a level that makes established congregations tremble:

> To develop a healthy community, the best approach can actually involve being clear that one is not starting a community at all and that there will be no pastoral support, that no one will be charged with the job of taking in money and distributing it on

people's behalf, and that no one will be responsible for calling
you up if you stop attending events. In short, it must be clear
that the group does not care about people's needs in the slight-
est. While this may sound deeply uncaring, the reason for stating
this is precisely in order to help provide a healthy soil for real
pastoral and financial support to grow. Providing a space with
no welcoming team or pastoral support group means that individuals need to take responsibility for welcoming and caring for
others themselves. Here the role of those setting up the group is
not to create a new priest / laity divide but rather to refuse to act
in the role of a priest precisely so as to encourage a priesthood
of all believers, offering relational, mutually dependent, pastoral
support. This does not mean that there is no place for leadership, for here the leader is the one who attempts to prevent any
one person, including the leader, from taking over the space.[32]

This is strong medicine for established congregations to take and
is likely too much for them to handle — it's too much for us to
handle! — but the point is well made. Though Rollins isn't trying
to state that all emergent collectives should take such an approach
(he's naming the convictions within his own context), his perspective
reminds us that not every community has to be bound to structures
that often reflect the culture more than the gospel.

We recognize, however, that many mainline congregations will
faithfully endeavor to start a new emergent gathering within the
established church. Though worship is not the only way to offer
hospitality to emergents and progressives, it still remains the primary
entry point most people make when considering ways to further their
faith. This is the approach that we have taken at Brentwood. We have
been fortunate enough to work with members who have empowered
worship leaders to develop an emerging approach to worship that
offers a Bible Belt alternative sorely lacking in this area. While we've

connected with many who otherwise would not have darkened the door of our church, we're also learning to live with the tension of various expectations from church members who don't recognize that not everyone is interested in assimilating to an already established church culture. Emergents are more interested in building community than in preserving institutions.

A third way to connect with emergents and progressives is for a new collective to be supported by one or more established congregations. When this is the case, established communities generally recognize that as much as they would love to offer the kinds of ministries needed under their own roof, their church culture is simply not conducive to such an endeavor. For instance, A House for All Sinners and Saints (Denver) is supported by the financial resources of established church structures. The point is to offer support to the collective without colonizing the space. Nadia Bolz-Weber (the pastor at A House for All) shares some insights offered by a friend: "People need to try and not see the emerging church as a resource which can be duplicated in your congregations resulting in young adults joining your church; instead folks should see these new communities as the growth of the church in a bigger sense, not simply a way to try and grow your own congregation." As Bolz-Weber writes:

> Established churches should support the people who are native to the postmodern culture and then walk away. Pray for the people who are appropriate to and equipped for this culturally specific ministry, see that this is a needed and a vital ministry that you are likely *not* equipped or appropriate for but which is in need of resources . . . give them money, prayer and blessing, . . . tell the kids who grew up in your churches, but who no longer are in Christian community to check it out.[33]

When we started writing this book, we thought that the above examples were basically the three ways that mainline communities could connect with emergents and progressives. However, the example of St. Luke United Methodist Church mentioned toward the beginning of this chapter shattered our preconceived notions of what was possible for established congregations. Never did we think that a rural parish in the middle of the Ozark Mountains (made up mostly of older members who worshiped the same way decade after decade after decade) would not only be willing to consider opening themselves to a bit of change so that others could be welcomed, but radically embraced an emerging approach to worship and ecclesiology that has served as a rebirth of this struggling congregation. By combining the depths of progressive mainline theology with a heart for mission and ancient-future worship, this congregation has experienced a convergence of emergents, progressives, and established members responding to the call of Christ in their lives and in their world. St. Luke United Methodist doesn't represent a denominational new church start, it's not an emergent collective supported by the funds of an established congregation, nor is it a second gathering meeting under the roof of an established church. It is nothing less than an unexpected emergence, unforeseen by all yet experienced by many.

Part Two

EMERGENT ETHOS

McLaren

Progressive
8 Points

Emergent Ethos

1. more concerned about what happens now, here on earth, than any "heaven"
2. partner w/ God in the work God is already doing in the world — transformative — missional — passion for social justice
3. life + teachings of Jesus
13. many faiths work together for healing of the world
4. takes issue w/ America being the country we want it to be and that God might want it to be —
   - against war in Iraq
   - against all violence and killing
   - against nuclear warheads
   - against US sanctions that hurt people
5. want to root out systemic injustice wherever the least are ruled by powerful (empire)
6. desire for new social order
12. intentional hospitality + welcome, open + inclusive — importance of right relationships + honor
7. concerned w/ living the questions than claiming answers
8. responding to Mystery of God takes precedence over explaining the Mystery of God
9. faith = being on the way — in conversation + on a journey
10. Searchers: wandering opens the door to faith — who may we become?
11. Interpret scripture responsibly seeking the piece of wisdom, the universal principle, applicable to situation — narrative / not literal interpretation of scripture

1. Approach to God through life + teachings of Jesus
   - do not call Jesus "Savior"
   - original blessings
   - No atonement theory
2. recognize faithfulness of people who have other names for the way to God; their ways are true for them as ours are for us
3. sharing bread + wine in Jesus' name is an ancient vision of God's feast for all people.
4. invite all + people don't have to become like us to be acceptable:
5. the way we behave toward one another is the expression of what we believe
6. the search for meaning is more grace filled than certainty; questions more than answers
7. communities where people work using gifts they have —
   - peace + justice
   - protect + restore integrity of earth
   - hope to be at nonviolent alternative
8. following Jesus is costly, entails selfless love, conscientious resistance to evil + renunciation of privilege

Chapter Four

A PASSION FOR JUSTICE

Jesus wants to save us from making the good news about another world and not this one. Jesus wants to save us from preaching a gospel that is only about individuals and not about the systems that enslave them. Jesus wants to save us from shrinking the gospel down to a transaction about the removal of sin and not about every single particle of creation being reconciled to its maker. Jesus wants to save us from religiously sanctioned despair, the kind that doesn't believe the world can be made better, the kind that either blatantly or subtly teaches people to just be quiet and behave and wait for something big to happen "someday." — Rob Bell and Don Golden[1]

The public discussion between evangelicals and progressives has been dominated by too many false choices and too much mutual misunderstanding. — Jim Wallis[2]

By offering an in-depth analysis of the theological shifts taking place within emergent culture, part two of this book helps mainline communities of faith recognize the ways that their theological approaches offer great gifts to emergents who are longing for more progressive approaches to faith. Understanding the theological ethos of emergents will help progressive communities of faith consider the ways they might develop emerging expressions of community that deeply resonate with emergents and progressives alike.

Broadly speaking, these shifts include the ways that emergents approach the Bible, the church, theology, and ethics. To once again return to Mark Driscoll's "four lanes" analysis of the four streams of emerging/emergent church culture, the characteristics named in this section will highly resonate with most of those from lane four and some of those from lanes one, two, and three (though each person will inevitably and importantly add his or her own nuances, perspectives, critiques, and appropriations). These theological perspectives aren't always identical to those generally held by progressives, but they are quite similar.

One last disclaimer: As we continue down this path loosely referred to as postmodernism, the last thing any of us need is to become fundamentalists in reverse: in other words, becoming those who think that our way is The Truth, The Whole Truth, and Nothing but the Truth, whether it happens to be conservative *or* liberal. A keen eye toward postmodernism recognizes that all of our dualistic tendencies — whether right or left, conservative or liberal — ultimately end up being flip sides of the same coin, and the postmodern turn (if such a thing exists) tries to maintain a sense of ambiguity that holds such either/or tendencies at arm's length.[3] Progressives are part of the conversation, but they don't represent The Answer any more than anyone can. We just happen to believe that emergents and progressives make good conversation partners.

WHY GOD INVENTED HIGHLIGHTERS

When the late Rich Mullins (an evangelical singer/songwriter who passed away in 1997) went on concert tours around the world, he often noticed that Christians from different parts of the world tended to underline or highlight different passages of scripture in their Bibles. For instance, he observed that Christians in Central America liked to underline the parts of the Bible that speak about Jesus blessing the poor and admonishing his followers to sell everything they have and give away the proceeds. By contrast, he noted that Eurocentric Christians in North America were much more likely to ignore those kinds of verses and highlight ones that — according to their interpretations — talk about securing a place in the afterlife. Mullins observed that in the few instances that Eurocentric Christians *did* highlight verses about the blessing of the poor, they almost always found a way to creatively interpret such passages in a spiritual fashion that robbed them of their material import.[4]

> You guys are all into that born again thing, which is great. We do need to be born again, since Jesus said that to a guy named Nicodemus. But if you tell me I have to be born again to enter the kingdom of God, I can tell you that you just have to sell everything you have and give it to the poor, because Jesus said that to one guy too. . . . But I guess that's why God invented highlighters, so we can highlight the parts we like and ignore the rest.[5]

For deeply systemic reasons, most Eurocentric white Christians have found it much easier to proclaim a savior who offers the safety of a comfortable afterlife than a savior who invites one to a challenging — though not necessarily comfortable — life of discipleship. However, emergents (like progressives) are trying to change this conversation by offering an alternative vision that highlights the ways that Christianity is about a lot more than just making it to heaven. They are beginning to affirm with John Dominic Crossan that "heaven's in great shape; earth is where the problems are!"[6]

Emergents consistently describe themselves as "missional," which generally means that those in emerging and emergent circles are deeply committed to God's will being done on earth, as it is in heaven.

As one of the most influential emerging churches puts it, missional Christians "believe that the church exists for the world and not for herself — she is to introduce and usher in the Kingdom of God into every part of this world."[7] In a manner reminiscent of what is often included in mainline liturgical practices, Tony Jones says that in an emergent church "you're likely to hear a phrase like 'Our calling as a church is to partner with God in the work that God is already doing in the world — to cooperate in the building of God's Kingdom.' "[8]

Emergents are articulating their faith in ways that are not centered solely around concerns about the afterlife but also carry just as much emphasis on the import of Christianity in the here and now. The theological turn emergents have made toward progressive articulations of Christian faith has especially been seen in a passion for social justice. When surveying the popular styles of music reflected in most contemporary worship settings, Brian McLaren makes a heartfelt request for Christian songwriters to consider what he calls an "eschatological" perspective that offers more focus on the mending and repairing of this world than in a passive waiting for the next. He draws on the thought of Walter Brueggemann and Jürgen Moltmann in order to offer "a whole new approach to eschatology" that "doesn't indulge in 'modern' charts or shaky predictions" but instead bathes itself in the poetry of biblical writers like Isaiah and Jeremiah. McLaren contends that such poetry, "when it enters us, plants in us a vision of a world very much different from and better than ours. And when this hope grows and takes root in us, we become agents of it."[9] As a result, emergents are on the front lines when it comes to issues like poverty, caring for the environment, and racial reconciliation.

Those within emerging and emergent circles like to appropriate the work of the highly acclaimed Anglican scholar N. T. Wright. According to Eddie Gibbs and Ryan Bolger, one of the central foci of the emerging church is rooted in Wright's interpretive analysis of Mark 1:15–16, in which "the good news was not that Jesus was to die on the cross to forgive sins but that God had returned and all were invited to participate with him in this new way of life, in this redemption of the world."[10] From this perspective, the gospel is not simply restricted to assurances about one's eternal destiny, but is radically reconstituted as a call to partner with God in the transformative work already being done in this world. "More than simply offering a message of personal salvation," Gibbs and Bolger observe, "Jesus invited his followers to participate in God's redemption of the world. Emerging churches have adopted this restored understanding of the gospel, and it has dramatically transformed the way they train new and not-so-new Christians in the faith."[11]

Dieter Zander has been on the frontlines of the emerging movement since its inception in North America. He was the founder of the first Gen-X church in the United States (New Song, Pomona, California), and then went on to Willow Creek Community Church to launch its emerging gathering (Axis). He left Willow Creek a few years ago in order to be part of a smaller, intentional Christian community in San Francisco. "All my Christian life," he reflects, "I had been abducted by an alien gospel." In reassessing his own approach, Zander says that "a lot of church people don't know the relationship between the gospel of Jesus and how we are to live. They are threatened by reevaluating that. Their belief is that they try to believe in Jesus so that when they die they get to go to heaven." In this scenario, "populating heaven is the main part of the gospel." Now, however, Zander believes that "the gospel is about being increasingly alive to God in the world. It is concerned with bringing heaven to earth. This really throws people off."[12]

Part of the shift emergents are making in this regard serves as a critique to the radical escapism of contemporary expressions of evangelicalism, especially as evidenced in the kind of popular "Left Behind" theology that Rob Bell and Don Golden roundly criticize in *Jesus Wants to Save Christians* (which we will discuss below). As emergents reflect on their call to work with God on this side of the grave, they echo progressive voices down through the ages that have recognized God's commitment to the transformation of this earth. When the nineteenth-century former slave Sojourner Truth became frustrated with those in her own day who claimed that Christianity was primarily about being taken up to some parlor in heaven in order to escape from the struggles of this world, she delivered one of the most powerful orations in modern Christian history:

> You seem to be expecting to go to some parlor away up some-where, and when the wicked have been burnt, you are coming back to walk in triumph over their ashes — this is to be your New Jerusalem!! Now I can't see anything so very nice in that, coming back to such a muss as that will be, a world covered with the ashes of the wicked. Besides, if the Lord comes and burns — as you say he will — I am not going away; I am going to stay here and stand the fire, like Shadrach, Meshach, and Abednego! And Jesus will walk with me through the fire, and keep me from harm.[13]

Sojourner Truth's words remind me of one emergent Christian who recently told me that if God planned on sending everyone who wasn't a Christian to hell, then she would have "no other choice than to go to hell as an act of moral protest against such a God." Furthermore, she said she wouldn't go to hell "in spite of Jesus, but in the name of Jesus."

Emergents are also changing the ways that they talk about the afterlife in general. Instead of thinking in terms of traditional images of heaven and hell that seem more cartoonish to them than anything else, many emergents — once again significantly informed by main-line scholar N. T. Wright — prefer thinking in terms of God's ultimate restoration of the world that brings heaven (the New Jerusalem) down to earth, and not vice versa. Wright tends to be a more conservative voice within mainline traditions, and that is part of the reason evangelicals from lanes one through three are especially drawn to his thought. Still, even his more conservative interpretation of Christ's death and resurrection leads him to emphasize God's full renewal of creation, and he goes to great lengths to make sure this isn't confused with the highly individualistic notions that place a premium on individual souls somehow living on after death in some disembodied (Platonic) state.[14]

As Peter Rollins has suggested (following Nietzsche), when the truth of Christianity is watered down to securing one's place in the afterlife, one can make the argument that this is "nothing less than a form of nihilism, for the belief in the eternal life robbed this life of its fragile, fleeting beauty." From this perspective, Rollins says, the point

> is not to argue for or against the existence of a heavenly eternity, but rather to help draw us away from the idea that such a belief relates to what Christianity offers as its transformative truth. Indeed, if one does believe in a literal heaven, it may even be important to suspend this belief in order to approach the truly good news of Christianity. For the original disciples the introduction of an afterlife arose only after they had already given up everything and followed Jesus — in short, after the good news had already been received.[15]

RETHINKING THE CROSS

In addition to the renewed emphasis that emergents are placing on the life and teachings of Jesus are christological questions of no small import, especially in relationship to theologies of the cross. Simply put, emergent Christians — as well as progressives — are increasingly uncomfortable interpreting the soteriological significance of Jesus' death in terms of popular versions of substitutionary atonement theologies that permeate the evangelical landscape. Phyllis Tickle has observed that, in the great emergence, "the actual nature of the Atonement . . . or the tenet of an angry God who must be appeased or the question of evil's origins are suddenly all up for reconsideration."[16] One emerging blogger summarizes the struggle felt by many emergents:

> I guess at the grassroots, this is the problem that remains for me. The God of the heavens is terribly angry at God's people for their many sins. . . . Yet John tells us that "For God so loved the world. . . . " Herein lies the problem, bound up nicely and theoretically in the penal substitutionary atonement theory, at least for me. God sends God's son to die so that God can keep Godself from killing the people, the object of God's anger. Father kills son (or has son killed, if you prefer the passive voice) so God won't kill (judge/pour out wrath on) others that God also loves. Doesn't this sound terribly pathological to anyone but me? Seriously, I picture Jack the Ripper (for the UK'ers in here) and Sam Gacy (for the stateside reader) when I think of this. It borders on Silence of the Lambs-esque for me, in all honesty. "I love you so I have to kill you. Wait! I will kill my kid instead to show you that I love you."[17]

These sentiments have been reflected most popularly in the highly controversial emergent book *The Lost Message of Jesus,* in which the authors try to rescue Jesus from interpretations of his death that, to them, hint of cosmic child abuse. According to authors Steve Chalke and Alan Mann, a vengeful God who punishes "his Son" for an offense not even committed makes those both inside and outside the church find "this twisted version of events morally dubious and a huge barrier to faith." Yet even deeper than this, these authors suggest, is that "such a concept stands in total contradiction to the statement 'God is love.' If the cross is a personal act of violence perpetrated by God towards humankind but borne by his Son, then it makes a mockery of Jesus' own teaching to love your enemies and to refuse to repay evil with evil."[18]

In a recent podcast interview, Brian McLaren adds an additional gloss to this subject by recalling the words of a popular Christian leader (McLaren doesn't cite this leader by name because he wants to "protect his reputation" in the evangelical world) who has trouble believing that God would ask us to do something unconditionally (forgive) that God is incapable of doing unless "He punishes somebody in place of the person He was going to forgive." This leader doesn't see how any of this makes sense, for "God doesn't say things to you [like] 'Forgive your wife, and then go kick the dog to vent your anger.' God asks you to actually forgive. And there's a certain sense that a common understanding of the atonement presents a God who is incapable of forgiving. Unless He kicks somebody else."[19]

It's not unintentional that writers such as Chalke and Mann frame this topic through language that evokes divine child abuse. We are reminded of progressive feminist voices like Rita Nakashima Brock and Rebecca Ann Parker who have pointed out that such understandings reinforce the myth of redemptive violence in extremely unhelpful ways. By being taught to identify with an image of Jesus that posits him as "obedient to the will of the Father," victims of a wide range of abuses are taught that their suffering is justified and/or redemptive. Furthermore, victims are conditioned to believe that they are powerless in the face of oppression. They are taught that Christ suffered passively and so should they. Perhaps most tragically,

victims are taught that the very oppression that binds them is redemptive, for they are to "count it as pure joy" to be able to suffer
as Christ suffered. And though Jesus' first public sermon recorded
by Luke states that he came to proclaim release to the captives,
recovery of sight to the blind, and to let the oppressed go free, the
theologies of redemptive suffering that have followed in his name per-
petuate the very structures of oppression that he so often struggled
against.[20]

While concerns about the atonement may appear new, they are as
old as the doctrine itself. Peter Abelard, a contemporary of St. Anselm
(who is largely responsible for solidifying the doctrine of substitutionary atonement in Christian tradition), critiqued Anselm's work
by asking, "Who will forgive God of killing his own son?"[21] In the
nineteenth century, Hosea Ballou was one of the most outspoken
Protestant critics of substitutionary atonement, and he shared many
of the same concerns that emergents and progressives bring to the
table. For Ballou, the doctrine of the atonement "is an idea that has
done more injury to the Christian religion than the writings of all its
opposers." Ballou believed that no matter how much sin and death
abounded, God's grace was greater. It's not that God doesn't take sin
seriously, but rather that God's love seeks to restore human beings
in spite of their sin. When Ballou posed the following scenario, he
named the thoughts and feelings of many emergents and progressives: "Your child has fallen into the mire, and its body and garments
are defiled. You cleanse it, and array it in clean robes. The query is,
Do you love your child because you have washed it? or, Did you wash
it because you loved it?"[22]

According to Marcus Borg, most mainstream scholars don't think
that atonement theology goes back to Jesus himself, and this is welcome news for emergents and progressives alike.[23] Though Christian
scripture articulates at least five ways of interpreting the death of

Jesus, most scholars agree that the most popular form of atonement theology voiced today — the one that says Jesus died on the cross for our sins so that God can forgive us — didn't fully develop until about nine hundred years ago, in other words, about a thousand years after the Christian scriptures were written.[24]

Generally speaking, those within the emergent conversation are drawn to at least one of three ways of rethinking their theologies of the cross. Some follow the lead of scholars like N. T. Wright by emphasizing the renewal of all things and their reconciliation to their maker. Others emphasize God's solidarity with human beings, even in the face of terrible suffering and tragedy. Somewhat connected to this view are emergents who embrace liberation theology's emphasis on Jesus as a fellow brother who comes alongside and suffers with those who are oppressed and marginalized. They point to the ways Jesus continues to be crucified, even today.

Emergents also find it increasingly helpful to understand the death of Jesus not as the preordained will of God, but rather as the consequence of following in the way of God. From this perspective, Jesus' death was the consequence of the way he lived his life, not the purpose of his life. To illustrate this idea through recent analogies, the deaths of prophetic figures such as Martin Luther King Jr. and Oscar Romero can be seen as the consequence of what they were doing, but not the purpose of what they were doing.[25] Like these heroes of faith, Jesus refused to compromise in the face of the powers that be, even if it cost him his own life.

As progressives Jack Nelson-Pallmeyer and Bret Hesla summarize, "The idea that God sent Jesus to die for our sins makes sense only if you embrace the punishing images of God rejected by Jesus." By contrast, an infinitely loving God, like the father in Luke's parable of the prodigal son — who forgives before being asked — doesn't need an atoning sacrifice.[26]

[handwritten: Jesus for President / Claiborne + Haw]

This isn't your grandmother's
evangelical publishing house

When it comes to a passion for justice, one of the most striking characteristics of emergent culture is seen in the ways it offers a prophetic critique of empire and systems of domination. Imagine our surprise when we learned that Zondervan, a long-time evangelical publisher, aggressively marketed Shane Claiborne and Chris Haw's biting critique of empire in the 2008 release *Jesus for President*. Through the incorporation of captivating imagery and prophetic words that challenge American forms of religious nationalism at their very core — the kind of nationalism prophetic progressives like Walter Brueggemann have continually warned us about — Claiborne and Haw open their newest book with a vignette that features brief sentences on each page juxtaposed with a stirring sequence of religious, national, and militaristic images. While we highly recommend viewing this book in order to experience its visual impact first-hand, we will try our best to describe the contents of its first few pages.

The opening sequence features a picture of a five-year-old daughter and her father happily sitting at a kitchen table. It looks like the picture was taken in the mid-eighties. The following words appear under the picture: "You grew up in a good family; hardworking dad and a mom who was there when you needed her." The next picture is also of a young daughter with her father; this time they are near the dad's pickup truck, circa 1980: "They taught you and your little brother to share and showed you how to pray every night before bed." The page turns to show a black and white photo of an all-white children's Sunday School class, circa 1950 or 1960, with the following caption: "In Sunday School, you learned about Jesus and sang all the songs with the rest of the kids. There was Noah and his ark, Moses and the Ten Commandments, and little baby Jesus asleep on the hay." You then turn the page and see a young girl pledging allegiance to a large U.S. flag directly in front of her: "You learned about the blessing that was America and were grateful to live in a country led by good Christian leaders. With a hand over your heart or above your brow, you pledged allegiance to God and Country, for the Lord was at work in this holy nation." But here comes the reversal. This time, the turn of the page reveals a gripping photo of what looks like a wounded young Iraqi boy, around ten years of age, being operated on in a makeshift hospital. The sheet is drenched in blood. The following words appear below the picture: "But lately you are beginning to wonder if this is really how God intended things to be. And you question if God is really working through places of power. Maybe, you wonder, God had a totally different idea in mind."[27]

At the conclusion of *Jesus for President,* the authors offer a selection of books for further reading written by progressive patron saints: Dorothy Day, Abraham Joshua Heschel, Walter Brueggemann, Oscar Romero, Leonardo Boff, Desmond Tutu, and Joan Chittister (just to name a few). Throughout this book, the hermeneutical tools Claiborne and Haw employ in their interpretations of scripture could easily lead one to believe that they are operating more as liberation theologians than as evangelical ones. For instance, instead of interpreting the book of Revelation as one full of magical codes and crystal ball prophecies that reveal the true identity of the Antichrist — which is what we expect to see on the shelves of most evangelical Christian bookstores — Claiborne and Haw follow mainstream scholarship by interpreting Revelation as a critique of the Roman empire.[28]

Jesus for President not only pushes the envelope further than many evangelicals are willing to go, but also runs up against the comfort zones of many progressives. One of the most powerful — and controversial — pieces is related to Claiborne's experiences of living in Baghdad during part of the Iraq war. On one of the first days that bombs were dropping in Baghdad, CBS broadcast a live interview with him and asked what his impressions of the United States were at the time. Within the first minute of the conversation, CBS thought his responses were too critical of the U.S. actions, and they immediately pulled the plug on the interview. Claiborne, a graduate of Eastern University (a prestigious evangelical school) and former intern at Willow Creek Community Church (one of the most influential evangelical megachurches in the country), penned the following poem in response to these experiences:

> If this bloody, counterfeit liberation is American...
>> I am proud to be un-American.
> If depleted uranium is American...
>> I am proud to be un-American.
> If U.S. sanctions are American...
>> I am proud to be un-American.
> If the imposed "peace" of Pax Americana is American...
>> I am proud to be un-American.
> But if grace, humility, and nonviolence are American...
>> I am proud to be American.
> If sharing to create a safe and sustainable world is American...
>> I am proud to be American.
> If loving our enemies is American...
>> I am proud to be American.

Regardless, I would die for the people of New York, but I will not kill for them...my kingdom is not of this world.

I would die for the people of Baghdad, but I will not kill for them...my kingdom is not of this world. I will stand in the way of terror and war...my kingdom is not of this world.

I will pledge an allegiance deeper than nationalism, to my God and to my family...my kingdom is not of this world. I will use my life to shout, "Another world is possible"...for my kingdom is from another place. "My kingdom is not of this world. If it were, my servants would fight... but now my kingdom is from another place" (Jesus; John 18:36).[29]

Penning such a poem might get someone like Jeremiah Wright "blacklisted" or censored, but it got Shane Claiborne published by Zondervan.

FROM NOOMA TO NONVIOLENCE

[handwritten: Rob Bell Nooma videos]

Perhaps no one is more influential among young evangelicals than Rob Bell. Bell is well-known for the highly creative "Nooma" videos that artistically feature his teachings in poignant and memorable ways. He is also the bestselling author of *Velvet Elvis: Repainting the Christian Faith* and the founding pastor of Mars Hill Bible Church,[30] one of the few emergent congregations that can be classified as a megachurch.[31]

Bell is a graduate of both Wheaton College and Fuller Theological Seminary, two well-known evangelical institutions. In 2008, Zondervan published *Jesus Wants to Save Christians: A Manifesto for the Church in Exile,* co-authored by Bell and Don Golden. While *Velvet Elvis* was "outside the usual evangelical box,"[32] Bell and Golden take things to another level in *Jesus Wants to Save Christians.* Like Claiborne and Haw, they interpret the Bible largely through the lens of liberation thought (though they offer their own twist on it and refer to it as "New Exodus" theology), saying that "the Hebrew scriptures have a very simple and direct message: God always hears the cry of the oppressed.... God gives power and blessing so that justice and righteousness will be upheld for those who are denied them. This is what God is like. This is what God is about."[33]

Bell and Golden highlight systemic injustice[34] and the myth of redemptive violence,[35] which are of course issues that progressives have been articulating for decades. Echoes of James Cone and Cornel West are heard as these young evangelicals acknowledge the complex history of the United States.[36] An explicit proclamation that "America is an empire"[37] leads to a manifesto of repentance and a call for Christians "in exile" to embody a nonviolent alternative deeply informed by the progressive biblical scholarship of John Dominic Crossan and Marcus Borg.[38] Crossan's influence is particularly evident when Bell and Golden note the ways that "the Roman Empire, which put Jesus on an execution stake, insisted that it was bringing peace to the world through its massive military might, and anybody who didn't see it this way just might be put on a cross. Emperor Caesar, who ruled the Roman Empire, was considered the 'Son of God,' the 'Prince of Peace,' and one of his propaganda slogans was 'peace through victory.' "[39] I can't get over the fact that just a few short years ago, Crossan and Borg were deemed virtual heretics in evangelical circles because of their historical Jesus research, yet now their scholarship is at the forefront of emergent hermeneutics.

Bell and Golden interpret the book of Revelation as a "bold, courageous, politically subversive attack on corrosive empire and its power to oppress people."[40] In what leads up to our favorite line from the entire book, they state that the original readers of Revelation were confronted with a fundamental question:

> "Who is Lord? Jesus or Caesar? Whose way is the way? The way of violence or the way of peace? The way of domination or the way of compassion? The way of building towers to the heavens or the way of sharing our bread with our neighbor? . . . The way of greed and economic exploitation or the way of generosity and solidarity? Who is your Lord? . . . " Were the people in John's church reading his letter for the first time, with Roman soldiers right outside their door, thinking, *"This is going to be really*

helpful for people two thousand years from now who don't want to get left behind?"[41]

Of course not, they imply. Their interpretation of Revelation is remarkably similar to one offered by mainline scholar Barbara Rossing, whose wonderful book *The Rapture Exposed* radically critiques the kind of thought that has been so popularized in and through the "Left Behind" series of books (whose authors have sold more books in the United States than anyone except J. K. Rowling[42]). Rossing is, of course, working out of mainstream biblical scholarship, and she observes that the early Christians resisted the claims of empire "by their patient and subversive lifestyle of love and welcome and community.... They lived in light of the vision of the Lamb that had changed their lives. And people around them marveled at their joy and boldness."[43]

KARL BARTH 2.0: THE REMIX VERSION

When considering the shifts that are taking place within evangelical culture, few theorists doubt the influential role postmodernism plays in this process. Nor do we. But without discounting postmodernism's influence, we think that another factor is just as responsible (if not more so) for the critiques of empire that have been passionately articulated by emergents like McLaren, Claiborne, and Bell. But in order to develop this theory, we need to go back in time approximately one hundred years and consider the life of a then not-so-well-known pastor by the name of Karl Barth.

Before Barth became a household name in theological circles (he is arguably the most influential theologian of the twentieth century), he was a parish pastor in Safenwil, Switzerland, the country of his birth. Like an increasing number of emergent leaders today, Barth's "extensive engagement with local social and political questions and his reading of leading Christian social thinkers led to his longing for a new world, a new social order that would put a stop to the oppression of the poor and disenfranchised and challenge the well-to-do to take seriously the social responsibilities of their privileged position."[44]

Barth had received a top-notch theological education in Germany before moving back to Switzerland. At first, he held his German teachers and mentors in high regard, as well as the theological foundations they had set before him. Yet the outbreak of World War I, especially the realization that his former teachers had signed a document pledging their support for the war and for the kaiser, led him to lose all confidence in the theological teachings that had been passed down to him. Barth reflected on this moment later in life:

> One day in early August 1914 stands out in my personal memory as a black day. Ninety-three German intellectuals impressed public opinion by their proclamation in support of the war policy of Wilhelm II and his counselors. Among these intellectuals I discovered to my horror almost all of my theological teachers whom I had greatly venerated. In despair over what this indicated about the signs of the time I suddenly realized that I could not any longer follow either their ethics and dogmatics or their understanding of the Bible and of history.[45]

The unflinching support for World War I on the part of Barth's teachers left his theological world in shambles, and he "considered the support of the war to be nothing less than a betrayal of Christian faith."[46] The modern theology that he inherited made God "function as one who simply sanctioned the values and norms that society had established," certifying them "with a divine seal of approval."[47]

Barth's disappointment with the church would only deepen upon the events that led to the outbreak of World War II. Once again, he felt like the church was in bed with the state. In 1933, he was bold enough to assert that anyone who wished to preach the gospel in Germany must also couple it with a stand against the disappearance and persecution of the Jews.[48] A year later, he was the primary person responsible for penning the now famous Barmen Declaration, in which he basically challenged those in Germany to determine whether or not they pledged their ultimate allegiance to God or to the state. Because he was teaching in Germany during the time, it's little wonder that the powers that be tried to silence him. In the latter part of 1934, after refusing to pledge an unqualified oath to Hitler, he was dismissed from his teaching duties in Germany. Being one of the more fortunate voices of dissent, he was allowed to return to his hometown of Basel.

Barth's thought usually receives mixed reviews in progressive circles. For many progressives, his Christology is too high and his God is too providential. This leads progressives to all too often dismiss the entirety of his legacy. We think this is unfortunate, for Barth remains a towering witness from the twentieth century who had the courage to put his very life on the line for the sake of justice. But that is a subject for another day.

For the purposes at hand, we would like to revisit some of Barth's most formative experiences, particularly regarding the way he lost trust in his teachers, and compare them to some of the formative experiences that are responsible for deeply shaping the thought of young emergents.

Before trying to traverse this ground, it's vitally important to add this disclaimer (we hope the italics got your attention): We do not for one second think that the context of two World Wars and the circumstances surrounding each compares to the context and circumstances that young emergents have faced in the latter part of the twentieth and the beginning of the twenty-first centuries. We are not equating these eras, nor are we equating the figures and events surrounding them.

What we *are* interested in considering is the way that, nearly a century ago, Barth lost all confidence in the theological, biblical, and ethical teachings that had been handed down to him. He felt burned by those he had trusted, and the bulk of his disappointment was rooted in the unflinching support that the most dominant voices of the institutional church gave to the affairs of the state, even when they led to war and oppression. For Barth, the will of God must never be confused with the will of the state. His theology pronounced a resounding "Nein!" to those in the highest seats of power who took the name of God in vain by advancing their own interests and affairs through the exploitation of religious images and discourse.

While young emergents are certainly in a different time and place, we wonder if it's possible that they are reacting to their environment in a similar fashion? Are they rejecting the teachings that have been passed down to them by the most dominant voices within evangelical and fundamentalists circles — the very teachings that led to the post-9/11 rush to war that was so championed by the Religious Right (as Pat Robertson put it, "to blow them all away in the name of the Lord")? Are they rejecting the religious teachers who have tried to tell them that torture can be justified and that preemptive war can be unflinchingly supported, even by those who follow the Prince of Peace? Young evangelicals were reared under the massive influence of the Religious Right, and we wonder if they are rejecting the brand of Christianity handed down to them — the kind of Christianity that baptizes war, greed, and exploitation in the name of the nation's "best interest." As John Caputo asks, aren't the poetics of the kingdom of God as announced by Jesus "in almost every respect the opposite of the politics that presently passes itself off under the name of Jesus?" Shouldn't the kingdom of God "turn on peace not war, forgiveness not retribution, on loving one's enemies and not preemptive war?"[49]

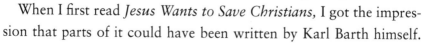When I first read *Jesus Wants to Save Christians,* I got the impression that parts of it could have been written by Karl Barth himself.

To quote Bell and Golden, Christians "should get very nervous when the flag and the Bible start holding hands," for "this is not a romance we want to encourage." They have the courage to provocatively ask, "When the commander in chief of the most powerful armed forces humanity has ever seen quotes the prophet Isaiah from the Bible in celebration of military victory . . . is this what Isaiah had in mind?"[50]

You can almost hear Bell and Golden pronounce a resounding "Nein!" to theologies that allow contemporary Christians in the United States to take the name of God in vain by confusing their own interests and pursuits with those of God. In the words of Bell and Golden, Jesus' followers are all too often "claiming to be the voice of God, but they are speaking the language of Caesar and using the methods of Rome, and for millions of us it has the stench of [Rome]."[51]

A few years ago, two college students from a nearby evangelical church attended one of Rob Bell's tour stops in Oklahoma City. Both of them loved *Velvet Elvis* and the "Nooma" video series, and they couldn't wait to hear Bell speak in person. They came back from Oklahoma City refreshed and inspired. It wasn't long until *Jesus Wants to Save Christians* was published, and both anxiously awaited their copy of the book to arrive in the mail.

Soon afterward, another opportunity to hear Bell speak in person came around, and one friend called the other to see if he wanted to hear him speak yet again. By this time, however, things had changed. The other friend refused to go, calling Bell a heretic and saying he "no longer had any desire to read or hear anything Bell has to say." It turns out that the church this person attended — which at one time used "Nooma" videos for its youth group meetings and held several discussion groups on *Velvet Elvis* for the adults — decided to ban everything Bell had written, for he had "crossed the line" with *Jesus Wants to Save Christians*. The first friend had to drive to the second tour stop all alone.

Which communities of faith will be there for emergents who are drawn to progressive approaches like Bell's, but don't know where to turn? To return to Carol Howard Merritt (Western Presbyterian Church, Washington, D.C.) and her prescient words offered at the beginning of this book: "The biggest change on the religious front is that young Evangelicals are leaving their roots. Can we put aside our elitism? Can we reach out to them? If we can, this could be a time of tremendous growth and renewal for our congregations."[52]

Chapter Five

POSTMODERN PATHS

We sing songs to the truth as if it were a source of comfort, warmth, and good hygiene. But in deconstruction the truth is dangerous, and it will drive you out into the cold. Nietzsche had it right when he said we lack the courage for the truth, that the truth will make us stronger just so long as it doesn't kill us first. We want the truth attenuated, softened, bathed, and powdered, like the smarmy depictions of Jesus.

—John Caputo[1]

In theology one has to keep talking, because otherwise somebody will believe your last sentence. —Douglas John Hall[2]

BEYOND CERTAINTY

I recently had the task of purchasing a Bible for a friend who had just graduated from seminary. Her ordination service was around the corner, and during the liturgy a Bible was being presented to her as one of the "Signs of the Office." As I made my way to the Bible section at a local Christian bookstore, I couldn't believe the number of possibilities before my eyes. Though I didn't purchase it, the edition that most caught my attention that day was *The Apologetics Study Bible*. It featured all kinds of commentaries, notes, and theories defending the reasons why the Bible is, without a doubt, the infallible, inerrant, inspired Word of God, and why affirming its "simple" and "plain" Truths unlocks the key to believing in God without any doubts whatsoever.

The Apologetics Study Bible reminded me of the days in my own life when I tried so hard to believe in God without any doubts whatsoever. I wanted stability, certainty, and absolutes from my faith. I was afraid of doubt, insecurity, and ambiguity. I believed that if I had enough evidence for the truthfulness of God and Christianity, then I would be able to remove these doubts and uncertainties from my mind. This, in turn, would bring stability to my world.

Indeed, the quest for certainty, stability, and absolutes has long been regarded as a central task of religion. Much of the appeal of evangelical culture has been its attempt to provide a message of security and certainty in what postmodern theorist Mark C. Taylor describes as "a world of frenzied flux and flow."[3] Such a quest is based on the hopes that our anxieties can be mastered if only we can secure the ground of absolutes. Now, as pluralism and globalization increasingly shape the postmodern context in which we live, our increased encounters with those other than us often give rise to even more forms of fundamentalism and conservativism that long for simplicity, clarity, and certainty in a world of difference.[4]

To be sure, this quest for certainty has hardly been expressed by religion alone. During the modern period (marked by the Enlightenment), when religion gave way to Reason, the quest for absolutes remained the same — except instead of a dethroned God being the source of certainty and stability, it became possible for human beings, through the use of reason, to provide stability, certainty, and absolutes that could stand the test of time. Indeed, the entire philosophy of René Descartes — the so-called father of the Enlightenment — can be understood "as an effort to overcome the insecurity brought by uncertainty and to reach the security promised by certainty." For Descartes, truth was equated with certainty.[5]

Throughout modernity, whether human beings have placed their faith in God (via religion) or in humanity (via reason), the primary quest of securing ground in "a world of frenzied flux and flow" has been of central importance. While fundamentalism and evangelicalism are generally viewed as reactions against the Enlightenment, they, like Protestant liberalism, are actually products of it.[6] As such, faith is often boiled down to what should be believed after surveying all of the evidence, and the promise is that ambiguities can be replaced by absolutes.

When emergent author and pastor Doug Pagitt reflects on some of his first encounters with Christianity (he is one of the few emergents who didn't grow up in church, but instead found his place in evangelical culture while in high school), he shares a story that took place during a meeting with two mentors who were assigned the task of "discipling" their new convert in the faith. While sipping milkshakes at Burger King, one of Pagitt's mentors started describing the primary tenets of Christian faith by writing them on one of the paper tray liners. According to the tray liner theology, the three essentials to salvation went from mind (facts) to feelings (faith) to will (repentance). In other words, facts backed up by evidence lead to faith. Pagitt struggled with this perspective. He felt like his life had already been transformed by an event of which he had little knowledge. For him, his faith was seeking understanding (Anselm), not the other way around. "I had jumped into Christianity," he reflects, "without any sense of the absolutes, without knowing the essentials, without a shred of assurance."[7] Pagitt's transformation wasn't the sort that can be proven in a laboratory. In the time since, he has recognized the modern, Cartesian influence on this model, and he has been one of the most influential voices attempting to offer an emergent alternative.

In modern forms of evangelical thought, the Cartesian love of certainty is seen most starkly in the school of apologetics, as reflected in the *Apologetics Study Bible* and by bestselling authors such as Josh McDowell, Lee Strobel, and Norman Geisler.[8] From this perspective, faith is not the result of any kind of Kierkegaardian leap, but rather is the result of cold, hard, indubitable facts, particularly as presented in the Bible. When certainty is the most highly regarded virtue of the modern world, doubt is viewed as a vice to be avoided at all costs. Yet this modern approach to Christian faith is one of the primary things that emergents are critiquing.

One of the main concerns that emergents have with definitive proclamations of Absolute Truth has to do with the ways in which such certainty can breed highly unethical practices. When someone wants to convince you that their foundations are Absolutely Right, derived from God without any doubts whatsoever, it's usually because they want to gain some sort of authoritarian ground. As philosopher Gianni Vattimo observes, "When someone wants to tell me the absolute truth it is because he wants to put me under his control, under his command." Vattimo is reminded of what Dostoevsky wrote a century ago, that, if forced to choose between Christ and the truth, he would choose Christ.[9] Brian McLaren affirms the same:

> The other side of the coin is to talk about the ways claims about knowledge and certainty are used to fight or perpetuate injustice.... The real issue, in my mind, is not simply an argument about truth; it's the need for repentance about the abuse of power — especially by white Christians who used the Bible to justify some pretty horrific things, whether we're talking about the genocide of native peoples, the African slave trade, the Holocaust, apartheid, or whatever. While we claim a high level of certainty in regards to truth, we have shown ourselves

to be relatively clueless about matters of justice. I'm not advocating uncertainty at all; I'm all for having a proper confidence, but I also want us to think about how we can be more gentle and humane in the way we treat other people, especially people whom we feel don't see the truth as we do.[10]

Emergents are distrustful of metanarratives (master stories that claim overarching access to universal Truth), and, as such, they aren't attempting to shift from one understanding of Absolute Truth to a different understanding of Absolute Truth (reverse fundamentalism), but rather to recognize that no one has access to Absolute Truth, and that is okay. Like the original cynics of old, Rollins suggests, emergents are more interested in living the questions than in claiming to have all of the answers. "The original cynics were a dusty group of people who questioned ethics, not because they hated ethics but because they loved ethics so much. They questioned God and religion, not because they were skeptical but because they were obsessed with God and religion."[11]

In recognizing the contingency of our beliefs, we are reminded of the mystic Meister Eckhardt, who prayed for "God to rid him of God," meaning of course his own understandings of God. Such a prayer has been made by theologians both past and present. It can be heard in Paul Tillich's prayer for the "God beyond God"; in St. Basil's confession that "knowledge of the divine involves sensing God's incomprehensibility"; and in Thomas Aquinas's conviction that "the highest human knowledge of God is to know that one does not know God."[12] From this perspective, responding to the Mystery of God takes precedence over trying to explain the Mystery of God. Emergents are quite comfortable embracing such mysteries, for if God can be comprehended, then whatever is comprehended can't be God (Augustine). This is similar to the wonderful Buddhist idea that basically says if you meet the Buddha on the road, kill it, because whatever you've met on the road can't be the actual Buddha. In other words, all of our interpretations of God (not to mention scripture) are finite. As Scot McKnight writes,

> The emerging movement tends to be suspicious of systematic theology. Why? Not because we don't read systematics, but because the diversity of theologies alarms us, no genuine consensus has been achieved, God didn't reveal a systematic theology but a storied narrative, and no language is capable of capturing the Absolute Truth who alone is God. Frankly, the emerging movement loves ideas and theology. It just doesn't have an airtight system or statement of faith. We believe the Great Tradition offers various ways for telling the truth about God's redemption in Christ, but we don't believe any one theology gets it absolutely right.[13]

While these approaches to faith carry their own nuances within emergent contexts, we can readily see their familiarity with postliberal thinkers such as George Lindbeck and William Placher. Each recognizes the limitations of modernism, particularly in relationship to the inability of human beings to adequately describe the nature of God, and both are responding to what theologians have traditionally referred to as revelation.[14]

Emergents remind people of faith that orthodoxy — the idea that we can readily possess all of the right beliefs about God — runs the risk of idolatry, the Bible's most oft-quoted sin. Emergents aren't as interested in speaking about God as they are in being the place where God speaks, a distinction that is seen in a provocative excerpt from Peter Rollins's blog:

> Without equivocation or hesitation I fully and completely admit that I deny the resurrection of Christ. This is something that anyone who knows me could tell you, and I am not afraid to

say it publicly, no matter what some people may think. . . . I deny the resurrection of Christ every time I do not serve at the feet of the oppressed, each day that I turn my back on the poor; I deny the resurrection of Christ when I close my ears to the cries of the downtrodden and lend my support to an unjust and corrupt system. However there are moments when I affirm that resurrection, few and far between as they are. I affirm it when I stand up for those who are forced to live on their knees, when I speak for those who have had their tongues torn out, when I cry for those who have no more tears left to shed.[15]

Mazing grace

Given the influence of postmodernism, emergents are drawn to "the conversation, not the conclusion; the journey, not the destination."[16] It's not a coincidence that the second book in McLaren's *A New Kind of Christian* trilogy is titled *The Story We Find Ourselves In,* for it privileges narrative forms of theology to systematic ones.[17]

As a result, emergents like to return to biblical language that describes faith as being "on the way." Such language deeply resonates with Christians throughout the ages, for this is not the newest way of describing Christianity; it is the oldest.

The idea of being on a journey also resonates with postmodern theorists like John Caputo, whose work has witnessed a meteoric rise in influence among emergents. Caputo's own thought has been deeply influenced by the restless searching of figures like St. Augustine, Søren Kierkegaard, and Jacques Derrida, and his willingness to translate theory with an eye toward the church has offered emergents (and others) life-giving water. In *What Would Jesus Deconstruct: The Good News of Postmodernism for the Church,* Caputo follows the image of Christianity as being "on the way" with a postmodern look at Charles Sheldon's famous book *In His Steps* (from which came the oft-quoted question, "What Would Jesus Do?"). He ventures the thought that "to be 'religious' in its deepest sense is to be a searcher, living in search of something, as opposed to being satisfied with the reality that sits under our noses, content with the present."[18]

Emergents have an idea of where they came from; they just aren't sure where they are going. This can lead to mixed reviews in emerging settings. Some emerging pastors, to recall Driscoll's words, assume those on journeys such as these have "totally gotten off the highway and are lost out in the woods."[19] And this may very well be the case. However, many emergents in lane four don't think that being "lost" is such a bad thing, and they are offended at the connotations of such a statement. It may require a bit of (Kierkegaardian) fear and trembling, but, from their perspective, being "lost" is precisely what opens the door to faith. As Caputo puts it, "Jesus is not the way unless you are lost, even as Jesus is not the answer unless you have a question." In a "dose of postmodern truth" that will send his "friends on the Right rushing for the doors," Caputo asks the question, "Are we not all a little 'lost,' like the people who crash-landed on that island in [the television show] *Lost,* looking for clues about where they are and frightened by the mysterious things going on around them? Is not that a figure of our lives? Are we not like people following an obscure clue, on the tracks, on the trail, in the trace of something-we-are-not-sure-what?"[20]

From a postmodern perspective, one of the challenges of faith lies in wrestling with a sense of uncertainty and recognizing that such doubts don't have to be viewed strictly as vices. As we come out of the modern era, in which truth was domesticated to incontrovertible Answers and Principles that could be empirically verified, postmoderns are trying to find a way to frame faith that is beyond the modern enterprise of "facts" and "proofs." Mark C. Taylor has radicalized this notion with his image of "Mazing Grace," in which

[handwritten margin notes: Mazing Grace ⟷ Labyrinth / wandering / unsure what direction to go / fixed entry, fixed destination]

those in the postmodern situation don't necessarily move from one fixed point of reference to another, but rather can be likened to those wandering (erring) in a maze, and they aren't sure which direction to go.[21] For Taylor, the point is not in returning to a mythic past or arriving at a certain destination. His image of "mazing grace" can be contrasted to a labyrinth, in which there is a fixed entry point and a fixed destination.

To be sure, many emergents (and progressives!) prefer the image of the labyrinth, for it offers a bit more solace than the rugged postmodernism offered by Taylor. Regardless, both images imply the sense of wandering that emergents and progressives are drawn to. On one hand, such wandering can feel threatening and daunting. But in returning to Caputo's appropriation of Kierkegaard and Derrida, we are reminded that wandering is also what opens the door to faith. Caputo speaks of the way that all of us wish to know the Truth and speak the truth, but we must admit that when it gets down to it, none of us can claim access to the Truth in any unshakeable, definitive way. We are not hardwired to some "spiritual global positioning system" that pre-programs our journey. What we do have to go on, he posits, are the several faiths shaped by centuries of experience, each of which carries great theological, liturgical, and ethical practices and traditions.[22] Emergents tend to recognize that if we have all of the Answers, then we are not acting on faith, but on knowledge, and we might as well just set ourselves on auto-pilot and await our destination. To draw on Caputo's imagery, we would be knowers (Gnostics) who have taken ourselves out of the game, like vacationers eager for an adventure, a journey into the unknown — but not without "an air-conditioned Hummer with four-wheel drive, an experienced guide, and reservations at a five-star hotel."[23]

Peter Rollins has noted the ways that the influence of modernism has led churches of all stripes to place primary attention on the destination: one *becomes* a Christian, *joins* a church, and *is* saved. This

has certainly been the case in most established churches, both evangelical and mainline. However, he says, those within emergent circles
are more interested in *becoming* Christian, *becoming* Church, and
being saved.[24] Therefore, it doesn't come as a surprise that emergents
appreciate the response attributed to Kierkegaard who, when asked
whether or not he was a Christian, was prone to say, "I'm trying
to become one every day." It's not a one-time affair, but a continual
work in progress. As Maya Angelou once said, "I'm always amazed
when somebody says, I'm a Christian. I think, already? You've got it
already? Trying to be a Christian is like trying to be a Muslim or a
Buddhist or a Shintoist: it's not something that you achieve and then
you sit back and say, now I've got it. I'm trying to be a Christian in
every moment."[25]

From *Archē* to archive

Postmodern approaches to faith have also significantly influenced the
ways in which emergents approach the Bible as a whole. One of
my favorite scenes from the stateside version of *The Office* is when
Michael and Dwight are driving a rental car with a GPS system.
They aren't sure where they are going, so they plug the exact coordinates into the system and trust the computer's lead. While they are
wandering in the middle of nowhere, the simulated computer voice
says, "Make a right turn." Michael and Dwight begin arguing over
whether or not the computer means to turn right then and there or
veer right on the upcoming highway. So at this crucial point in the
journey, in a moment of frantic decision making, Michael turns right
onto the gravel road and promptly drives the car into a pond.

Many contemporary appropriations of scripture are similar to this
scene. As mentioned previously, the journey of life leads to a desire
for certainty, especially when it feels like one is lost, wandering in the

middle of nowhere. Those who aren't comfortable with such wandering often point to the Bible as the tool which provides them with the certainty they so desire. It is thought that the Bible can serve as a certain GPS system that stands the test of time. If a person has a question, they can use the Bible like an encyclopedia in order to find the right answer. The questions can range from whether or not it's okay to break the speed limit or drink a glass of wine or even invade a sovereign country. Whatever the question, the Bible, like an encyclopedia, contains every answer to every possible question — as long as one knows how to properly interpret (that is, decode) its "true" meaning. From this perspective, human beings can uncover the "real" meaning of scripture and then plug in the proper coordinates for their daily lives. As Doug Pagitt explains, this approach has maintained that "inside of all that narrative, behind all the context and culture, [is] a nugget of truth." It is the reader's responsibility, he says, "to find that timeless piece of wisdom, that universally applicable principle, and drop it into the situation at hand." If readers want to really dig into the truth hidden in the words and sentences of scripture, Pagitt says, they can learn to decode the secret languages — Hebrew, Greek, Aramaic — that hold "the real key to the mysteries of the Bible."[26]

Of course, this is where readers run into the same kinds of problems that Michael and Dwight ran into. At some point along the way, we realize that the Bible — like their GPS system — demands decision making that is not based upon a surplus of knowledge, but still yet a lack of knowledge. While the GPS system gives the impression of rock-solid certainty, one is still left to interpret its precise directions. In the same way that the GPS system doesn't anticipate each and every turn (the map is not the territory), the Bible doesn't anticipate each and every question we bring to it. Plus, even topics that are covered in the Bible — slavery or war or divorce, for instance — still require our own finite interpretations. "What exactly qualifies as honoring thy father and mother?" Tom Cathcart and Daniel Klein playfully ask. "A Mother's Day card? Marrying the boring son of the family dentist, as thy honorable mother and father want you to do?"[27]

Postmodern thought emphasizes the way that all of our knowledge is filtered through particular interpretive lenses. When Nietzsche said "there are no absolute truths, only interpretations," he too was making an interpretation.[28] As Gianni Vattimo writes, *"There is no experience of truth that is not interpretative. I do not know anything that does not interest me. If it does interest me, it is evident that I do not look at it in a noninterested way."*[29] All of that may sound rather abstract, but Pagitt highlights the ways this plays out on the ground by looking at the way modern Christians have approached some of the most controversial elements within scripture:

> I struggle with the Bible as a weapon, the Bible as an encyclopedia.... I know this is going to raise some hackles, but I think there are people who argue for an "inerrant" authoritative understanding of the Bible to support their prejudiced feelings about homosexuals. I know they would deny it, and they have done so to me many times.... It just seems so odd that their beliefs on other biblical topics are not so pronounced. I have rarely had a conversation about the ills of gossip based on the authority of the Bible. I've had even fewer conversations in which people suggest the church should be actively working to eliminate obesity as a form of gluttony because the Bible clearly condemns it.... And despite the Bible's deep and continual concern for the poor, I rarely have conversations in which people use the authority of the Bible to make a case for economic justice. But on the issue of homosexuality, something strange happens. If the subject at hand is the authority of the Bible, someone invariably asks what I think about homosexuality. If the subject is homosexuality, someone invariably asks what I think about the authority of the

Bible. There must be some connection. It makes me wonder if people would argue about the authority of the Bible if it had nothing to say about homosexuality."[30]

Numerous interpretive variables are at work when any person approaches the Bible. Christians who want the Bible to speak absolutely and universally for all time are left to determine who has the "right" interpretation. The question is not whether the Bible can be trusted, but rather whose interpretation can be trusted. While the Bible is supposed to give the definitive answer, we see that decision making still abounds, and the much desired certainty once again gives way to ambiguity. This approach to scripture thinks that it is possible to find the original (*archē*) meaning of the text and then apply it to each and every situation, absolutely and universally.

However, as Pagitt has expressed, emergents are hardly comfortable with this perspective. Like progressives, emergents highlight the contextual nature of scripture. Rather than viewing the Bible as a divinely authored document neatly sent down from heaven, emergents recognize that Christian scripture represents a diverse number of interpretations about God, religion, life, faith, ethics, and so on. From this perspective, the Bible contains an archive of interpretations about God (and in response to God), but shouldn't be confused with the voice of God. After all, when believers are convinced they have God contained in a book, they have once again found themselves content with an idol that passes for God. This is what mainline theologian Douglas John Hall has repeatedly called "bibliodolatry,"[31] and here the United Church of Christ's slogan that reminds us "God is still speaking!" becomes particularly apropos. As John Caputo observes, "The New Testament is an archive, not the *archē*, and to mix up the two, as the fundamentalists do, is to make an idol out of an icon."[32] When asked to defend this approach, Caputo not only draws on Derrida's distinction between *archē* and archive,[33] but also on feminist theologian Elisabeth Schüssler Fiorenza's distinction between viewing the Bible as a "timeless archetype" or as a historical "prototype."[34] Schüssler Fiorenza's work is, of course, a staple in mainline seminaries, and this general approach is widely valued by progressive voices across the board.[35]

Emergents, like progressives, are hesitant to embrace the Bible as God's infallible, inerrant, literal word. Instead, they view Christian scripture as an invitation to enter into an ancient conversation that continues to this day, stepping into the stories "not as observers, but as participants in the faith that is alive and well and still to be created."[36] Here again we see the emergent interest of interpreting Christian faith through the lens of narrative theology.

Within the United States, perspectives on biblical literalism have significantly shifted over the past forty years. According to a Gallup Poll taken in 1963, 65 percent of respondents agreed with a statement affirming biblical literalism: "The Bible is the actual word of God and is to be taken literally, word for word." However, in 2001, this figure had dropped to 27 percent.[37] The question becomes, Which communities of faith can respond to those who are changing the way they view the Bible? Perhaps progressive communities of faith were born into the world for such a time as this.

One of my professors from seminary is a highly sought-after speaker for conferences and conventions throughout the United States. He often talks about the way the Bible should be taken seriously, but not always literally. He points out that there are actually two creation stories in Genesis, and neither offers a scientific account of the origins of the cosmos. He shows how the Bible has been written in specific contexts that sometimes reflect the biases and prejudices of its respective authors. He compares what a given text likely meant to its original listeners, as well as the way in which it's been interpreted through the centuries. He also tries to assure listeners that approaching the Bible from a contextual, historical, and metaphorical perspective isn't done in order to destroy the value and meaning of the Bible, but in order to help the Bible come alive in ways in which its truth isn't confined to literal-factual accounts of what "really happened" (which of course represents a modernist convention anyhow).

At each of his speaking engagements, he always offers a time for questions and answers. Invariably, he says, there is always someone who asks something to the effect of, "How can you call yourself a Christian?" His approach is threatening to their faith, and they are afraid that if they doubt one thing or ask one question, then their whole house of cards will come falling down. But time and again — even though there are always a handful of people who wish to throw stones at him — lines will form at the conclusion of the conference and people will come up to him and quietly say things like, "Thank you, thank you, thank you. I didn't know I was allowed to believe these things. Thank you, thank you, thank you."

Where are the churches that will connect with those who have felt alienated by the most conventional — though not necessarily the most traditional — approaches to the Bible and Christian theology? Where are the churches that will offer an alternative for progressives and emergents who don't wish to discard their faith, but are looking for new ways of cultivating it?

Chapter Six

EXTRAVAGANT HOSPITALITY

So if it seems to you that you have understood the divine scriptures, or any part of them, in such a way that by this understanding you do not build up this twin love of God and neighbor, then you have not yet understood them. —St. Augustine[1]

Every time Jesus eats, he seems to be eating with the wrong people, at the wrong table, or saying the wrong things, or not washing his hands ahead of time. By doing so, Jesus redid the social order and this upset both church and state. That we would forget such a message and make the Eucharist itself some kind of measuring of worthiness is pretty much turning Jesus' teaching absolutely on its head. —Richard Rohr[2]

MISTY'S STORY

One of the most prominent ways emergents reflect progressive approaches to Christianity is in their desire to be places of intentional hospitality and welcome. In the course of writing this book, we were given the privilege of hearing several different stories of faith. Perhaps none was more moving than the one shared by a graduate student from the Midwest. The following is her story in her own words, unedited by us.

121

"Where do I start? I was four when my family first started attending church. It was a small independent charismatic church. I can't really remember what it was like not to go to church as a kid. For the most part I enjoyed being with everyone on Sundays and Wednesdays. I am kind of a shy person so being around people was a nice change. I played the game quite nicely. I learned that at church people would like me more if I said or did certain things and didn't do others. I became the perfect youth. The one the parents wanted their kids to be. I did well in school, I went to church every week, I didn't get into any type of trouble. The only problem was that I was miserable inside. Years of trying to live up to other people's standards for my life had taken its toll.

"When I was in high school I became very depressed. I began to cut myself and think about what it would be like to just not wake up in the morning. No one ever really took notice, and to me the depression just became another means of beating myself up. In addition, it was around this time that I began to question my sexuality. This just became another aspect of my life that I had to hide. I sat through many sermons telling me how horrible homosexuality was, how no one could be gay and go to heaven. My response to this was to overcompensate. I became super Christian.

"Over the next few years, I decided to become a missionary; I went through the process of becoming an ordained minister and was pursuing my undergrad degree in languages so that I could teach English in Africa. It was around this time that my best friend came out to me. I lived in a fairly conservative city so this was the first real experience I had with someone telling me he was gay. He wasn't a Christian nor did he claim to be, but the conversation I had with him that night shook up my life. Here was this man that I have known for as long as I can remember. We have been through a lot together. I can say that I truly love him. That night, I realized that him telling me he was gay didn't change how I felt about him. For the first time homosexuality became human. It wasn't a huge evil sin. It was something that described my best friend.

"I did go to Africa, but my heart wasn't in it. I came back home defeated. I was depressed and miserable. I didn't know what do with my life. I felt like a failure. More importantly I felt as if God had forgotten me. I felt that because I struggled because I was beginning to think differently from other people that went to my church that I was wrong. I could only think in terms of right and wrong, black and white, and if those at my church were right then I was terribly wrong. I began searching for a way to escape. That escape came in the form of a job in China. For a year I taught social studies at an international school. I found out, however, that my problems wouldn't go away simply by leaving the country. My problems were with me.

"My last month in China, I attempted suicide. I didn't want to live anymore. I was tired of always feeling guilty, always thinking that there was something wrong with me. I came home a month later. Only a couple of people knew what had happened, and that was the way I kept it. But there was something different. I was now committed to my life. I began to seek therapy and began the process of learning to accept myself for the person God created. I haven't determined my sexuality; I am still questioning. But whatever it is, I believe I will be okay with it.

"The last year and a half has been one of the most difficult and most rewarding of my life. I have had to make some tough choices in my life. I decided to leave the church I was raised in, and I decided to go back to school to pursue what I always wanted to do: a career in law. Those were both huge steps in my life. I still have a long way to go, but at least now I am willing to take this journey."[3]

Cultivating unambiguous inclusion

According to Tony Jones, some of the most common words emergents use to describe their communities of faith include "open," "nonjudgmental," and "inclusive."[4] One is reminded of the popular tagline that follows the wonderful commercials of the United Church of Christ: "No matter who you are or where you are on life's journey, you are welcome here."[5] The focus of connecting with those who have felt left out — and letting them know that other options are available — runs through the veins of Jesus' ministry, the emergent church, and progressive theological traditions. It is what Presbyterian pastor Carol Howard Merritt has called cultivating unambiguous inclusion.

Like mainline theologian Douglas John Hall, emergents confess that their faith in Jesus makes them more inclusive of others, rather than less. While this shift can hardly be relegated to just two aspects of emerging Christianity, it is especially seen in the ways that emergents approach (1) conversations in relationship to the affirmation of those within the GLBTQ community and (2) questions of religious diversity. When A House for All Sinners and Saints describes itself as "a group of folks figuring out how to be a liturgical, Christo-centric, social justice oriented, queer inclusive, incarnational, contemplative, irreverent, ancient-future church with a progressive but deeply rooted theological imagination,"[6] they tend to be representative of emergents in general.

One of the distinctive aspects of the Awakening is its welcome, which remains the same every week. By conveying a sense of hospitality that is at the heart of progressive and emergent approaches to faith, the welcome is by far the most meaningful aspect of the liturgy for virtually all of the participants. It simply reads:

We come from many different paths to gather here,
for wide is God's welcome, and you are welcome here:

If you are young or old, you are welcome

If you have brown skin, black skin, white skin, yellow skin,
or red skin, you are welcome

If you are married or single, you are welcome

If you are sick or well, you are welcome

If you are gay or straight, you are welcome

If you cannot hear or see, you are welcome

If you are a man or a woman, you are welcome

If you are happy or sad, you are welcome

If you are rich or poor, powerful or weak, you are welcome

If you believe in God some of the time or none of the time
or all of the time, you are welcome....

So come, let us stand and worship our welcoming God.[7]

In the words of one evangelical college student from the Awakening who now attends a mainline seminary on the East Coast: "When I sat down in the sanctuary and heard the welcome for the first time, I immediately knew I had found my new church."

When you pay attention to the most popular phrases in emergent circles, you will soon hear about a desire for participants in emergent collectives to "belong before believing." From this perspective, hospitality, community, and welcome precede affirmations of faith. This is one of the most controversial aspects of the emerging church, and it certainly stands in the face of traditional approaches to Christianity in which certain beliefs are necessary before one can be an official member of the community.

Though emergents may be accused of throwing orthodoxies (right beliefs) out the window, they haven't come to these convictions lightly. First of all, they contend, Jesus welcomed those who had a wide variety of beliefs and backgrounds, going so far as to place reconciliation above sacrificial expressions of worship.[8] From this perspective, emergents reflect the thought of progressive theologians like Carter Heyward, who continually remind us that right relationships are more important than right beliefs. As Emergent Village's Values and Practices succinctly state, "We firmly hold that living in reconciled friendship trumps traditional orthodoxies — indeed, orthodoxy requires reconciliation as a prerequisite."[9]

Second (as we discussed in chapter 5), emergents tend to emphasize the inherent limitations of historic doctrines and creeds. Even though they view them as beautiful affirmations of faith, they also recognize that such expressions necessarily reflect particular social locations and historical contexts. As such, emergents don't wish to confuse them with Absolute Affirmations of Universal Truth.

As reflected in Misty's story, emergents often come from communities of faith that have largely been exclusive of those who don't fit a particular mold, and those still holding on to the faith wish to chart a new direction that doesn't reflect what they view as the prejudices of contemporary society (especially in the United States). In *They Love Jesus but Not the Church*, Dan Kimball has documented six reasons that emerging generations are highly suspect of the church, and four of the six are directly related to matters of hospitality. In addition to believing that the church "arrogantly claims all other religions are wrong," emerging generations describe the church as "judgmental and negative," "homophobic," and "dominated by males and oppressive of females."[10] They are longing for a more inclusive approach to Christianity than the one they've found in most of the churches they are familiar with, and they believe cultivating such approaches aren't unfaithful to their interpretations of the message of Christ, but are *faithful* responses to it.

Carol Howard Merritt has noted that when the church fights over whether or not to accept gay and lesbian people into the church, churches often think they're fighting over a relatively small percentage of the population. In actuality, however, they're deciding whether or not they'll dismiss the roughly 72 percent of younger generations in the United States who no longer deem homophobia an acceptable form of prejudice. "The majority of young adults in our country," Merritt writes, "embrace a variety of cultures and religions, and they know that faithful, loving relationships can grow up between two adults of the same sex. They see their duty as spiritual people as being to treat others as they would like to be treated, and that means that they don't tolerate intolerance."[11]

In the words of the Rev. John Gage (United Church on the Green, New Haven, Connecticut), "Gays and lesbians have been rejected by the church time and time again, and if we want to minister to our whole community, we need to confirm our stance as clearly as possible. We have to welcome them time and time again."[12] Explicitly and unambiguously.

When it comes to the affirmation of gay and lesbian people within the church, we recognize that there is still significant disagreement that is shared among faithful Christians, both mainline and otherwise. From time to time, we experience this tension in our own congregation. Many within the first three lanes of the emerging conversation feel conflicted regarding this matter, and several emergents and progressives have been branded as heretics for choosing to be open and affirming. Emergents and progressives are often labeled as unbiblical and heretical, but perhaps the following discourse can highlight some of the complexities and nuances involved in the conversation.

WRESTLING WITH SCRIPTURE

When it comes to cultivating communities of unambiguous inclusion, there is a wide range of perspectives among faithful Christians from all four lanes of the emerging and emergent movement, as well as mainliners, Catholics, and others. No topic is more divisive and none harbors more potential for discord. We can readily see this in the Episcopal Church, which is currently going through the painful struggles that became especially prominent since the 2004 installment of Gene Robinson (an openly gay man) as bishop of the diocese of New Hampshire. The fallout has been so strong that Rowan Williams, the head of the worldwide Anglican-Episcopalian church, now views his job not as trying to get everyone to agree, but rather to keep everyone in the same room so that a conversation can at least be had.

The questions are not just about whether or not gay men and lesbian women should be ordained as ministers, installed as bishops, or, in some cases, whether they should even be allowed membership in a church. Even more basic are questions whether same sex relationships are even permissible by biblical standards. Should communities of faith be welcoming but not accepting? accepting but not affirming? Is it possible to welcome while at the same time exclude or condemn, as in the well-intentioned but hurtful phrase "love the sinner but hate the sin"? Faithful Christians from a variety of perspectives sincerely wrestle with such questions.

While the implications of these questions are usually guised within the context of the church, let us not forget that the major impact of these dynamics play out much closer to home — in our families and in our friendships. Disagreements may abound in the church, but the same differences of opinion that threaten churches are threatening to divide families as well.

Within the Bible, there are at most eight references to what our culture might refer to as homosexuality, and only five to be sure, and none at any extended length.[13] But even more difficult than having so few biblical references is the recognition that same-sex activity referred to in the Bible does not refer to what we generally mean today when we talk about many of the relationships that are shared between two people of the same gender. There were certainly sexual activities that took place among men or women of the same gender back then, but there wasn't an understanding of what we would today call an "orientation."

Scholars tell us that in the Hebrew Bible, primarily Leviticus, such behavior was condemned for a handful of reasons that were particular to the context of ancient Israel, especially in relationship to the Holiness code.[14] Some of the most significant concerns were related to fertility and population, as well as the maintenance of gender superiority. The Israelites needed to be strong in number in order to fend off their enemies, so many of the codes in the Hebrew Bible were intended to increase the Israelite population as rapidly as possible through as many births as possible. As a result, it was strictly forbidden for men to "waste" opportunities of fertilization in any way whatsoever. Sexual activity was intended to be used with wives who could give birth to as many children as possible as quickly as possible, thus increasing the population and hence the strength of the Israelite defenses. But today, we live in a world where overpopulation is the concern, not underpopulation. Such reasons don't seem to make sense in today's culture.

Another reason sexual activities among those of the same gender were prohibited in the book of Leviticus had to do with ritual impurity, much in the same way that having relations with a woman during her menstrual cycle deemed one ritually "unclean." The struggle here, as has often been noted, is that there are many Levitical cleanliness laws we've thrown out. For instance, most of us don't mind wearing two kinds of fabric sown into one garment, we love eating barbecued pork, and millions love watching Sunday afternoon football while person after person handles a dead pigskin — a true Levitical taboo. Such a lack of consistency makes it difficult to justify our reasons for condemning one thing as taboo while ignoring other taboos that lie side by side in the text.

Things get even murkier when we turn our attention to Christian scripture. In ancient Greco-Roman societies — the context in which

St. Paul was situated — same-sex activity was quite common. Often, as a rite of passage, adolescent boys were subjected as passive partners to older men of power and prestige. The older men would display their power by relegating these adolescent boys to the passive role of women — further establishing the patriarchies of Greco-Roman culture. When the boy became an adult, he would switch roles, and then he would marry a woman and have children. This practice was so common that the legendary Greek philosopher Plato took all of this for granted and praised the virtues of courage and honor that resulted from such relationships. And while these practices were common, they are once again in stark contrast to the kinds of relationships that are shared today among mutually consenting adults, so we're left wondering. The late Presbyterian scholar William Placher takes into consideration St. Paul's writings and says that

> ... though some scholars argue the point, [it seems] fairly clear that Paul considered these practices sinful. Some Christians conclude that that settles the matter [while] others feel that Paul simply reflected the prejudices of a Jew who had come into contact with [Greco-Roman] culture.... Paul condemned what he saw ... [but] we are not sure why Paul condemned what he saw. Would he have felt differently if everyone involved had been an adult? If the relation had been understood as between equals? ... Such questions have no obvious answer.[15]

One thing Paul does say is that such activity is unnatural — that it goes against the created order — and this is one of the strongest arguments that is still made today, especially in relationship to the first chapter of Romans. But appealing to natural law is a dangerous path to tread. After all, Paul's writings have also been used to argue that slavery and patriarchal structures are natural. As John Caputo comments, "Natural law *theory* is notorious for serving the interests of the natural law *theorists,* for starting with a conclusion and then working back to the idea of 'nature' that provides them with a suitable cover.... The word 'natural,' like the question 'What would Jesus do?' often functions as a club to pound what is different, to smash anything that falls outside the tolerances of the powers that be or the historical prejudices of the day."[16]

In the cases of slavery and patriarchy, it's quite convenient for men who already have the power to define what nature means, isn't it? And when it comes to such situations today, don't we gladly admit that Paul reflected an ancient bias that no longer holds? All of which raises the unavoidable question: If Paul got the "natural law" wrong when it came to slavery and women, who's to say he got it right when it comes to homosexuality? Critics often object at this point and say that the only way to populate the species is intercourse between a man and a woman, so the natural law is clear. But if the only purpose for sexual activity is the procreation of the human race, should we then condemn sexual activity between married senior citizens or younger couples who are infertile?

Furthermore, those who criticize Christians for affirming gay men and lesbian women often remark that such an emphasis is an accommodation to culture. But many emergents and progressives emphasize precisely the opposite. When it comes to biblical interpretation, Placher states:

There is something very wrong in current attitudes in many churches, where condemning homosexuality appears to be the most important of all ethical topics.... Any honest reading of the Bible will make clear that it takes sins like greed, hatred, and lack of compassion much more seriously than [it takes homosexuality].... If a denomination singles out [gay men and lesbian women] for judgment ... but doesn't speak and act forcefully on other matters where the Bible is far more forceful, it looks as though its motive is not faithfulness to Scripture, but accepting the prejudices of contemporary society. In such cases, while Christians may claim to stand up against the values of our culture, in fact they are yielding to them.... As I write this, the top-selling album in the country, by a young white rapper named Eminem, includes songs that talk vividly about beating up and killing those who are gay. An [edited] version of the album for sale in chain stores... has the worst of its profanity eliminated, but leaves these references to violence unchanged.[17]

While several nuances remain, Caputo has summarized his perspective in a way that resonates with a high number of emergents and progressives who wish to cultivate communities of unambiguous inclusion. Again, contrary to prevailing assumptions, these perspectives aren't grounded in some sort of unbiblical accommodation to culture, but rather in what emergents and progressives view as the heart of the biblical message:

My own view is that the outcome of a careful debate about these matters would be to show that there simply are no arguments to show that homosexual love is of itself anything else than love, and that therefore, since the essence of the Torah is love, it hardly falls afoul of the law. To be sure, when it is not love, when it is promiscuity, or infidelity to a sworn partner, or rape, or the sexual abuse of minors, or in any way violent, then it is indeed not love, but that is no less true of heterosexuality.[18]

One of the emergents who attends the Awakening reflects on the way that he has changed his mind on this matter. He relates his struggle of accepting his friends who are gay and lesbian to a scene out of Mark Twain's novel *Adventures of Huckleberry Finn,* in which Huck went back and forth wondering what to do about his friend Jim, a slave who Huck helped escape. Huck knew it was his responsibility to return Jim to his owner.

Therefore, Huck also knew he was going against what he had been taught. He said that "the plain hand of Providence [was] slapping me in the face, letting me know my wickedness was being watched from up there in heaven." He recalled the Sunday School class where he learned that people who treat slaves the way he's treating Jim "goes to everlasting fire."

So out of fear, in order to do the "right thing and the clean thing," Huck wrote a letter to Jim's owner, telling her where she could pick Jim up. Huck said that after writing the letter he "felt good and all washed clean of sin for the first time, and I knowed I could pray now. I was thinking how good it was all this happened so, and how near I come to being lost and going to hell. . . . But then I went on thinking. And got to thinking about our trip down the river; and I see my friend Jim before me, all the time . . . and somehow I couldn't seem to strike no places to harden me against him."

Huck thought about his friendship with Jim, and he thought about the letter he was supposed to send to Jim's owner. He went back and forth, back and forth, wondering what to do. Then Huck took the letter and held it in his hand. "I was atrembling, because I'd got to decide, for ever, betwixt two things, and I knowed it. I studied a minute, sort of holding my breath, and then says to myself: 'All right, then, I'll go to hell' — and I tore up [that letter because I couldn't betray my friend]."[19]

EMBRACING DIVERSITY

Though emergent approaches to religious diversity are still controversial in some lanes of the emerging conversation, they are much less of a lightning-rod than conversations on sexuality. Brian McLaren echoes the thought of mainline theologians like Douglas John Hall by stating that because he follows Jesus, he is "bound to Jews, Muslims,

Buddhists, Hindus, agnostics, atheists, New Agers, everyone."[20] Similar to the South African concept of "Ubuntu," in which none of us are complete unless all of us are complete, or to Martin Luther King Jr.'s emphasis on the inescapable web of mutuality in which injustice anywhere is a threat to justice everywhere, McLaren emphasizes that his Christian faith leads him to recognize a shared world that demands that those from many faiths (and no faiths) work together in its healing.[21]

McLaren has consistently recognized that highly individualistic expressions of modern Christianity diminish possibilities for embracing diversity, for they are primarily concerned with looking out for one's self, no matter what happens to others. He locates this dynamic — among other places — in popular songs used in worship: "Too many of our lyrics are embarrassingly personalistic, about Jesus and me," he writes. "If an extraterrestrial outsider from Mars were to observe us, I think he would say either (a) that these people are all mildly dysfunctional and need a lot of hug therapy (which is ironic, because they are among the most affluent in the world, having been blessed in every way more than any group in history), or (b) that they don't give a rip about the rest of the world, that their religion/spirituality makes them as selfish as any non-Christian."[22]

Emergent approaches recognize that the individualism that pervades North American culture greatly inhibits God's work being done in this world, and their faith in Christ challenges them to reconsider such perspectives. They are trying to make moves toward hospitality and welcome, but this doesn't come easily, especially for those from Eurocentric "privileged" classes. In most of Christian history, efforts have been made to colonize and convert, sometimes because of fear of that which is different, and other times for political or material gain. As a result, emergents and progressives are trying to cultivate communities in which differences are honored and respected, as opposed to being merely tolerated. Hall reminds us that the biblical exhortation of hospitality is not to "smother others," but to "welcome others." All of which means, among other things, "Let them be themselves!"[23] Emergents and progressives prefer the image of a salad bowl over that of a melting pot.

Critics of emergents and progressives will say that such notions smack of relativism. As a result, they are often accused of not taking ethics very seriously. Strikingly, however, an emergent approach to ethics isn't all that different from Christian traditions that have come before. Instead of drawing up grand metaphysical absolutes, they prefer focusing on what Gianni Vattimo refers to as the oldest and most orthodox way of approaching Christian ethics: namely, that of love. "If you read the gospels or the fathers of the church carefully, at the end, the only virtue left is always that of charity. From Saint Paul we learn that the three greatest virtues are faith, hope, and love, 'but the greatest of these is love.' Even faith and hope will end at one point or another. As Saint Augustine instructs, 'Love and do what you want.'"[24]

From this perspective, the "truth" of love cannot be contained to any metaphysical system, no matter how much modern Christians wish to fall back on one. This is the beauty of its excess. To paraphrase St. Augustine, "If love is the measure, the only measure of love is love without measure." It's no wonder that our good friend and colleague Jon Bormann (First Christian Church, Petersburg, Illinois, and First Christian Church, Tallula, Illinois) often ends his sermons by saying, "Christ doesn't call us to be right. Christ calls us to be faithful."

As emergents and progressives strive to cultivate unambiguous inclusion, it is their faith in Christ that makes them more inclusive of others, not less.

Part Three

Emerging Worship

Chapter Seven

WHY EMERGING WORSHIP IS
GOOD NEWS FOR PROGRESSIVE
COMMUNITIES OF FAITH

Despite all the talk about worship styles in the emergent church — the return of the ancient Celtic prayers; the grungy music; the dialogical sermons — it's really the theology under- neath the styles that is most important. —Tony Jones[1]

There is no prescription — there is no one model.
—Martha Grace-Reese[2]

EMERGING WORSHIP POINTS TO THE QUESTION,
NOT THE ANSWER

Throughout the course of the so-called worship wars — those that have dominated conversations on worship for the past two decades — congregation after congregation has fallen for the myth that says the key to connecting with younger generations through the act of worship is based solely on the implementation of a specific style. While churches have been busy asking whether they should go with a traditional, contemporary, or blended style of worship, emerging movements have come along challenging churches to reframe the whole way in which worship is cultivated and planned. Emerging forms of worship are much more concerned with grounding worship experiences that reflect specific contexts and theological convictions than they are with any specific style. This is good news for progressive communities of faith.[3]

For the better part of twenty-five years, thousands of church leaders have flocked to worship seminars led by church growth gurus who promote particular styles of worship. The emphasis has usually been on contemporary implementations of music, drama, media, preaching, and the like. These kinds of seminars often address questions like: "How do church leaders put together a dynamic praise band?" "How can your congregation make drama even more effective than traditional preaching?" "What kind of lighting or media is needed to communicate the gospel most effectively?"

In the midst of all these discussions are the tired arguments that pit "old hymns" versus "praise and worship" choruses, and these infamous worship wars have led to the pervasive myth that says if you want to connect with postmodern generations, you need to decide whether to replace the organ with a rock band or hymnals with screens.

Now, as the face of postmodern worship increasingly turns toward emerging models, more and more mainline congregations are trying to get their hands on an alternative worship "starter kit with candles, a glue on goatee, and an icon for $49.99 that is guaranteed to attract young adults."[4] In their hurried effort to connect with younger generations, all too many mainline congregations worry more about being trendy and fashionable than on articulating their deepest theological convictions. It's as if established congregations believe it possible to find a magical formula — be it contemporary, emerging, postmodern, alternative (or whatever other happening description you want to give it) — that automatically appeals to emerging generations. When this is the case, church leaders operate as if the answer to their worship woes lies in securing state-of-the-art screens, creating flashy videos, or hiring a musician who also, quite conveniently, has a nose ring which all of the students think is cool.

But such an approach trivializes the deeper theological hunger emergents and progressives bring to the table by turning worship into a game of smoke and mirrors that has more to do with superficial preferences than deeply seated convictions. While emergents are shouting from the rooftops (via blogs, artwork, collectives, etc.) for their theological convictions to be taken seriously, established congregations of all stripes and sizes have been scrambling to figure out what gimmick will next lure younger generations into the church.

I'm reminded of Pastor Skip from the film *Saved*. As the forty-something principal of American Eagle Christian High School, Pastor Skip went to great lengths developing a sense of style and personality that he hoped would make him appear hip in the eyes of his students. He made such drastic efforts to learn the pop-lingo his students were using that during daily chapel services at American Eagle High his favorite call to worship was "Let's get our Christ on, let's kick it Jesus-style!" When he wanted to converse with students, he'd say things like, "I know that she's a part of your posse" or "I was thinking of something a little less gangsta."

Pastor Skip's over-the-top quest to be cool led him to substitute a canned style for a lived authenticity, and the students could see through it in a heartbeat. Underneath all his superficial veneer, Pastor Skip — like several students at American Eagle High — was a much more complicated, broken character that struggled getting past the surface level. Similarly, many congregations — including mainline progressive ones — who have wanted to connect with emerging generations have focused more on style than on substance, and as a result they have offered worship services focused much more on what they believe is fashionable than on what is authentic to their deepest theological convictions. As a result, they, like Pastor Skip, have struggled getting past the surface level.

Considering this
opening
at Lent 2011

Not long ago, I was asked to speak at an informal worship service at a local university sponsored by a mainline campus ministry. The group — which had attracted several emergents — was excited about the progressive "Living the Questions" spiritual formation curriculum they had studied over the past semester, and they prided themselves on being a progressive alternative to the dominant Bible Belt voices that were so prevalent in their area. Even though the students gathered for worship were those who valued inclusivity and diversity, the leadership team picked out praise songs that set up very strong "us vs. them" polarities. Much of the contemporary music was catchy, but the lyrics conveyed a message that was far from consistent with the vision, mission, and purpose of this particular campus ministry. Whether or not participants are consciously aware of it, such expressions of worship leave emergents and progressives feeling confused as to their mission and identity, and they wonder why it's so difficult to find a worship service that resonates with their deepest theological convictions.

A friend of mine recently called to vent. She works as the associate minister at First Christian Church, a downtown congregation that used to be the largest mainline church in its city. Members of First Christian are proud to have been on the frontlines of the civil rights movement of the 1960s and to have been charter members of the community's interfaith network. To this day, they have continued to be a consistent advocate for the oppressed and marginalized.

Despite this rich history, First Christian now struggles to hit the two-hundred mark in worship on Sundays. Like many other mainline congregations, most of the people in the pews are over the age of sixty-five. The ministerial team is at a loss, and they simply don't know what step to take next. Several voices from the congregation are urging them to connect with emerging generations simply by adding a contemporary worship service. "It worked for Jones River Fellowship down the road," they say. "I'm sure it will work for us!"

Such a suggestion by these well-intentioned members of First Christian fails to take into consideration at least two things. First of all, contemporary worship doesn't attract emerging generations like it attracted baby boomers, and what worked well for Jones River twenty years ago offers no guarantee of "success" in today's context. (If you start a contemporary worship service in order to connect with postmoderns, more than likely you'll end up connecting with their parents.) But that is hardly what concerns us.

Much more importantly, those from Jones River have a very different theological approach than most of those who sit on the pews of First Christian. As a mainline congregation that values social justice, inclusivity, and peace, First Christian's adaptation of Jones River's resources would fail to connect with the theological approach held dear by many at First Christian. What resonates in one context is hardly a guarantee of what will resonate in another context, and even though most of the contemporary worship resources like the ones used at Jones River are geared toward those with a fairly exclusive approach to Christianity, the desperation and panic felt by many progressive mainline congregations has led them to substitute style for substance time and again. The resulting inauthenticity leads to a lack of passion and connection, and participants within the congregation are left to believe that their deepest theological convictions don't have a place at the table.

It is precisely here that emerging approaches to worship become good news for progressive communities of faith. Because emerging approaches (notice the plural) encourage congregations to dig deeply within their own traditions to develop worship gatherings that are authentic to their theological convictions and their cultural contexts, progressives are freed to embody liturgies that match, rather than detract from, the core theological convictions that define their community of faith. From an emerging perspective, the emphasis is not placed on a particular style inasmuch as it is placed on an authentic ethos that connects with the theological convictions of the worshiping community within a given context. When progressive communities of faith dig deeply into their traditions — instead of trying to find superficial gimmicks that will somehow lure others in — both progressives and emergents are offered the opportunity to encounter expressions of worship that not only resonate with their faith but also help them find fresh ways of cultivating it. These emergences aren't contrived; they are authentic. They aren't manufactured; they are organic. They aren't afraid of their traditions, they embrace them.

To state it most succinctly, emerging forms of worship don't point to the answer as much as they point to the question: Namely, why have progressive mainliners chosen to water down their worship by continually substituting style for substance? In a disappointing irony, mainline congregations wanting to connect with emerging generations have all too often abandoned the very theology that emergents and progressives are longing to see embodied the most. Emergents and progressives wish to drink from deep wells, but superficial concerns regarding style have all too often inhibited them from doing so.

It would be nice to think that emerging worship offers a one-size-fits-all strategy that can be nicely and neatly implemented in a formulaic fashion, but emergent experiences lead one to conclude that liturgies operate on different levels within different contexts. What works really well in one setting, for instance, may not work well when transplanted to another time and place. As creatures of postmodernity, emerging generations have a keen sense that recognizes the ways in which every context is different. Therefore, instead of asking whether or not the particular style should be traditional, contemporary, alternative, or blended, emerging approaches to worship beg us to consider whether or not the liturgy, aesthetics, music, space, message, and so on support and strengthen the theological approach within the cultural context of the gathered community, no matter what the style might be.

With a mainline background in mind, you can almost hear Nadia Bolz-Weber pleading to established congregations: "Please don't try to have your Easter vigil in a Goth club like Church of the Apostles. Please don't try to have a 'Tomb Show' during Lent like Mercy Seat. That would be just as silly as them [starting] a quilting circle because it works in your community." Instead, she says, "Pay attention to the questions that the [Emergent Church] is asking and then ask those same questions in your community. . . . Ask 'is our worship service culturally appropriate to our context?' and 'Does the language we use in our community reflect our core values?' "[5]

The result of asking questions like these gives form to the style and liturgy that shapes a given congregation's worship, whether it be contemporary, traditional, alternative, or emerging, if such a thing even exists.

EMERGING WORSHIP IS BEYOND EITHER/ORS

One of the major concerns prevalent in mainline churches today is that many of its leaders are not even aware that possibilities for worship exist beyond the styles that have generally been referred to as traditional and contemporary. When mainline congregations look at most of the worship planning resources that are available to them, they are led to believe that their choices are limited to the kinds of either/or options that most emergents tend to resist.[6] When a local pastor from a progressive mainline congregation recently stopped by my office, he was disappointed to learn that I didn't have music to a particular song by Amy Grant. He was hoping to use the song in his church's worship service, and he thought that our church (having what he understood to be a "contemporary" worship service) was just sure to have such a piece. It is difficult for mainliners to understand that the word "emerging" is not synonymous with the word "contemporary," and the last thing it should be confused with is a revised or spiced up version of contemporary worship.[7]

Perhaps this is part of the reason why, when mainline leaders are resourcing worship they hope will connect with emerging generations, they are aware only of the standard kinds of praise and worship choruses: those that focus more on "me" than on "we"; those that tend to water down Christianity to nothing more than making sure one is ready for the afterlife (no matter what happens to this world); those that make sure Jesus' way of the cross is understood only as a transaction to be believed in rather than a pattern of life to be followed; those that care much more about one's own personal relationship with Jesus than with one's own personal relationship with the structures of oppression that Jesus critiqued; those that like to keep Jesus crucified so that he isn't able to speak to the injustices so prevalent in our society today. Such approaches hardly reflect the depths of progressive mainline traditions, yet because many congregations remain unaware of faithful possibilities that lie beyond the scope of contemporary worship, many of their best efforts intended to connect with emergents and progressives all too often ring hollow.

One of the hardest questions asked about the Awakening concerns style of worship. We certainly don't want to say it's contemporary, because contemporary worship represents much of what we want to get away from. Part of us wants to tell people that the Awakening is traditional, because, like many other expressions of emerging worship, it actually follows a pattern of traditional liturgy that goes back centuries. Even though the closest representation of the Awakening is probably seen in the aesthetics and structure of the Orthodox church's Divine Liturgy, few people would even begin to associate what they experience at the Awakening as traditional worship, simply because of the typical associations that come up in their mind when the phrase "traditional worship" is used (organ, choir, robes, etc.). At times we've tried referring to the Awakening as "emerging worship" or "alternative worship," but those phrases break down because the very nature of emerging worship recognizes that each gathering is deeply rooted in its own specific context (plus, the words "emerging" and "alternative" are so unfamiliar in general vernacular that people wouldn't know what we mean by them anyhow). So to tell a person that we have an emerging worship service doesn't help move the conversation forward.

All of these responses have prompted too many quizzical looks than we care to remember, so we've found ourselves telling people that the Awakening is much better experienced than described. About the only thing we consistently describe is the theological approach of the Awakening, because our experiences indicate that participants are drawn to it because of its approach to faith more than its approach to worship. Therefore, instead of getting bogged down in stylistic concerns, our website (*www.SpringfieldAwakening.com*) simply describes the Awakening as a "new, emerging worship experience in the Springfield area for those seeking an open and inclusive approach to the Christian faith that values both the mind and the heart. We are committed to social justice, peace, and the welcoming of all people; and these commitments are at the heart of our worship and our community of faith." At the website it is possible to follow several links in order to learn more about the general ethos of the Awakening's style of worship, but style is certainly not the first thing we try to communicate. As we said, the Awakening is much better experienced than described.

When it comes to considering the best ways to connect with emerging generations, Martha Grace-Reese has said that the least helpful thing for mainline congregations to think is that there is some kind of seven-step formula that will all of the sudden attract young adults into the church. This mindset, Grace-Reese says, is far too simplistic: "I am stunned by the differences around the country in what church looks like and what works well. One of the biggest, fastest growing churches in the country is in Kansas City. Church of the Resurrection serves about twenty thousand people after sixteen years. They have a traditional Methodist service with a pastor in a robe. No one would say do that. But it's working because the congregation is context-related and Spirit dependent."[8]

I'm reminded of an experience I had a few years ago when I was out of town for the weekend and didn't have any idea where to go to church. I was visiting a relatively small town, so there weren't many options to choose from. I decided to attend the local United Church of Christ congregation simply because it was the closest to my faith tradition (and its service didn't start until eleven o'clock, which gave me the chance to sleep in a bit later — something I'm always a fan of doing).

When I entered the sanctuary, I could tell this church had fallen on some difficult financial times. The white paint was peeling from the walls in some pretty obvious places, and the red carpet was in dire need of replacement. You could see where the roof had leaked by noting the places where the walls were discolored. While the sanctuary could have seated around four hundred people, there were about fifty present. The average age of the worshipers was around sixty or seventy. To be honest, I didn't expect much.

Not incidentally, the service took place in March of 2003, just a few days after the bombs started to fall in Iraq, and there was a cloud of sadness that enveloped not only myself, but many others who had gathered for worship that day. I expected to trudge through worship with my mind weighed down by other concerns.

However, in what felt like a pure, unexpected gift, the music, prayers, and sermon were seamlessly woven together in a manner that intentionally addressed the very concerns that the gathered congregation had brought to the table. Instead of blessing the war unflinchingly (as was the case in most of the other Bible Belt pulpits and pews that Sunday), the liturgy blessed the peacemakers and remembered the words of Jesus of Nazareth and Martin Luther King Jr. We were given space to weep for the lives that had already been taken, and we remembered those who had beloved ones in danger, no matter which side of the conflict they were on and no matter which uniform they wore. At the same time, the sermon reminded us not to demonize and vilify the president of the United States. We were reminded that evil isn't nearly as black and white as we make it out to be.

It wasn't a state-of-the-art service by any stretch of the imagination. There were no screens, projectors, tea lights, icons, or prayer stations, but none of that mattered. It deeply resonated with those of us in the pews, and it could not have done so at a more important time. Due to the depth of the liturgy, I didn't pay attention to the peeling paint or the worn carpet. This church didn't carry the glitz and glamour of the bigger churches in town, but it was an oasis for those hungering for a different approach than the one commonly found in the Bible Belt. The ambience, setting, and style were secondary; the theology was primary.

Another one of the most transforming worship experiences I've ever shared in took place in a graying mainline church that held an emerging worship gathering on Friday nights. The setting was a traditional downtown sanctuary located amid the bars and night clubs of the city. While the sanctuary was huge, only a smattering of people occupied it on Friday nights. Most of those in attendance were college students and young adults who gathered for worship before heading off to the night clubs. I attended worship this particular evening because I was interested in observing the congregation's approach to emerging worship. The power of this service, however, quickly moved me from the role of an observer to the role of a participant.

It was clear that the worship leaders made every effort to set the ambience for this service, and, to be sure, the setting was very cool. The sanctuary was dimly lit, with most of the light coming from the candles that lined both sides of the center aisle. Ancient icons were projected on several screens near the front. At the same time, the pulsating rhythms of Moby's blend of electronica and ambient sounds played over the sound system.

Worship began with a reading from the book of Job, which immediately opened up the age-old difficulty of reconciling faith with suffering. Being in observer mode at this time made me think about the ways that such a topic might be addressed, and I cringed as I thought about the ways I've heard it addressed in the past. Usually, it seems, the music and liturgy try to offer answers to the problem of the theodicy. We're told that there are some things we simply can't understand, that God's ways are above our ways, that God can always work for a greater plan and purpose that we are unable to see. I've rarely been content with these pat answers in my own life, and they are precisely the kinds of responses that have led emergents to reject many of the beliefs that have been passed down to them.

I expected the same pat answers to quickly take over this worship gathering. Even though it was led by a mainline congregation and was billed as alternative, I had been burned by so many Bible Belt worship services that it was hard for me to expect anything different. And my worst fears were nearly confirmed. Just after the problem of suffering was addressed via scripture and invocation, the musicians started to crank out the popular contemporary Christian anthem "Shout to the Lord" (for readers who aren't familiar with the lyrics to this song, suffice it to say that they serve as a major disconnect for those who feel angry and frustrated with God). I was immediately turned off. I considered walking out of the service right then and there. Here I am, I thought to myself, fooled yet again by another bait-and-switch, smoke-and-mirrors approach to worship.

But it turns out that I was in for a surprise. I didn't realize that after singing the original version of "Shout to the Lord," we would be invited to sing two additional verses along with a new chorus.

Instead of singing "Shout *to* the Lord" yet again, we were given the opportunity to "Shout *at the Lord*." A subtle switch had been made, and the lyrics to "Shout at the Lord" offered space for us to voice the frustrations we sometimes feel with God.

The music deeply resonated with the struggles that were such a part of my own faith, and I couldn't help but be caught up in song and in prayer. Instead of offering a candy-coated gloss on the deepest incongruencies in my own life and faith, these incongruencies were given a space to breathe. The loose ends didn't have to be tied up, and that was okay. Following the worship service, I realized how few times worship has given me a place to lament.

In both of these examples, the strength of each worship service wasn't in their stylistic approaches — it was in their substance. It didn't matter that one was a traditional service and the other was an emerging service. What mattered was the theology that supported each.

The emergent movement reminds worship leaders that we would be wise to quit worrying about what particular style of worship our congregations offer and pay more attention to the theology our worship services convey.

All of this leads to a couple of pressing questions: If traditional expressions of worship are able to convey the kind of theological depth to which emergents and progressives are drawn — as the case has been in several of our own experiences — then what is wrong with traditional worship? Why should congregations even consider doing something different? Perhaps they shouldn't.

Some traditional worship services in established congregations already convey the depth of theology for which emergents and progressives are crying out. This is certainly the case with one of the most prominent mainline congregations in Springfield. They offer a rich, vibrant, high church tradition that is coupled with progressive theology, and a large number of emergents and progressives find a home

[handwritten marginalia: NSC make our own authentic context]

there. We wouldn't begin to ask them to change their approach to worship, for they are doing what fits their respective context in an exceptional manner. The same can be said for hundreds of progressive mainline congregations throughout North America.

At the same time, however, the emergent conversation highlights the ways that all of our worship services reflect particular cultural contexts. It points to the myopic perspective that believes culturally conditioned styles actually point to the way it was in the beginning, is now, and ever shall be. When Nadia Bolz-Weber calls attention to the arrogance that often accompanies established apologists who thumb their noses at alternative expressions of worship, she speaks for many emergents who are tired of such elitism:

> One red flag that goes up for me when a church wants to try and attract young adults is that there is the implication that traditional congregations are normative Christian communities which everyone SHOULD want to be a part of. I tend to resent the idea that the current manifestation of traditional church (building, pews all in a row, nicey-nice people, hymns, organ, Sunday worship, aurality as the primary sensory experience of the liturgy, etc.) is NOT a single cultural expression of Christian community but the normative expression to which all deviations are judged.[9]

Sometimes, emergents call attention to systemic concerns deeply embedded within various expressions of traditional liturgies. While reflecting on "the gems of the tradition," Stephanie Spellers says that "lots of us have identified what's essential, and what we love and desperately want to see survive for more generations. But right now, the traditional...liturgy speaks from a very white, educated, monied, owning-class cultural context. If that's the only way of self-expression that we have, the only thing that can receive the label 'authentic'...then the church deserves to be marginalized and to shrink away."[10]

When emergents critique mainline worship, it's often because they observe traditional services as supporting and maintaining a sense of hierarchy — with the "privileged" or "educated" elite running the show — that betrays the kind of mutuality that progressives and emergents value. They certainly don't like the way the pastor gets so much of the attention in contemporary evangelical services, and they aren't convinced that the power dynamics are all that different in traditional mainline services (just look at pulpit placement). Therefore, instead of reinforcing these structures through sacred ritual, they prefer using ritual to subvert them.

Perhaps less subtle are some of the more overt theological trappings that are part of several established worship services. When theorists such as Marva Dawn rightly point out that using shallow materials in worship will shape shallow theology and form us superficially,[11] it's easy to assume they are picking on contemporary styles of worship, and oftentimes they are. But let's be honest. Sometimes traditional expressions of worship lack just as much substance as any other approach, including contemporary ones. While in seminary, I attended worship at a church known for the strong nonviolent stand it had taken in the community. I had specifically visited this church because I was inspired by a newspaper article the church's minister had written about the myth of redemptive violence. So I was surprised to learn that even in this context, two of the hymns sung that morning were laced with violent imagery. As I lifted my voice in song, I couldn't help but feel a major disconnect, and I wondered how and why a congregation so committed to peace with justice would plan worship that went against the grain of what they held so dear.

To this congregation's credit, I understand that singing old favorites may help build bonds of community. Even though the language is highly individualistic at times, singing these hymns in worship creates a sense of community that unfamiliar songs are unable to do. However, in times like these, emergents drawn to progressive theological approaches aren't going to experience the same sense of community. Being new to these settings, they are likely going to feel like the congregation's theology is schizophrenic, which in turn makes them feel confused and disoriented.

At the same time, progressives who have grown up in established services (or have spent significant time in them) often grow immune to liturgies and hymns that don't consistently speak from the progressive approaches they hold dear. They might appreciate the quality of the music, but not necessarily its theological undertones. In these instances, they are usually drawn to the sermon because it is the most likely place in the worship service in which progressive thought is articulated in an explicit manner. When Jack Nelson-Pallmeyer and Bret Hesla wrote *Worship in the Spirit of Jesus,* one of the main things they critiqued was that progressives often find themselves in worship singing songs about things they simply don't believe. Why must this always be the case? Why not develop liturgies that speak to the depths of what progressives hold most dear?

For instance, I (Emily) grew up in church, but my experiences were very different from those of emergents who grew up in the shadow of fundamentalism. As long as I can remember, Sunday morning worship has been as much a part of my week as sleeping, eating, and going to school. Thanks in large part to the influence of my church, as I grew older I began to cultivate a deep passion for social justice and peace.

But admittedly, when sitting in mainline congregations on Sunday mornings, I often find myself disappointed. While it may not seem like an important issue to a lot of people, much of the language I hear in worship now grates on my ears like nails screeching on a chalkboard. Whether it's by singing the Gloria Patri (Patri is Latin for "to the Father") or by consistently hearing prayers addressed to the "Heavenly Father" — I'm disappointed that God must always be referred to as a male.

It makes me wonder: where are the churches that can help children learn to value diversity, even in the most subtle of ways? Where are the churches that won't alienate others my age, but might even encourage them to give Christianity a chance?"

One of the advantages of emerging worship — especially for progressive communities of faith — is that it pays incredibly close attention to detail and continually asks the question of what is being communicated theologically via every aspect of the liturgy, no matter how large or small. From the perspective of emergents, all forms of worship are subject to deconstructive critique. This is viewed as a good thing, for it keeps worship gatherings alive and open to reform, which is precisely what should happen when congregations are open to the Spirit.

EMERGING WORSHIP RESPONDS TO THE EVENT OF GOD

Another gift that emerging worship offers progressive communities of faith is the reminder that the depths of Christian tradition help us break free from the all too modern mindset that relegates Christian worship to a series of cognitive ideas communicated through liturgy, word, and song. An ancient-future approach to worship, coupled with the overall value that emergents place on mystery and wonder, challenges progressives to reconsider passive forms of worship that place much more emphasis on matters of the head than on matters of the heart. When worship is domesticated to cognitive ideas — and the door is shut on the Mystery of God — then it's all too easy for worship to become a passive gathering in which responding to the Sacred takes a back seat to merely *talking about* responding to the Sacred.

This isn't to say that intellectual concerns don't matter — hardly at all — but it is to say that intellectual concerns don't necessarily lead to the transformative event that is at the heart of Christianity and is beyond the scope of rational categorization. To use a simple example, progressives can debate until kingdom come whether or not the resurrection of Jesus was a literal or metaphorical event, and they are notorious for doing so. However, debates like these remain locked in our minds, and they have nothing to do with becoming the site (embodiment) where the resurrection actually takes place. Peter Rollins has articulated this problem theoretically and liturgically:

> The problem with so much religious communication is that it aims at changing our minds. The result is that we can hear the message of the preacher without necessarily heeding the message; we can listen to the "truth" and agree with it, yet not change in response to it. To use an example, many of us have had a conversation with someone about how accumulating wealth does not bring happiness, about how working all the hours God sends is not healthy, and that owning bigger and better cars is damaging, not only to the soul, but to the world. But then, after the conversation, those involved turn around and act *as if they believed these things*.[12]

When worship is relegated to cognitive ideas — indeed, when progressives worship at the altar of the modern God of Reason — they mistakenly assume that rational comprehension of the Divine is primarily responsible for transformation. In contrast, however, emergent approaches remind progressives that the way out of this trap is not in the ability to rationally comprehend the event of God — nor to manufacture the event of God — but rather to be transformed by the event of God. From this perspective, the only evidence of having "heard" the message is in the fleshly incarnation of it, and not in the ability to wax poetically — or intellectually — about it. That is why emerging approaches to worship aren't nearly as interested in understanding the event of God as they are in responding to the event of God. From this perspective, emerging worship attempts to cultivate experiences of the Sacred as opposed to attempts that are merely aimed at explaining the Sacred.

To be sure, such experiences should be distinguished from the kind of experiences that many contemporary expressions of worship attempt to cultivate, precisely because emergents are interested in transformative experiences of God that are otherwise — in other words, encounters with the Wholly Other that aren't equated with the feel-good ego trips that are usually the focus of most contemporary services. This is much of the reason that Dan Kimball prefers emphasizing emerging worship *gatherings* as opposed to emerging worship *services*. While Kimball recognizes that Christian worship has historically been understood as a "service" that we perform, he believes that our consumer culture associates the word service with something that is performed for us. He illustrates this idea by calling attention to the proverbial image that compares worship attendance with going to a gasoline station for a fill-up. Kimball believes this image should be done away with, for it reinforces the mistaken idea that the focus of worship should be on ourselves instead of on God.[13]

When we say that emerging worship privileges experiences to explanations, we don't mean the wishy-washy, touchy-feely, make-me-feel-good experiences that have been rightly criticized by a wide range of scholars.[14] We wholeheartedly agree with such critiques. Instead, we mean to highlight the ways that emergents wish to move past the modern domestication of God in order to encounter the *Mysterium Tremendum* that is rendered intelligible only as unintelligible — or, in the words of Catholic theologian Jean-Luc Marion, is incomprehensible yet not imperceptible. Like Moses hiding in the cleft of the rock — or like Isaiah's vision in the temple — the event of God leads human beings to hide their faces before the Holy and to tremble in awe and wonder. From a biblical perspective, encountering the Holy doesn't change minds as much as it changes lives; it doesn't make us feel warm and fuzzy inside as much as it demands something — everything — of us.

In short, emergents wish to join with other voices in emphasizing that worship at its very best — no matter the style — leads to transformative acts in which participants become the site (embodiment) of God's love and action, as opposed to merely talking about God's love and action. While worship planners can't manufacture such experiences, it is possible to create an appropriate context in which such experiences might take place.[15] Within our own community of faith, an emerging approach to worship has been the most effective vehicle for creating the context in which participants are best able to respond to the event of God and, thus, experience an alternative mode of being in which the action of God is incarnated on the ground. Perhaps such an approach will be helpful for your community as well. In the next chapter, we turn our attention to exploring the dynamics of emerging worship for progressive communities of faith.

Chapter Eight

EMERGING LITURGY FOR PROGRESSIVE COMMUNITIES OF FAITH

These temporary spaces will likely appear as much in art galleries, on street corners, in bars and basements, as they will in churches and cathedrals. They may involve rituals and creeds that have survived millennia, or they may have been dreamed up moments before they are acted out. The liturgies may be printed in hymnbooks or scrawled on the back of beer mats. They may be accompanied by angelic choirs or by someone beating out a rhythm on a battered, beer-soaked tabletop. They may be confessions of belief or affirmations of doubt. But everything, absolutely everything, will be designed to invite, encourage, solicit, seek out, recall, remember, reach out to, bow down before, and cry out to that unspeakable miracle testified to by faith — that miracle beyond miracle that dwells, quite literally, beyond belief.

— Peter Rollins[1]

EMERGING RITUALS

On a cold January morning, I sat in front of the television and began to watch a historic day unfold in front of my eyes as the forty-fourth president of the United States was sworn in to office.

159

Throughout the inauguration day, I kept hearing things like "The Obamas and the Bidens are attending services at St. John's Episcopal church down the road from the White House, a tradition going back to previous presidents-and-vice presidents elect..." or, "As is tradition, the president-elect and his wife will join the president and first lady for tea in the White House..." or, "Traditionally the president and the president-elect ride to the Capitol building together..." or, "Mr. Obama will read a letter written to him by President Bush and placed in the desk of the Oval Office, a tradition begun with President Reagan...." It was a day of traditions and rituals, and each offered a sense of continuity even in the midst of party changes and bitter rivalries.

Rituals hold us together. "They are like the bones of a body's skeleton," Rita Brock and Rebecca Parker comment, "the framework that holds things into a shape, giving form to a community's values and relationships."[2] From a Christian perspective, worship as ritual serves as a foretaste of the reign of God. As professor of worship Scott Haldeman writes,

> Worship provides Christians with an opportunity to leave behind, for momentary and fragile periods, the structures of inequality and violence that pervade our lives and to imagine — even more, to experience — an alternative mode of being, a place and time where justice and peace are known.... Political organization, action, and protest will always be necessary if we desire to reform society, but we must pursue ritual action as well — where in an environment of beauty and abundance, in gathering with neighbors and strangers, in the encounter of the Holy, we know a joy that makes us dissatisfied with anything less in our everyday lives.[3]

Kathleen Norris has said that we go to church in order to sing, and theology is secondary.[4] In many respects, we think she is right. The problem, however, is that emergents and progressives have trouble singing songs and hymns that run up against the grain of so much they hold dear. When emergents have experienced rituals that haven't served as a foretaste of the reign of God nearly as much as a foretaste of life under the Religious Right, they are in need of rituals that serve as liberating rites so that they might be able to reimagine their world.[5] Too many Christian rituals, Peter Rollins has said, "have become mired in the project of an exclusivist, violent expression of Christianity and thus need to be renewed and rethought."[6] This isn't, of course, an insight unique to emergents, but it is one they are intentionally responding to.

Similarly, when progressives have experienced rituals that have, for instance, reinforced the myth of redemptive violence, or focused solely on a heaven that is light years away, or sold their soul to the idol of modern rationality, they are in need of rituals that — among other things — help them reimagine nonviolent ways of being in the world that are deeply grounded in the present and are open to the Mystery that ultimately can't be comprehended, no matter how hard one tries.

Norris is right in stating that we come to church in order to sing, and theology is secondary — *as long as people of faith are able to participate in communities that incarnate their shared hopes, dreams, and visions.* Worship is an incarnational expression of Christian theology, and it demands the very best that we have to offer. Those who plan worship are responsible for helping the gathered congregation to remember how to sing, or perhaps for helping them learn how to sing for the first time.

Though each emerging worship service has its own flavor and feel, there are a few characteristics that are generally, though not uniformly, shared within emerging expressions of worship. The most popular descriptions of emerging worship often draw on the acronym EPIC: experiential, participatory, image driven, and connected.[7] They tend to be creative, artistic, multisensory, non-hierarchical, and content rich. They bridge deeply rooted Christian traditions with postmodern expressions of faith and life. Gatherings tend to be casual, and there is a significant emphasis on community and social justice.[8]

To help progressive communities of faith get a feel for what emerging worship might look like from a progressive perspective, we begin with a description of the gathering we know best, the Awakening at Brentwood Christian Church. Keep in mind that this is what has developed within our own context. Feel free to adapt anything you find helpful, but remember that emerging gatherings are organic by their very nature and demand the creativity of each respective community. What works well in one context doesn't necessarily translate well to other contexts, and part of the joy (and challenge) of cultivating emerging gatherings is envisioning what works best in your particular community. Indeed, no two emerging gatherings are alike.

◆ ◆ ◆

WELCOME TO THE AWAKENING

As you enter to worship, the sanctuary is bathed in warm light, with tea lights flickering serenely. Gentle music washes over you, offering space for contemplation and reflection. The communion table, which occupies the central space of the sanctuary, is covered with a purple cloth that catches and reflects the different lights of the room. You are reminded it is the season of Lent. Set on either side of the table are earthenware candle holders, each with a white pillar candle. On that table, a Celtic cross holds central space. While there may not be any one thing in the sanctuary that demands your focus, you nevertheless find it to be a feast for the eyes. At one moment you are drawn to the two children who walk up to the votive candle stand and light a candle as an act of prayer for a loved one. The next moment the movement of the gently flowing stream projected on the screens catches your eye. Icons at the base of the chancel remind you that you are part of the communion of the saints. After a while you find yourself content to close your eyes and let the sounds of the music envelop you as you open yourself to the Holy Other.

The background music gently fades and gives way to the simple chord progressions of a Taizé chorus. The gentle pulse of "Veni Sancte Spiritus" draws the attention of the congregation. As the texture of the chords is enriched with each added harmony, a solo voice floats over the chorus, invoking the Holy Spirit in this place. After several repetitions, the piano accompaniment drops out and eventually the voices fade away as "Let Us Build a House" begins. Led by piano, this song brings with it a procession of symbols that are brought in by children and adults, men and women. First, a high school student brings forward an open pulpit Bible and places it on the communion table. Next, an earthenware plate holding freshly baked bread is brought forward, then a matching carafe accompanied by two chalices. The table is set, and the procession ends with a woman carrying forward a pitcher filled with water. Her feet bare as she treads upon holy ground, she arrives at a basin that has been placed on a small table at the front of the communion table. There she pours the water into the basin, beginning with the pitcher held close to the rim, then drawing it up high as the water pours forth, giving all a chance to see the living water that is present in this place of worship. The mystery of worship is unfolding.

As the last processor returns to her seat, one of the worship leaders proclaims the words of welcome. As you look around the room, you see some worshipers sitting with their eyes closed, allowing the words to flow over them. Others utter the words with the worship leader, all being drawn to the importance of this sacred ritual:

We come from many different paths to gather here,
for wide is God's welcome, and you are welcome here:
    If you are young or old, you are welcome
    If you have brown skin, black skin, white skin, yellow skin,
      or red skin, you are welcome
    If you are married or single, you are welcome
    If you are sick or well, you are welcome
    If you are gay or straight, you are welcome
    If you cannot hear or see, you are welcome
    If you are a man or a woman, you are welcome
    If you are happy or sad, you are welcome
    If you are rich or poor, powerful or weak, you are welcome
    If you believe in God some of the time or none of the time
      or all of the time, you are welcome....
So come, let us stand and worship our welcoming God.[9]

The music that plays as background to the words grows along with them, reaching a high point at the invitation for all to stand. At this point, the music from the worship leaders takes on a different feel, moving away from the meditative quality of the gathering songs and into the more driven quality of songs and hymns of praise. The lights in the room are now fully raised.

Following this time of praise, the congregation sits and a voice from the gathered body rises up to offer words of sacred scripture, further setting the stage for the time with children, the passing of the peace, and the sermon, all of which take place on the floor (rather than on the chancel), in the midst of the people. All that we have heard and experienced up to this point waits to be woven into our very beings as we enter a time of prayer following the sermon. As the lights are again dimmed, the congregation joins their voices in song, preparing us for the silence and reflection that awaits. One of the worship leaders introduces the prayer stations, and then the worshipers are left free to spend the following minutes in whichever way is most meaningful for them. Music from the film *Whalerider* plays in the background as one or two make their way to an area on the east side of the sanctuary, light a candle on a small table at that location, and sit on a cushion in solitude, sometimes with heads bowed in prayer, sometimes with eyes focused on the ever moving and always changing light of the candles. Children gather on the west side of the sanctuary at a bench covered with a cross, a prayer garden, finger labyrinths, paper, and crayons for them to express their prayers. One person stands at a lectern halfway down one of the side aisles and pours her heart out as she writes in the book of common prayers. A few people walk up to the votive candle stand toward the front of the sanctuary and quietly light a candle, pausing for a moment as they lift up a joy or concern in their lives. On this particular Sunday, a handful of others take the opportunity to paint their own Salvadoran crosses, using rich colors that reflect the beauty and diversity of creation. Most remain in their seats and reflect on the words and images that appear on the screens, words and images that speak to the brokenness in our world and lives, the longing we have for the reign of God, and the hope we place in the One who calls and sustains us.

We are drawn back together as we make our way to the table, first in offering, and then in communion. After simple offering baskets are passed by the people, two participants from the congregation move behind the communion table to break the bread and pour the wine while a worship leader shares these Words of Institution:

We gather at this table and remember how on the night when Jesus was handed over, he gathered with his disciples in the upper room and together they shared in an ordinary meal that had extraordinary implications. For at this table, Jesus broke bread and shared wine with one who betrayed him. At this table,

Jesus broke bread and shared wine with one who denied him. At this table, Jesus broke bread and shared wine with those who fled from him in his time of need. At this table, Jesus broke bread and shared wine with people from all walks of life. And so whenever we gather at this table to share the bread and the cup in this community of faith, we proclaim Jesus' life, which affirms there is a place at the table for all people, for the love of God transcends every power that tries to contain it.

The lights in the sanctuary again brighten as we respond as the one body of Christ, walking forward to receive communion, joining our voices together, eating from the one loaf. Nourished by the communion feast, we rise together, ready to go out into the world as the hands and feet of Christ. The final words of benediction pour over the congregation, reminding us of God's steadfast love and presence in and through and around our lives:

And now, may the Sacred Spirit made known to us in Jesus Christ: go before you to show you the way, go behind you to push you into places you wouldn't necessarily go yourself, go beside you to be your companion, and dwell inside you to remind you that you are not alone, and that you are loved beyond your wildest imagination. And may the fire of God's blessing burn brightly upon you, and within you, now and always. Amen.[10]

AESTHETICS AND SPACE

As reflected in the Awakening, emerging worship services pay significant attention to aesthetics and space. In a reaction against contemporary seeker-sensitive movements (and perhaps Protestant iconoclasm in general) that removed sacred symbols from their churches and turned their sanctuaries into theaters, emerging gatherings draw heavily on Christian symbols throughout the ages. Every aspect of the space conveys a sense of awe and reverence, and every single detail is intended to help participants feel as if they are entering sacred space. This is not unlike the immaculate attention to detail experienced in Roman Catholic and Orthodox traditions.[11]

In order to keep participants from feeling like spectators, the arrangement of most emerging worship spaces conveys a sense of participation, community, and belonging. A variety of visuals are often used, including icons, crosses, paintings, and other images projected on one or several screens, which in many ways can be seen as emerging expressions of stained-glass windows. Sometimes these visuals are video loops; other times they are stills. Crosses — often with a raw, ancient feel — are regularly seen throughout the room.

Candles have been used in churches throughout the centuries to represent hope, life, and light, and emergents follow in a long line of worship traditions by incorporating their use. In order to convey an added sense of mystery, lights are often turned down very low, and the candles help foster a beautiful atmosphere. A lot of emerging expressions — including the Awakening — have votive stands similar to what is found in Roman Catholic and Orthodox traditions, and a wide array of candles is used to evoke a sense of awe and wonder. Candles are often set up in sets of three, seven, or twelve.

We can't underestimate the importance of considering what space says about theology. How does it convey immanence and transcendence, for instance? Where is authority located? Are flags more prominent than crosses? Do screens cover sacred symbols that should be seen? As Scot McKnight observes,

> Some emerging Christians see churches with pulpits in the center of a hall-like room with hard, wooden pews lined up in neat rows, and they wonder if there is another way to express —

theologically, aesthetically, and anthropologically — what we do when we gather. They ask these sorts of questions: Is the sermon the most important thing on Sunday morning? If we sat in a circle would we foster a different theology and praxis? If we lit incense, would we practice our prayers differently? If we put the preacher on the same level as the congregation, would we create a clearer sense of the priesthood of all believers? If we acted out what we believe, would we encounter more emphatically the Incarnation?[12]

At the Awakening, worship leadership is shared among a wide range of participants. Musicians are not "center stage," but are off to the side. Readings and prayers are generally shared by those within the gathered assembly. The focal point of worship is the communion table and the cross. Worship leaders at the Awakening never lead from the chancel, but always from the floor. Indeed, the only time worship leaders step onto the chancel is when the worship elements are brought forward and placed on the communion table, as well as when the bread is broken and the wine is poured as we prepare to celebrate communion. In both of these instances, by the way, it's not the clergy who step onto the chancel, but laity — women and men, young and old, married and single, gay and straight. In emerging worship settings, leaders rarely take center place. This reflects the mutuality valued by emergents and reflects the priesthood of all believers.

We've been fortunate in the sense that Brentwood's sanctuary is designed in the round, which lends itself well to fostering a sense of community and intimacy. Whether emerging worship space is a sanctuary, gymnasium, coffee house, or any other venue, efforts are usually made to convey a feeling of interconnectedness that fosters a sense of belonging and participation. This is harder to do in large settings (the larger the setting the more creativity needed), as well as in sanctuaries in which all of the rows are parallel with the chancel. Sometimes lighting can be effectively used to create a participatory feel, and other times bolts of fabric utilized in the form of drapery or streamers hanging from the ceiling work quite well. Be creative so you can avoid placing stilted signs on pews that say things like, "Please sit in center sections."

POWER CORRUPTS AND POWERPOINT CAN CORRUPT ABSOLUTELY

Within the context of worship, the use of screens is often a double-edged sword. Most emerging gatherings use one or more, and we've found that using screens in the Awakening is extremely conducive to the overall flow of the liturgy, *provided they don't get in the way.* Those who use technology in worship — which is a central feature of most emerging gatherings — need to have a good idea what they are doing. We compare the use of screens in worship to referees in sporting events. If they're doing their job well, then they don't get noticed. They move the event along, seamlessly. When they become the center of attention, however, something has gone wrong. As such, multimedia presentations that draw too much attention to themselves — through gaudy displays of textual movement to pictures that are way too pixilated to computer operators who forget to hit the right button — can end up being the bane of an otherwise well-planned service.[13]

We may be old school, but our multimedia presentations are very simple, and this reflects the meditative quality of the Awakening.[14] We like to use video loops during the gathering time of worship, and then we transition to one main image that occupies the screen when text is not needed. The same image is covered with a transparent screen when we need song lyrics so that the image is always there, a subtle reminder of the unifying theme. In our context, black backgrounds work best for both images and text, and we use white text in simple fonts that are easy to read. Whatever you do, make sure people don't have to squint at the screen. Put in a hundred more slides than you'd like before running the risk of distracting worshipers because they can't read the text. More than anything, however, don't let text dominate your multimedia presentations. The best part about screen usage in emerging settings has much more to do with images than words (cultural shifts are moving away from print-based media). Remember that a worship service is not a board meeting (just as you wouldn't want to replace ancient icons with paintings by Thomas Kincade, you don't want to replace creative multimedia for what is found in lecture halls and corporate board rooms). Worship is not the time to try to get fancy with fonts and the million different ways they can dance in a PowerPoint presentation! And please, please, please, whether the presentation is simple or complex, practice it as many times as necessary to make sure everyone responsible for running technology in worship is adequately prepared and ready to go. Practice in advance so you aren't rushed right before worship. In other words, don't plan on running through things fifteen minutes before the service starts. Few things do more liturgical harm that multimedia presentations that call attention to themselves — either because they're too gaudy or too full of glitches. No multimedia is much better than bad multimedia, and emergents are hungry for theological depth much more than fancy presentations.

With all of those disclaimers in place, we do think the usage of screens serves as great tools in worship for a number of reasons. At the Awakening, we seek images that express a variety of ethnicities and cultures, as well as art from around the world. It allows us to use videos and other non–print driven forms of media, and also helps participants sing out in worship rather than down into a book. Screens also allow worshipers to experience the full atmosphere of the worship space while singing (including visual images) as opposed to only staring at a book.

Music and language

Thomas Long has noted that vital congregations feature music that is both excellent and eclectic, and the same holds true for most emerging gatherings.[15] One is reminded of Kim Bechtel's advice: "Don't do everything different; do everything better."[16] As you might expect, emerging gatherings use a wide range of music in worship. You might hear jazz, grunge, electronica, or Taizé, just to cite a few examples. A House for All Sinners and Saints sings modal choruses from the sixteenth century, while Church of the Apostles incorporates techno-trance from the twenty-first. St. Andrew Christian Church (Olathe, Kansas) holds a folk mass that lends itself well to emerging expressions, as does Scottsdale Congregational United Church of Christ's (Scottsdale, Arizona) improvisational jazz. Like all things emergent, there isn't a set style that can be formulaically implemented in any given context. Congregations interested in developing emerging approaches to worship need to consider what works best within their own respective context.

At the Awakening, we keep things simple and eclectic. We use piano, acoustic guitar, and bass (all three aren't always playing at the same time), and sometimes add percussion (for example, congas, shakers, tambourines, but never a drum set). Whether it be a jazz version of the "Kyrie," a blues version of "We Are Walking in the Light of God," or a syncopated rhythmic version of "Joyful, Joyful," we are lucky enough to have a band that gets the feel and flow of the liturgy, and they are able to seamlessly transition us from one element in the liturgy to the next so that worship feels like one inclusive whole, rather than several chopped up pieces thrown together.

Another thing that has helped build a sense of energy in our worship service is the use songs from Africa and Latin America. These songs demand energy and are written in ways that lend themselves to building and growing as the song is repeated over and over. For this reason, they work especially well as calls to worship (why speak what can otherwise be sung?). Percussion is a must for songs like these, starting off, for example, with a simple beat on the congas and then adding maracas and other shakers, a tambourine, and clapping.... It is not uncommon for children to dance in the pews during these songs. Plus, as a bonus of sorts, it's vital for progressive communities of faith to be multicultural in our liturgical expressions if not in our makeup. We live in a world that has incredible diversity, yet all too often our worship doesn't reflect it. While the majority of participants from the Awakening are European American, songs in Zulu, Swahili, or Spanish help take us out of our comfort zones, and we are reminded that we are not the only ones on this journey.

When it comes to selecting hymns and songs for the Awakening, we hold fast to progressive approaches in general by making sure the music is grounded in nonviolence, justice, hospitality, and mutuality, and we try our best not to lose sight of the mystery and wonder of God. Like emergents in general, we focus on music that is neither highly individualistic nor concerned with pie in the sky. In short, we try to make sure that every element of the liturgy — especially our music — reflects the theology held dear by progressives and emergents so that they can joyfully sing their faith without sensing a bunch of disconnects in the process. More than anything else, it is the music that stays with people, it is the music that seeps into their bones and reimagines their world.

We also make an effort to select music that allows people to bring their full feelings to worship, including those of lament. From this perspective, musicians are best viewed as worship leaders and not praise leaders. As one church puts it, "Although many come to worship to praise God in song, others come to look, to question, and even to express anger and confusion with God. Praise is an important expression towards God, but worship encompasses all of our emotions that we bring before God."[17]

Additionally, we try not to ritualize subtle reminders of patriarchy or racism. We always use inclusive language; in the few instances that God is referred to as a male, we balance this with female imagery for God. We are also trying to be mindful of language that reinforces white or light as "good" and black or dark as "bad." "Joyful Is the Dark" is a great song that subverts this tendency in our language, and we are trying to reimagine worship (and hence our world) along these lines. For these reasons, we are very appreciative of the efforts of the United Church of Canada's *More Voices* and the United Church of Christ's *Sing!* as well as the *Chalice Hymnal* and the *New Century Hymnal.*

Not long ago, I received an e-mail from the One Campaign (a progressive organization I fully support), and I was excited to hear that they offered some new resources for worship. I followed the links, but I was disappointed to discover that none of their resources used inclusive language. The prayer of confession was addressed to "Father," and we were called upon to feel our "brother's" need.[18] But what about our sister's need? Ruth Duck points out the problems of using predominantly patriarchal language:

Language that identifies a dominant group (e.g., males, masters, or parents) with God and makes others invisible or submissive (e.g., women, slaves, children) shapes the way we think. It makes it seem as if members of the more "godlike" group are worthy to control the others, even through coercion and violence. Jesus demonstrated mutual respect and not domination between males and females. Language that values men more than women is not consistent with a gospel ethic. The imagery of worship should provide alternatives to cultural values that do not reflect God's love and justice for all.[19]

I know that it is just common convention, but it would be nice for organizations committed to social justice to not ever so subtly reinforce the very systems they wish to change. Some may smile to themselves when they hear God referred to as Mother instead of Father, thinking, "All right, I see what they're doing. Good for them!" but many more experience a visceral reaction of no longer recognizing the God to which they have been singing. This points to the reality that we still live in a patriarchal culture, and the language used in worship usually reinforces it. Emerging worship from a progressive perspective recognizes that "using a broader range of imagery — including female imagery and pronouns for God along with more traditional imagery — witnesses to the Gospel more effectively. It demonstrates the all-inclusive love of God and opens new pathways to nurture relationship with God."[20]

don't just reflect culture/society // image what society can be

SCRIPTURE AND PRAYER

Worship in the Spirit of Jesus features a cartoon that captures the tension that progressives sometimes feel in relationship to scripture. The setting is a congregation at worship on Sunday morning, with the pastor sharing a series of verses from scripture that read like this: "See, the day of the Lord comes, cruel, with wrath and fierce anger, to make the earth a desolation, and to destroy sinners from it....So four angels were released to kill a third of humankind....And these will go away into eternal punishment...and there will be weeping and gnashing of teeth."

After finishing the scripture reading, the pastor begins the common liturgical response by proclaiming, "This is the word of the Lord," to which the congregation responds, "Thanks be to God."[21]

Progressives struggle reconciling these kinds of liturgical responses with their understanding of God and the Bible. On the one hand, they don't affirm the wrathfulness of God as perceived through the lens of such scriptures. In turn, they don't want to affirm what they don't believe — especially in the context of worship. Given the way that progressives view the Bible more as an archive of interpretations about (and in response to) God as opposed to the original voice of God, it's helpful to use other liturgical options.

When scripture is read at the Awakening, we avoid this pitfall by using alternative statements following each reading, for example: "Herein we seek wisdom" or "May we hear what the Spirit is saying to the church." Neither of these responses equate the literal words on the pages of the Bible with the definitive Word of God, and so open the possibility to hearing how God might speak to us through interpretations of the archived text. This honors both the Bible and the Spirit, and it doesn't make progressives cringe in the pews after hearing some of the "terrible texts" that the Spirit of God leads many faithful Christians to critique.

When scripture is read at the Awakening, designated participants from the congregation simply stand and read from the place they are sitting. We ask a wide range of people to read, including children and adults, women and men. We prefer using the New Revised Standard Version of the Bible and *The Message*. We love the way that *The Message* makes passages come alive in ways that — even though it's not a translation per se — remain faithful to the original text; we just wish it used inclusive language.

One of the most powerful ways to experience scripture in emerging gatherings is through the practice of "incarnational translation."[22] This approach usually involves a small group of individuals who

Start a way of writing up to group. t. interpret. over time

research a particular text and creatively consider how it might be heard in today's context. Attention is given to the integrity of the passage and its possible import for today. One of the most powerful moments of the Awakening occurred when a participant stood up in worship to read Psalm 137. Here is the text as it appears in the NRSV, followed by the incarnational translation that was shared in worship in 2007.

Psalm 137: NRSV

By the rivers of Babylon—there we sat down
and there we wept when we remembered Zion.
On the willows there we hung up our harps.
For there our captors asked us for songs,
and our tormentors asked for mirth, saying,
"Sing us one of the songs of Zion!"
How could we sing the LORD's song in a foreign land?
If I forget you, O Jerusalem, let my right hand wither!
Let my tongue cling to the roof of my mouth,
if I do not remember you,
if I do not set Jerusalem above my highest joy.
Remember, O LORD, against the Edomites
the day of Jerusalem's fall, how they said,
"Tear it down! Tear it down! Down to its foundations!"
O daughter Babylon, you devastator!
Happy shall they be who pay you back
what you have done to us!
Happy shall they be who take your little ones
and dash them against the rock!

Psalm 137: Incarnational Translation

wow!

By the blue bay of Cuba — we were humiliated.
We received orange jump suits.
Our beards were shaved.
We wept as we remembered our families.

We hung up our prayer rugs
on the chains of confinement.
For there our captors mocked us,
putting hoods over our faces,
spinning us around,
laughing, saying,
"Now turn toward Mecca and pray."

But we are proud, O God,
too proud to forget our past:
We will not forget how our lands have been
    exploited so their cars could run,
    manipulated so their bases could be built,
    silenced, lest the balance of power be changed.

We remember when their smart bombs killed our sons and
    daughters.
We remember when their sanctions starved thousands of
    children on our streets.
We remember.
We remember.
We loved, yes we loved, those whose name is collateral damage.

Happy shall they be who pay you back,
Happy shall they be who fly airplanes into your skyscrapers.

When experienced in worship, incarnational translations often create
palpable connections between worshipers and text in ways that are

not easily forgotten. Incarnational translations approach the Bible as a living document — an archive as opposed to the *archē* — continually asking what the Spirit is saying to the church.

The images of God that progressives bring to the table also affect their approaches to prayer. For many of them, it is awkward to imagine God as some sort of supernatural, metaphysical Being living up in the heavens who occasionally intervenes in the affairs of human beings. From this perspective, our former worship professor describes an approach to prayer much better than we can:

> When I use the word *prayer,* for example, I understand it to be first and foremost a verb, an alternative form of discourse, an activity through which God — who calls us to an alternative reality — is construed. Prayer (like the work of poetry and fine art) imagines or construes the alternative reality in which God dwells; prayer *speaks* it into being. Prayer relies upon imagination, where, of course, the Holy Spirit lives, and breathes, and enjoys.[23]

This is part of the reason that the Prayers of the People aren't spoken by clergy, but appear on the screens, and it also speaks to the way that emerging worship gatherings are drawn to artistic expressions of prayer through the use of prayer stations (see the appendices for further treatment of emerging approaches to prayer, including several detailed examples of prayer stations).

PREACHING

Most emerging gatherings in North America still incorporate a sermon of some sort. It may go under the guise "message" or "teaching" or "reflection," but it is, for all practical purposes, a "sermon." Emergents (and many progressives) are hesitant to use the word sermon because of the connotations it raises in their minds. For them, sermons are generally associated with authoritarian figures trying to get everyone to conform to a particular way of viewing the world, which tends to be rather exclusive and arrogant.

Emerging gatherings incorporate a wide range of approaches to the sermon. Sermons can be surprisingly long in emerging contexts, sometimes up to forty minutes. Most are around ten to twenty minutes. As you might expect, preachers from an emergent perspective tend to draw on inductive methods of preaching, with a particular emphasis on narrative and conversation. Doug Pagitt's homiletic reflects a theology (and ecclesiology) of mutuality, which leads him to consider how sermons might be an organic, shared experience among participants.[24]

Video clips, props, screens, visuals, flip charts, and the like are sometimes used (though rarely by us), and the sermon is a communal event. While at Jacob's Well, Tim Keel usually opened his sermon with several minutes of unprogrammed conversation on particular topics or texts, and the responses of the participants significantly shaped the flow and content of the sermon itself. Dialogical approaches to the sermon are fairly common in emerging circles, though by this we don't mean to say that two ministers take turns reading prepared manuscripts. Instead, it means there is a genuine give-and-take going on among preachers and the congregation, for it is a shared, conversational, interactive event.

In addition to these stylistic concerns, emerging gatherings remind established communities of faith that good preaching is supported by good liturgy. Unfortunately, preachers from established congregations often feel the weight of the worship service rising or falling on the quality of their sermon. Perhaps that's the preacher's ego talking a bit too much, but perhaps also it's a sign that liturgies don't always support sermons as much as they should. In our particular context, there are several times when we feel as if the strength of the Awakening's liturgy and music can stand on its own. Good sermons preached at the Awakening certainly add to the overall experience shared by worshipers, but the worship service can be incredibly meaningful without them.

A TABLE OF LOVE

At the Awakening, the entire liturgy builds to the banquet feast that is communion, in which everyone is explicitly welcomed to Christ's table. Divisions fall away, walls are knocked down, and boundaries are transcended. It is precisely here that we most fully catch a glimpse of the reign of God.

At this table, we most explicitly confess what we don't believe, in order to make room for what we do believe. We don't confess that we are saved by a man being brutally crucified according to the divine will of his Father. We don't confess that we are saved by the violent silencing of a man who lived his life out of nonviolent principles. We don't confess that we are saved through a blood sacrifice that pays the price for our or anyone else's sins.

However, we do find hope in a man who lived a God-filled life by reaching out to the least of these no matter what the consequence. We do, however, find hope in a man who preached the inbreaking of God's kin-dom by turning traditional understandings on their heads. We do find hope in a man who taught that we see the very face of God in the poor, hungry, naked, homeless, sick, and imprisoned. We do find hope in a man who broke bread with people from all walks of life, who did not let society dictate who was in and who was out, but instead welcomed all with extravagant hospitality so that we could, in turn, extend that hospitality to those in our time in the hopes of building the kin-dom of God in our midst. It was from these convictions that I (Emily) developed the following words to serve as alternative Words of Institution for progressive communities of faith:

> We gather at this table and remember how on the night when Jesus was handed over, he gathered with his disciples in the upper room and together they shared in an ordinary meal that had extraordinary implications. For at this table, Jesus broke bread and shared wine with one who betrayed him. At this table, Jesus broke bread and shared wine with one who denied him. At this table, Jesus broke bread and shared wine with those who fled from him in his time of need. At this table, Jesus broke bread and shared wine with people from all walks of life. And so whenever we gather at this table to share the bread and the cup in this community of faith, we proclaim Jesus' life, which affirms there is a place at the table for all people, for the love of God transcends every power that tries to contain it.

As it turns out, such convictions have deeply resonated with those in our worshiping community as well. It's not that we ignore the harsh reality of Jesus' death, for it carries a haunting power that speaks ever more powerfully of his embodied love and at the same time exposes the powers that be for what they are. We don't, however, interpret it as God's pre-ordained will, but rather the result of following in the way of God. When we celebrate at the communion table, we proclaim a feast of love, welcome, and hospitality that is stronger even than death.

We close this chapter with a story that reflects the hunger for such an approach to faith. Mark is in his forties. He grew up in a fundamentalist tradition where communion was associated with a blood sacrifice demanded by a vengeful God, and he views such symbolism as repugnant. Mark got used to well-meaning people in the pews who often whispered to their neighbor, "Oh, he must be Catholic" as he regularly passed the communion tray to the person next to him without partaking himself.

When we started the Awakening, Mark and his family decided to try it instead of the established service. After attending the Awakening for about three months, a curious dynamic developed, and it caught both of us off guard. He had told us before that he would come to church, but he didn't have any desire to participate in communion. We knew that. So imagine our surprise when one Sunday morning at the Awakening we noticed Mark among those who came forward for communion, breaking off a piece of the bread, and dipping it into the chalice. After the service, we asked him what changed his mind. He simply said, "The whole time I've been coming to the Awakening, I've been waiting for the other shoe to drop. I knew that sooner or later communion would turn into the blood of the lamb for the sins of the world for the sake of heaven later. It always turns into that. But I waited, and I waited, and I waited. And it never happened. All I heard was love and welcome, love and welcome. And after a life of searching, that's what faith in Jesus means to me: love and welcome. This was a feast I could no longer miss."

Every so often, Mark helps lead worship at the Awakening. On some Sundays, he even stands behind the communion table, breaks the bread, and pours the wine. He then walks forward and offers to regulars and newcomers alike a symbol of the extravagant hospitality of Jesus Christ.

When we think of people like Mark, we are reminded why a little church like ours in the heart of the Bible Belt was called to start the Awakening. We give thanks to God for alternative communities of love, hospitality, and grace in the midst of a very fragile world. And we pray that unexpected emergences like our own might be cultivated in communities of faith where they are needed the most. For the healing of the world, and to the glory of God.

Appendix One

A GUIDE TO THE RESOURCES
IN THIS BOOK

When we started the Awakening in August of 2006, our biggest struggle was finding the right structure and flow for the service. We had a good idea of what music would work well within our context, and we were blessed with some outstanding musicians. We had a state-of-the-art multimedia system and a strong network of volunteer support. We loved the idea of planning worship from scratch without any preconceived boxes or limitations. We had several creative ideas we wanted to implement. We just couldn't figure out how to put it all together.

In the time since, we've come to believe that in order for worship to flow seamlessly, no matter the style, it's helpful to learn how to dance. And learning how to dance isn't easy. It requires thinking about what steps you are going to make and how you are going to make them. It requires thinking about steps, counting steps, and keeping up with steps. All of which means you are not yet dancing, but are still learning how to dance.[1]

When we started the Awakening, we were learning how to dance. We were thinking about the steps and counting the steps. Everyone was so worried about making sure everything happened as it needed to happen that it sometimes felt like we were transported back to

183

middle school, trying to somehow make it through the awkwardness of a first dance. And sometimes we wanted to escape to the punch bowl.

In time, however, things would change. Over the course of the next few months, we finally found a rhythm. For the first time, we didn't have to think about the steps and we didn't have to count the steps. We were simply able to enjoy the steps. We had finally learned how to dance.

The image of worship as a dance wasn't given to us from the emergent community, but rather from Thomas Long, a mainliner who has also given serious consideration to finding a way "beyond the worship wars." In worship, Long says, "Vital and faithful congregations have a relatively stable order of service and a significant repertoire of worship elements and responses that the congregation knows by heart."[2] Such an approach offered worshipers the opportunity to learn the dance steps, and it actually opened up the creativity of the Awakening as opposed to limiting it.

Like many other emerging communities, we draw on the fourfold pattern of worship: Gathering, Word, Table, Dismissal. It's certainly not the only approach that emerging communities find helpful, but it has worked quite well for us. The dance steps that we've learned by heart, that we know "in our bones," you might say, are the Welcome, Words of Institution, and Benediction, which stay the same from week to week.

When participants know the major dance steps, it's possible to do more improvisation in the midst of the dance. This lends itself well to the creativity that is significantly valued in emerging contexts. If you consider emerging forms of worship, learn how to dance. And know that it might take some time.

EMERGING WORSHIP IS A COLLABORATIVE EFFORT

Emerging worship services are usually planned by several participants within the community. This approach offers the possibility for each worship gathering to reflect the diversity, mutuality, and creativity reflected within the gathered community, as opposed to the ideas and thoughts of just one or two individuals (which usually leads to colonized space that reinforces the kinds of hierarchical concerns that are deeply embedded in modern institutions of the church). Ideally, those who help plan emerging forms of worship can bring different gifts to the table, including but not limited to art, music, technology, and an eye for aesthetics and space.

This endeavor requires collaborative work, and we don't recommend that pastors and staff members try to plan emerging gatherings on their own. One of the beauties of emerging worship is the creativity that is generated through a wide variety of participants. Plus it is simply too draining for pastors to go it alone.

Developing prayer stations is a task that requires creativity, attention to detail, and theological integrity, and it's not a task to be taken lightly. It's easy for prayer stations to become fairly gimmicky or "cheesy," and it's vital for worship leaders to develop prayer stations that don't trivialize the theological content of the worship gathering. If your community of faith can develop prayer stations that maintain theological integrity, we highly recommend them. Just be careful that they don't become overly trite or superficial.

When planning emerging gatherings, there are usually at least four or five bad ideas for every good idea, so don't be too hard on yourself if good ideas don't consistently roll off the top of your head. One of the beauties of cultivating emerging worship is that there is room for failure — especially given the innovation such a task demands. While we encourage communities of faith to do all they can to learn the dance steps that best suit their given context, we also know that, theologically speaking, worship also leaves room for grace. We hope that communities will try to do all they can to create palpable atmospheres of expectation and excellence, but we also like the way that emerging collectives value participation more than perfection. Sometimes transitions will be rough and sometimes music will be off-key, but this is just a reminder that we are all trying to make it along life's way and that none of our journeys go exactly as we'd like. We do the best we can, and we give thanks to God for gifts of grace.

One of the most helpful ways to plan emerging gatherings is by convening all of those interested in being part of the creative process on a regular basis. A few groups meet weekly, but most meet monthly or quarterly. It's usually most effective to do large brainstorming sessions that meet every so often (you can invite anyone who wants to attend) to come up with general themes and ideas, and then a smaller, more focused group can work together weekly in order to hammer out the details. Networking via the Internet can be extremely handy.

When it comes to planning ahead, lectionary-based communities have some decided advantages for obvious reasons, but nonlectionary based approaches can also lead to significant creativity. Many emergents are drawn to keeping track of time via the church calendar, so there are many collectives that prefer the lectionary. However, some of the most vital emerging services have focused on precisely what the lectionary has left out, which is no small number of biblical texts. These communities are particularly adept at asking questions about the privileging of certain texts over others, and why certain parts of the Bible have been off limits in a wide range of Christian traditions. These are concerns lectionary-based progressives might wish to explore as well.

Within established congregations, when it comes to opening the floor for shared leadership, gate keeping becomes a major concern, especially for pastors who like to be in control. There are some valid concerns that such pastors share, especially in relationship to making sure that the theological content of each gathering is consistent with the ethos of the congregation. One of the best ways to facilitate creativity is by taking into consideration all of the ideas that are shared in large brainstorming sessions, then working with a smaller group in order to determine which ideas the smaller group thinks are most conducive to the overall purpose of the gathering. There will be some ideas, from both laity *and* clergy, that won't work and need to be thrown out. Pastors need to recognize that they don't have the monopoly on good ideas for worship, and they need to help foster an environment in which creativity is encouraged and ideas are welcomed.

Thou shalt not break the law!

There are a number of things to keep in mind when using music from a variety of resources. Simply buying hymnals or songbooks does not grant you the rights to use the music within them however you please. Hymnals and songbooks are meant to be sung out of by holding them in your hand as you read them. Once you photocopy the music or reprint the lyrics to put in the bulletin or on the screens, you are stepping outside the bounds of copyright laws. This is where it becomes necessary to purchase licenses that grant you the rights to utilize the music in ways beyond simply reading them out of the books you purchased. The copyright licenses generally allow you to reprint lyrics for bulletins or onscreen use, to photocopy the songs, or to even compile songs from the books you have purchased into your congregation's own songbook. There is a reporting method that allows the companies to pay the correct royalties to those who own the copyright to the songs you use.

⌐ ᴵegally use the songs that we use in the Awakening, we have had to purchase licenses from three different companies: LicenSingOnline (*licensingonline.org*), OneLicense.net (*onelicense.net*), and Church Copyright Licensing International (*ccli.com*). All three companies provide easy online reporting.

Sᴀᴍᴘʟᴇ ᴏʀᴅᴇʀ ᴏꜰ ᴡᴏʀsʜɪᴘ
ᴡɪᴛʜ ᴇxᴘʟᴀɴᴀᴛɪᴏɴs

Our worship service is rooted in the tradition of a fourfold order: Gathering, Word (Engaging), Table (Responding), Sending (Extending). In each of the resources in Appendix 2, we have suggested songs and hymns that have worked well in our context on the particular Sundays of the church year. Here are the basic tenets of what worship at the Awakening looks like on a general basis. This background will help you further understand the liturgies in Appendix 2. Feel free to adapt these however you like, but remember that emerging worship is contextually rooted. These resources offer an idea of what emerging worship from a progressive perspective looks like in one particular location, but they are intended to get the ball rolling and keep the conversation going. We have used songs and hymns from a variety of progressive resources to show you that several options are available.

◆ ◆ ◆

✚ *Gathering*

For ten or fifteen minutes before worship begins, we play music over the speakers to set the tone for worship. We have provided suggestions from various CDs for prelude music that can be accessed online at *www.uccresources.org*. During this time, as people gather for worship, they are invited to come forward and light a candle at the front of the sanctuary to symbolize whatever is on their hearts and minds. They can also walk around the sanctuary and reflect on the images around the room or spend time in reflection at one of the prayer stations. We fade out the music that is playing over the sound system and then begin the gathering songs. We usually have the lights dimmed quite low during the gathering.

"Gathering Song" #

We generally use a repetitive song, such as a Taizé song, as the first gathering song. The repetitive nature of the song helps focus people coming from the hustle and bustle of our busy world. It aids a spirit of reflection and contemplation.

"Gathering Song" #

During the second gathering song various symbols of faith are taken in procession to the front of the sanctuary. We ask different participants to bring forward one of the following items: a Bible, the bread, the juice, the chalices, and a pitcher of water. All items but the water are placed on the communion table. The water is the last thing brought forward. It is a nice touch to pour the water into a basin at the front of the sanctuary to mark the end of the procession.

✚ *Engaging*

Welcome

The Welcome is the same every week:

> We come from many different paths to gather here,
> for wide is God's welcome, and you are welcome here:
>> If you are young or old, you are welcome
>> If you have brown skin, black skin, white skin, yellow skin,
>>> or red skin, you are welcome
>> If you are married or single, you are welcome

If you are sick or well, you are welcome
If you are gay or straight, you are welcome
If you cannot hear or see, you are welcome
If you are a man or a woman, you are welcome
If you are happy or sad, you are welcome
If you are rich or poor, powerful or weak, you are welcome
If you believe in God some of the time or none of the time
    or all of the time, you are welcome....
So come, let us stand and worship our welcoming God.[3]

Generally, we play music from a CD as a background to the Welcome to give it some added energy. We make sure that the music does not dominate the space but rather serves as a subtle undercurrent of support for the words being spoken. We have provided suggestions from various CDs for music that has a good beat for the Welcome; it can be accessed online at *www.uccresources.org*. At the end of the welcome, we fade out the music and invite people to stand and join their voices together in songs of praise. Because the lights are lowered at the beginning of worship, we gradually raise the lights to evoke a feeling of praise as the following songs are sung.

"Song of Praise" #
"Song of Praise" #

Invocation

We like to start the introduction to the next song quietly as background to the invocation. We invite the congregation to sit down after the invocation.

"Song of Reflection" #

Scripture Reading

At the end of the scripture reading, we say "May we hear what the Spirit is saying to the church" or "Herein we seek wisdom."

Welcoming the Children

For congregations who like to have a time with children in worship, this is an excellent place to have it.

Passing the Peace

We invite the congregation to stand and pass the peace of Christ to those around them.

Building the Community

We welcome first-time visitors and guests and highlight any upcoming events — especially those that are mission/justice oriented.

Reflection

This is the time for the sermon. It doesn't always have to be in the form of a traditional sermon. There are a variety of ways to engage the congregation at this time. We've incorporated dialogues, *Nooma* videos, movie clips, music, all sorts of things. Even our own renditions of Stephen Colbert's "The Word." The words spoken after this time move the congregation into a time of prayer. We usually say something like "And now let us join our hearts, minds, and voices in prayer" as a transition.

✠ Responding

"Song of Prayer" #

We dim the lights during this time.

Prayers of the People

In addition to one-time prayer stations (see Appendix 2 for examples), we have a number of "fixed" prayer stations that are set up around the sanctuary. Going clockwise around the room, starting in one of the back corners, we have a station set up for children. It is a long bench with cushions setting in front of it for the children to kneel on. The bench has a prayer garden filled with sand the children can make designs in, a couple of finger labyrinths, and paper and crayons for the children to draw or write their prayers. Not too far away from that space, we have a podium set up with a couple of journals. We call this the book of common prayers. There are a number of prayers written in these books by participants of the Awakening and people are invited every week to reflect on the prayers that have already been offered or to add prayers of their own. We also have tape on the podium for those who wish to keep their prayers private by folding the page over and taping it shut. Towards the front of the sanctuary, just in front of the baptistery, we have a votive candle stand. These candles are available for people to light as a sign of someone or something they are lifting up in prayer. The final prayer station is on the other side of the sanctuary. It consists of a low table that has a lit candle in the midst of a sculpture of community. There are unlit tea lights around the central candle, available for those who wish to light them. Around the table, there are cushions for individuals to sit on. This prayer station is meant for those who wish to pray in solitude.

We recognize that not everyone will want to participate in the prayer stations, so we also have words and images that alternate on the screens through our PowerPoint presentation. We keep it really simple, with a prayer broken up into about seven different slides with a different image between each set of words. We try not to fill the entire screen with words and keep the font to a size that is easily read. We find that it is overwhelming and not conducive to reflection to have too much text on the screens. We have included prayers that you can use for this time in the worship service, as well as a list of images that will work in conjunction with the prayer. The best way to find these images is to do a Google or Flickr image search for the different words listed and just see what you come up with. (Make sure the ones you use are not copyrighted.) For an example of one of our PowerPoint presentations visit *www.brentwoodchristianchurch.com/multimedia.html*. Throughout the entire Prayers of the People, reflective music is quietly playing from a CD over the sound system. We also have a list of background music that is conducive to this time of prayer online at *www.uccresources.org*.

Outreach

Each Sunday, we highlight the chance for us to give in response to what God is calling us to do. Generally, the words are an extension of the reflection given earlier, but here is a sample of something that might be used:

And now, as we think about the ways we are the hands and feet of Christ in this world, the ways in which our lives can be reflections of the Sacred, we consider the ways we might partner with God as we endeavor for God's will to be done on earth as it is in heaven.

One of the most tangible ways we can make a difference is through outreach — the giving of ourselves through our time, our talents, and our resources. Giving also frees us from the materialism and consumerism of our culture that imprisons us, often on a personal level.

As we receive this morning's offering, we encourage you to think about the ways God's Spirit is calling you to make a difference in this world. As you give, know that every gift, both large and small, works together to make God's kin-dom an ever increasing reality in our area and around the world.

We collect our offerings in small baskets that are passed around the sanctuary and then brought forward and placed on the communion table.

Communion

As one worship leader reads the words of invitation for communion, someone from the congregation comes up and breaks the bread and pours the juice into the chalices. We do this to highlight the mutuality of all those gathered in that space, as well as to lift up the fact that, as Disciples, we believe that you do not have to be clergy in order to serve at the table. We use the same words for communion each week:

> We gather at this table and remember how on the night when Jesus was handed over, he gathered with his disciples in the upper room and together they shared in an ordinary meal that had extraordinary implications. For at this table, Jesus broke bread and shared wine with one who betrayed him. At this table, Jesus broke bread and shared wine with one who denied him. At this table, Jesus broke bread and shared wine with those who fled from him in his time of need. At this table, Jesus broke bread and shared wine with people from all walks of life. And so whenever we gather at this table to share the bread and the cup in this community of faith, we proclaim Jesus' life, which affirms there is a place at this table for all people, for the love of God transcends every power that tries to contain it. We invite you to come forward in two lines, to break off a piece of the bread, and to dip it into the cup, as we join together in this communion feast.

"Communion Song" #

We bring the lights back up as people come forward for communion. Communion is done by intinction.

✣ *Extending*

"Closing Song" #

As the introduction to this song begins, one of the worship leaders says, "And now as we prepare to go from this place as the hands and feet of Christ, I invite you to stand and join together in song."

Benediction

We use the same words every week for the benediction, alternating lines between the two ministers:

> And now, may the Sacred Spirit
> made known to us in Jesus Christ
> go before you to show you the way;
> Go behind you to push you into places
> you would not necessarily go yourself;
> Go beside you to be your companion;
> And dwell inside you to remind you
>   that you are not alone,
>   and that you are loved
> beyond your wildest imagination.
> And may the fire of God's blessing
>   burn brightly upon you,
> and within you, now and always.
>   Amen.[4]

Going Forth

We like to play music from a CD over the sound system. We have provided suggestions from various CDs for postlude music that can be accessed online at *www.uccresources.org*.

Abbreviations for the song books we use
in the Awakening are as follows:

CH	*Chalice Hymnal*
CP	*Chalice Praise*
MV	*More Voices*
NCH	*New Century Hymnal*
SPT	*Songs and Prayers from Taizé*
TSP	*Taizé: Songs for Prayer*

Note: As a Disciples of Christ congregation we generally use hymns from the *Chalice Hymnal*. However, sometimes the words in the *Chalice Hymnal* are not inclusive enough (meaning God is still referred to as male), and in those cases, we've gone to the partner hymns found in the *New Century Hymnal*.

Appendix Two

WORSHIP SERVICES

REFORMATION SUNDAY, TWENTY-SECOND SUNDAY AFTER PENTECOST, Year C

Prayer Station: I Do Not Believe

Materials needed for this prayer station

An old door, a large nail (almost like a spike), a hammer large enough for that nail, a piece of parchment, and some black Sharpies.

Setup

I went to an art supply store and bought a twenty-three-inch by thirty-five-inch sheet of off-white paper. In order to make it look aged and weathered, I crumbled the paper up and kept crunching it down to soften it, spread it back out, and poured tea on it. I let the tea set on it for a while, collecting in pools in some places, making trails in others. After some of it had soaked into the paper, I hung it up to dry in my shower. The paper was rolled up like a scroll for use in the worship service.

Set the door up in the worship space before worship begins. We put it against the back wall of the chancel, behind the communion table. Have a hole prepped in the door so that when someone goes to hammer the parchment to the door, the nail will go in successfully. Start a hole in the parchment as well (nothing ruins a dramatic moment in worship more than something not working the way it is supposed to!).

Presentation in Worship

The parchment should be put on the door during worship. There are a number of different ways you can do it. It works well to have it done after the sermon because then there can be a setup for Martin

Luther hammering his Ninety-Five Theses on the door of the Castle Church in Wittenberg. Since we picked a song that affirms questioning and seeking and discovering new life to introduce the prayers of the people, we feel that it works well to put the parchment on the door as soon as the song is finished. In fact, the person (it can be anyone from your congregation who is able to handle a heavy hammer and nail) can begin walking down the aisle, with the hammer, nail, and parchment in hand, just as the song is completing. Then, in the silence following, the person approaches the door and very deliberately hammers the parchment to the door. Take care to ensure a sense of drama and intrigue at this moment. After the parchment is nailed to the door, the person sits down and another person walks up to the door and begins writing on the parchment. The words being written also flash on the screen. The ideas for this portion of the service came from an affirmation of faith found in *Seasons of the Spirit* from Lent, Easter RCL Year C, 2007, on the Sunday that includes the story of doubting Thomas.[1] There was a whole list of "I do not believes." We drew from these to get people started and then let people on their own after that. Some examples:

"I do not believe God wills children to go hungry."

"I do not believe God is opposed to us asking questions."

"I do not believe that God approves of what we have done to religion."

After this is completed, one of the worship leaders introduces the prayer station:

When Martin Luther hammered his Ninety-Five Theses on that church door almost five hundred years ago, he was proclaiming a new vision for the church. We are "a reformed church, always reforming," and so we do not simply sit back and let things be. As long as the church has life in it, it will be changing and reforming. We live in a culture of faith in this part of the country that hammers certain beliefs into our heads. And quite often, they are beliefs in which we have a hard time believing. Habakkuk was called to write the vision, to make it plain on tablets. Today, we are called to write our vision and make plain on this parchment what we do *not* believe. Already you will see things written on the parchment stating things some do not believe. We invite you to add your own "I do not believe" statements as we join our hearts and minds together in a time of prayer.

After reflecting on what people had written on the parchment, we realized what a wonderful thing had happened. This prayer station was incredibly freeing. There were some great things that people wrote on the parchment, things that maybe they had only thought in secret before.

I do not believe that people should fear God.

I do not believe homosexuality is a sin in any way, shape, size, or form.

I do not believe in predestination; when death and wrong doings occur, it is *not* God's fault.

I do not believe God belongs to anyone, or any group.

I do not believe God loves anyone less because of race, sexual orientation, or religion.

I do not believe people *must* come to church to know God.

I do not believe you must dress nice to praise your Lord. He loves you even when you wear sweats or boxers.

I do not believe God would create differences only to say we should abhor them.

I do not believe God speaks only to Christ, and I do not believe God stopped speaking and speaks only through the Bible.

I do not believe that people who are different are bad or evil.

I do not believe in a God who condemns most people on this earth.

I do not believe God is the creator of evil.

I do not believe God wills human suffering.

I do not believe that all people have to worship the same way.

I do not believe that God is only in churches.

I do not believe there is only one way to heaven.

I do not believe that when terrible things happen, "It is God's will."

I do not believe God places humans higher than the rest of creation.

I do not believe that science is not in religion.

I do not believe that *only* Christians make it to heaven.

Prayers of the People

O God, sometimes it is easier to say what we do *not* believe. In a world that struggles to make sense of the chaos, many turn to creeds and doctrines as reassurances of your presence. And yet no words can fully grasp what it is we are longing for. O God, remind us not to confine you to our own mere words or within a narrow box.

God, your ways are mysterious and unknown to us. Each day of our lives is a day in which we can learn more of you, and yet in all of our learning, there is still much we do not know. At times we use our lack of understanding to explain the evils of this world. Forgive us. At times we barrel along with our own plans that destroy and harm, and then we claim your divine blessing on our actions because our lack of understanding makes it possible to do so. Have mercy on us. At times we give up hope because we don't experience you in ways we expect. Renew us.

God, may your unknowable ways keep us on our toes. May your unnamable presence give us strength. Keep us from creating you in our own image. We rejoice that you are in our belief and unbelief. Amen.

Images for Prayers of the People

• different kinds of doors

— ORDER OF WORSHIP —

✚ *Gathering* (see p. 188)

"With You, O Lord" #31 TSP
"God of Still Waiting" #20 MV

✚ *Engaging* (see p. 189)

Welcome (see p. 189)

"Uyaimose" #3 CP
"Be Thou My Vision" #595 CH

Invocation (see p. 190)

God of constant change, your Spirit fills our lives, pushing us ever onward, keeping the church a living church. Stir us from complacency, compel us to question, and dare us to vision a new way of believing in this world of challenge and strife. We come to this place, God, asking to be re-formed. Amen.

"Love Knocks and Waits" #94 MV

Scripture Reading: Habakkuk 1:1–4; 2:1–4 (see p. 190)

O Lord, how long shall I cry for help,
>and you will not listen?
Or cry to you "Violence!"
>and you will not save?
Why do you make me see wrongdoing
>and look at trouble?
Destruction and violence are before me;
>strife and contention arise.
So the law becomes slack
>and justice never prevails.
The wicked surround the righteous —
>therefore judgment comes forth perverted.
I will stand at my watch-post,
>and station myself on the rampart;
I will keep watch to see what he will say to me,
>and what he will answer concerning my complaint.
Then the Lord answered me and said:
>Write the vision;
>make it plain on tablets,
>so that a runner may read it.
For there is still a vision for the appointed time;
>it speaks of the end, and does not lie.
If it seems to tarry, wait for it;
>it will surely come, it will not delay.
Look at the proud!
Their spirit is not right in them,
>but the righteous live by their faith.

Welcoming the Children (see p. 191)

Passing the Peace (see p. 191)

Building the Community (see p. 191)

Reflection (see p. 191)

✝ *Responding* (see p. 191)

"This Is a Day of New Beginnings" #518CH

Prayers of the People (see pp. 191 and 202)

Outreach (see p. 193)

Communion (see p. 194)

"All Are Welcome" #159 CP

✝ *Extending* (see p. 195)

Benediction (see p. 195)

"You Are Holy" #45 MV

Going Forth (see p. 195)

Worship Service 2

FIFTH SUNDAY AFTER EPIPHANY, Year A

Prayer Station: Naming Injustice

Materials needed for this prayer station

A large wooden cross (one that would be difficult for a person to carry, but made of simple, unadorned wood), nails, a hammer, small pieces of paper, and writing utensils.

Setup

Hand a piece of paper to all those who enter the sanctuary. Place the cross near the front of the sanctuary with a bowl of nails and the hammer set beside it.

Presentation in Worship

The congregation sings the song that leads into the Prayers of the People and then one of the worship leaders introduces the prayer station for the week:

> The growing gap between the rich and the poor is an ever-increasing reality in our world. There are systems currently in place that trap people in desperate circumstances: minimum wage is not a living wage, health insurance costs are on the rise, and cycles of poverty make it nearly impossible for some to break out. As the Rev. Dr. Martin Luther King Jr. once said, as citizens of this world, it is important for us to recognize that injustice anywhere is a threat to justice everywhere. At the front of the sanctuary you will find a wooden cross. You are invited to take the piece of paper you were handed on your way into worship, write the injustices of which you are aware, and nail the paper to the cross.

Prayers of the People

God, we cry out to you! Where is justice? Why is there suffering?

There are many people on our minds this morning and we lift them up to you in prayer, O God of compassion. We pray that you may surround those in need. Be in the hands that administer medicine and give care. Be in the arms that embrace the afflicted. Be in the feet that carry food and supplies to the hungry and war-torn. Be in the minds that work together to find ways to bring clean water to countries languishing in poverty. Be in the mouths that tell of the love that includes *all* people. Be in the hearts of all people who help make peace a reality in this world.

Empower us to loose the bonds of injustice and to let the oppressed go free. Help us share our bread with the hungry and bring the homeless into your house. Give us the strength to step out in faith. Give us the hope that your love will prevail. Give us the courage to do the things the world may shun, the things that will make your realm, the kin-dom of all people, a tangible reality in this life, so that justice can roll down like waters. Amen.

Images for Prayers of the People

- Parades for justice
- Protesters
- Poverty

− ORDER OF WORSHIP −

✣ *Gathering* (see p. 188)

> "Lord God, You Love Us" #100 MV
> "Wind Upon the Waters" #247 CH

✣ *Engaging* (see p. 189)

Welcome (see p. 189)

> "Through These Hands" #126 CP
> "Hear Our Praises" #41 CP

Invocation (see p. 190)

> Our voices cry out to you, O God. We cry out, naming the injustices we see running rampant in our world. We cry out as children go hungry, families go homeless, the poor go naked, and we long for things to be different. We cry out! Transform us in our acts of worship, in our singing and our praying and our listening, that we may seek justice in your holy name. Amen.
>
> "Come Touch Our Hearts" #12 MV

Scripture Reading: Isaiah 58:3–9a (see p. 190)

> "Why do we fast, but you do not see?
> Why humble ourselves, but you do not notice?"
> Look, you serve your own interest on your fast-day,
>   and oppress all your workers.
> Look, you fast only to quarrel and to fight
>   and to strike with a wicked fist.
> Such fasting as you do today
>   will not make your voice heard on high.
> Is such the fast that I choose,
>   a day to humble oneself?

Is it to bow down the head like a bulrush,
  and to lie in sackcloth and ashes?
Will you call this a fast,
  a day acceptable to the Lord?
Is not this the fast that I choose:
  to loose the bonds of injustice,
  to undo the thongs of the yoke,
  to let the oppressed go free,
  and to break every yoke?
Is it not to share your bread with the hungry,
  and bring the homeless poor into your house;
  when you see the naked, to cover them,
  and not to hide yourself from your own kin?
Then your light shall break forth like the dawn,
  and your healing shall spring up quickly;
  your vindicator shall go before you,
  the glory of the Lord shall be your rearguard.
Then you shall call, and the Lord will answer;
  you shall cry for help, and he will say, Here I am.

Welcoming the Children (see p. 191)

Passing the Peace (see p. 191)

Building the Community (see p. 191)

Reflection (see p. 191)

✢ *Responding* (see p. 191)
"Sisters Let Us Walk Together" #179 MV

Prayers of the People (see pp. 191 and 207)

Outreach (see p. 193)

Communion (see p. 194)

"I Saw the Rich Ones" #127 MV

✠ *Extending* (see p. 195)

Benediction (see p. 195)

"What Does the Lord Require of You?" #661 CH

Going Forth (see p. 195)

Worship Service 3

THIRD SUNDAY OF LENT, Year A

Prayer Station: Brokenness

Materials needed for this prayer station

A few broken mirrors that are secured so that no one can get hurt.

Setup

Have the mirrors set up in a place where people can look at themselves in the mirror and reflect on what they see. We have a shattered mirror that is glued to the front of a large Celtic cross that was made out of a polystyrene-like material. In this case, it worked to have people kneel before the cross and gaze at themselves in the broken mirror. It also works to have mirrors that can be held in a person's hand.

Reflection

The reflection was offered as a story of the woman at the well. It explored what her life might have been like, what would have driven her to have so many husbands, why she would currently be living with a man who was not her husband.

Presentation in Worship

The congregation sings the song that leads into the Prayers of the People, and then one of the worship leaders introduces the prayer station for the week:

> We are broken, all of us. Just like the woman at the well, we are more than just a face. We all have a story that forms who we are and that informs how we experience life. During this time of prayer, you are invited to look at yourself in the broken mirrors

at the front of the sanctuary. Look deep inside yourself, see the broken places, the cracks that make you who you are, the part of you that you may not show, but that nevertheless makes you who you are. Where is God in the broken places?

Prayers of the People

God, we cry out to you! We thirst for living water! At times it seems there is no comfort, no relief from heartache. We wrap our pain around us like a shield, closing us off from the cries of the many throughout creation. We hear the cries of the grief stricken, the sick, and the abused: We thirst for living water! We hear the cries of the poor, the homeless, and the hungry: We thirst for living water! We hear the cries of the hiding, the conflicted, and the war-torn: We thirst for living water! We hear the cries of the invisible, the forgotten, and the forsaken: We thirst for living water! Is there no comfort in our pain? Is there no one with eyes to see, ears to hear, and a heart to care? Is there nowhere to turn?

Gentle Whisper of Presence, you are the living water to a thirsting soul. We pray you open our hearts to recognize the brokenness of the world around us, the wounds we often glance over because they don't seem to affect us. Remind us of our interconnectedness to one another. Your loving Spirit binds us all together, making us, every single one of us, an integral part of this global village.

God, tune our hearts to your presence. You are in the hand that pats our knee reassuringly. You are in the sympathetic glance given when another recognizes our pain. You are in the card we receive in the mail reminding us we are loved and appreciated. You are in the strong arm that reaches out to keep us from stumbling. You are in the care that gives dignity to the dying. You are in the embrace of a loved one. You are here. You are the living water. Heal our broken places. Amen.

Images for Prayers of the People

- Broken pots
- Mended Cracks
- Shattered Mirrors

— ORDER OF WORSHIP —

✠ *Gathering* (see p. 188)

"By Night" #46 SPT
"Healer of Our Ev'ry Ill" #506 CH

✠ *Engaging* (see p. 189)

Welcome (see p. 189)

"River of Mercy" #105 CP
"All Who Are Thirsty" #4 MV

Invocation (see p. 190)

God, sometimes we come to this place broken and in need of healing. Sometimes we just need to know that you are here, with us. Fill us, this morning, with your comforting presence and your strengthening love. Remind us that you are with us, even in the broken places. Amen.

"You're Here" #109 CP

Scripture Reading: John 4:5–26 (see p. 190)

So he came to a Samaritan city called Sychar, near the plot of ground that Jacob had given to his son Joseph. Jacob's well was there, and Jesus, tired out by his journey, was sitting by the well. It was about noon.

A Samaritan woman came to draw water, and Jesus said to her, "Give me a drink." (His disciples had gone to the city to buy food.) The Samaritan woman said to him, "How is it that you, a Jew, ask a drink of me, a woman of Samaria?" (Jews do not share things in common with Samaritans.) Jesus answered her, "If you knew the gift of God, and who it is that is saying to you, 'Give me a drink,' you would have asked him, and he would have given you living water." The woman said to him, "Sir, you have no bucket, and the well is deep. Where do you get that living water? Are you greater than our ancestor Jacob, who gave us the well, and with his sons and his flocks drank from it?" Jesus said to her, "Everyone who drinks of this water will be thirsty again, but those who drink of the water that I will give them will never be thirsty. The water that I will give will become in them a spring of water gushing up to eternal life." The woman said to him, "Sir, give me this water, so that I may never be thirsty or have to keep coming here to draw water."

Jesus said to her, "Go, call your husband, and come back." The woman answered him, "I have no husband." Jesus said to her, "You are right in saying, 'I have no husband'; for you have had five husbands, and the one you have now is not your husband. What you have said is true!" The woman said to him, "Sir, I see that you are a prophet. Our ancestors worshipped on this mountain, but you say that the place where people must worship is in Jerusalem." Jesus said to her, "Woman, believe me, the hour is coming when you will worship the Father neither on this mountain nor in Jerusalem. You worship what you do not know; we worship what we know, for salvation is from the Jews. But the hour is coming, and is now here, when the true worshippers will worship the Father in spirit and truth, for the

Father seeks such as these to worship him. God is spirit, and those who worship him must worship in spirit and truth." The woman said to him, "I know that Messiah is coming" (who is called Christ). "When he comes, he will proclaim all things to us." Jesus said to her, "I am he, the one who is speaking to you."

Welcoming the Children (see p. 191)

Passing the Peace (see p. 191)

Building the Community (see p. 191)

Reflection (see pp. 191 and 211)

✤ *Responding* (see p. 191)

"Out of the Depths"#510 CH

Prayers of the People (see pp. 191 and 212)

Outreach (see p. 193)

Communion (see p. 194)

"Table of Love" #168 CP

✤ *Extending* (see p. 195)

Benediction (see p. 195)

"You Have Called Me" #455 CH

Going Forth (see p. 195)

PENTECOST, Year A

Prayer Station: For the Healing of the Nations

Materials needed for this prayer station

Chicken wire fence, wire cutters, paper towels, duct tape, strips of material.

Setup

Cut some chicken wire into two four- or five- foot sections. Then use the paper towels as edging that you will then duct tape over in order to prevent the wires from cutting anyone. Place the two fences at the front of the sanctuary.

Reflection

This prayer station was used on a Sunday during a time when immigration reform was being widely debated in Congress. As we reflected on the ways in which the Spirit broke down the misunderstanding among the people on that day of Pentecost, we also remembered the walls of separation that are springing up between our country and Mexico.

Presentation in Worship

The congregation sings the song that leads into the Prayers of the People, and then one of the worship leaders introduces the prayer station for the week:

> Walls and fences have too often divided nation from nation, neighbor from neighbor, and even loved ones from loved ones. At the front of the sanctuary, you will find some wire fences. Just as the fences that line the border between the United States and Mexico have beautiful and colorful artwork on sections of

the Mexican side (artwork that stands in stark contrast to the brokenness communicated through such walls), you are invited during this time of prayer to wrap and weave the strips and leaves of cloth provided through the wire. If you wish, you may also write words of brokenness and words of healing, recognizing the imperfection of the ways of this world and our call to follow and make a new way.

Prayers of the People

Great and loving God, the air outside these walls is fairly still today, but within this place, the winds of your spirit wend their way among us. Breathe into us now, giving life to the ailing, hope to the despairing, strength to the weakened, voice to the oppressed, courage to the abused.

Like a great wind, you blow through us, O God. Like a gentle breeze, you stir our sometimes stagnant spirits into action. Your spirit comes to us and through us in infinite varieties and on every occasion, but on this day of Pentecost, we especially remember the ways in which your Holy Spirit rested upon the first apostles so many centuries ago. As we recall that moment when misunderstanding fell away and people from all areas of the known world were united in your one spirit, we pray for such unity now. We live in a fractured, broken world where unity seems elusive. Work in us, healing God, to bind us together in your one spirit of love.

Images for Prayers of the People

- ◆ Dove
- ◆ Flames
- ◆ Unity
- ◆ Pentecost
- ◆ The wall lining the border between the United States and Mexico

− ORDER OF WORSHIP −

✚ *Gathering* (see p. 188)

"Veni Sancte Spiritus" #41 SPT
"Spirit" #249 CH

✚ *Engaging* (see p. 189)

Welcome (see p. 189)

"O God, Send Out Your Spirit" #25 MV
"She Is the Spirit" #255 CH

Invocation (see p. 190)

Spirit of life, blow your winds of renewal over us this morning.
Pour the fire of your love on this worshiping body. Stir a fire
within us that moves us beyond words. Set our hearts on fire to
go out into the world doing the work you call us to do. Amen.

"Come and Seek the Ways of Wisdom" #10 MV

Scripture Reading: Acts 2:1–21 (see p. 190)

When the day of Pentecost had come, they were all together in
one place. And suddenly from heaven there came a sound like
the rush of a violent wind, and it filled the entire house where
they were sitting. Divided tongues, as of fire, appeared among
them, and a tongue rested on each of them. All of them were
filled with the Holy Spirit and began to speak in other languages,
as the Spirit gave them ability.

Now there were devout Jews from every nation under heaven
living in Jerusalem. And at this sound the crowd gathered and
was bewildered, because each one heard them speaking in the
native language of each. Amazed and astonished, they asked,
"Are not all these who are speaking Galileans? And how is it

that we hear, each of us, in our own native language? Parthians, Medes, Elamites, and residents of Mesopotamia, Judea and Cappadocia, Pontus and Asia, Phrygia and Pamphylia, Egypt and the parts of Libya belonging to Cyrene, and visitors from Rome, both Jews and proselytes, Cretans and Arabs — in our own languages we hear them speaking about God's deeds of power." All were amazed and perplexed, saying to one another, "What does this mean?" But others sneered and said, "They are filled with new wine."

But Peter, standing with the eleven, raised his voice and addressed them: "Men of Judea and all who live in Jerusalem, let this be known to you, and listen to what I say. Indeed, these are not drunk, as you suppose, for it is only nine o'clock in the morning. No, this is what was spoken through the prophet Joel: 'In the last days it will be, God declares, that I will pour out my Spirit upon all flesh, and your sons and your daughters shall prophesy, and your young men shall see visions, and your old men shall dream dreams. Even upon my slaves, both men and women, in those days I will pour out my Spirit; and they shall prophesy. And I will show portents in the heaven above and signs on the earth below, blood, and fire, and smoky mist. The sun shall be turned to darkness and the moon to blood, before the coming of the Lord's great and glorious day. Then everyone who calls on the name of the Lord shall be saved.' "

Welcoming the Children (see p. 191)

Passing the Peace (see p. 191)

Building the Community (see p. 191)

Reflection (see pp. 191 and 216)

✤ *Responding* (see p. 191)

"Holy Spirit, You're Like the Wind" #5 MV

Prayers of the People (see pp. 191 and 217)

Outreach (see p. 193)

Communion (see p. 194)

"Beyond the Beauty and the Awe" #80 MV

✤ *Extending* (see p. 195)

Benediction (see p. 195)

"Dance with the Spirit" #156 MV

Going Forth (see p. 195)

Worship Service 5

EIGHTH SUNDAY AFTER PENTECOST, Year A

Prayer Station: Caring for Creation

Materials needed for this prayer station

A tarp, two planter boxes, a bag of soil, flowers (pansies work really well for this), small hand shovels, and a small basin of water with a towel. On this particular Sunday, we also had an additional option that gave people the opportunity to sign a petition to put a clean air initiative on the ballot. (Of course, you would adapt this to your own context.) This would require a small table and writing utensils.

Setup

Have two stations set up at the front: one for the planting and one for the petition. At the planting station, set up a tarp on the ground at the front of the sanctuary. Place the planter boxes, the bag of soil, flowers and shovels on the tarp (the tarp is meant to keep the dirt off the floor). Put the small basin of water and the towel nearby for people to rinse off their hands after planting the flowers.

Presentation in Worship

The congregation sings the song that leads into the Prayers of the People and then one of the worship leaders introduces the prayer station for the week:

Our earth is suffering because of the careless ways we use our resources. Today we have a station for those of you who like to get your hands dirty by working in the garden. You are invited to come up and plant some pansies in the planters.

These flowers will add beauty to the entrance of our church and serve as a reminder of the magnificence of God's creation.

We also have an opportunity to lift up our voices on behalf of the environment. There are many people in town who are working together to get a clean air initiative on the ballot. If any of you would like to add your voice to theirs, we have a petition for anyone who is registered to vote to sign.

Prayers of the People

Creator God, we see your fingerprints on the world around us. In the patterns of birds in flight, in the steady rhythm and gentle music of the cicadas, in the wildflowers that color the meadows, you show us your beauty and your radiance.

We rejoice as the mountains and hills burst forth in song, and the trees of the field clap their hands. And yet today we see the tops of mountains removed and deposited in the rapidly filling valleys, and too many trees are being cut down.

We are told of your love for us in the stories of creation. The care expressed within those words speaks volumes to us. And God, we are humbled by the reminder that we are created in your image, filled with your breath of life.

Humbled because too often we forget what this means and abuse this gift given to us.

Remind us again and again how you intend for us to be your hands and feet on this earth. May the power of love overcome the love of power in our hearts. May we learn that to have dominion over something does not mean to dominate and destroy that thing.

We pray our time in this place propels us to speak out for creation. We pray our actions on this earth bring forth new growth. We pray our connection with the earth inspires us to conserve and nurture the resources that were once so plentiful on this planet and are now dwindling. Empower us to be good stewards of creation. Amen.

Images for Prayers of the People

- ◆ Landscapes of mountains, fields, forests, etc.
- ◆ Environmental devastation
- ◆ New things growing in freshly tilled earth
- ◆ People planting trees

– ORDER OF WORSHIP –

✚ *Gathering* (see p. 188)

"Come and Fill" #28 SPT
"Each Blade of Grass" #37 MV

✚ *Engaging* (see p. 189)

Welcome (see p. 189)

"To You O God All Creatures Sing" #17 NCH
"Mother Earth, Our Mother Birthing" #39 MV

Invocation (see p. 190)

All of creation cries out in praise to you, Creator of Life. As our voices rise up in song, open our eyes to the beauty in the world around us and remind us of our role in caring for all you have given us. Help us understand what it means to be partners with you in our stewardship of the earth. Amen.

"Creator God You Gave Us Life" #27 MV

Scripture Reading: Isaiah 55:10–13 (see p. 190)

> For as the rain and the snow come down from heaven,
>> and do not return there until they have watered the earth,
>>> making it bring forth and sprout,
>> giving seed to the sower and bread to the eater,
> so shall my word be that goes out from my mouth;
>> it shall not return to me empty,
>>> but it shall accomplish that which I purpose,
>>> and succeed in the thing for which I sent it.

> For you shall go out in joy,
>> and be led back in peace;
> the mountains and the hills before you
>> shall burst into song,
> and all the trees of the field shall clap their hands.
> Instead of the thorn shall come up the cypress;
>> instead of the brier shall come up the myrtle;
> and it shall be to the Lord for a memorial,
> for an everlasting sign that shall not be cut off.

Welcoming the Children (see p. 191)

Passing the Peace (see p. 191)

Building the Community (see p. 191)

Reflection (see p. 191)

✠ *Responding* (see p. 191)

"Touch the Earth Lightly" #693 CH

Prayers of the People (see pp. 191 and 222)

Outreach (see p. 193)

Communion (see p. 194)

"Walk in the Light" #155 CP

✠ *Extending* (see p. 195)

Benediction (see p. 195)

"Called by Earth and Sky" #135 MV

Going Forth (see p. 195)

Worship Service 6

SECOND SUNDAY OF ADVENT, Year B

Prayer Station: Nonviolence

Materials Needed for the Prayer Station

A chair that needs to be put together, tools, clear contact paper, crayons.

Setup

Place the dismantled chair at the front of the sanctuary, where it is visible during worship. Make sure the tools are placed near the chair. I used a chair from my home for this prayer station. I covered the seat with clear contact paper so people could write on the chair with crayons and it would not damage the chair. If you have a chair available that is okay for people to write permanently on, it would be great to use for this prayer station.

Presentation in Worship

The congregation sings the song that leads into the Prayers of the People and then one of the worship leaders introduces the prayer station for the week:

This is the season of Advent, the season of waiting, of longing, of anticipation of the Messiah, the one who is to come into our world as the Prince of Peace. In Scripture we read of how the Messiah will put an end to violence and injustice, and so we make a place for the Messiah here in our midst. We work and await his coming.

At the front of the sanctuary, you can see a chair in pieces. During our time of prayer, you are invited to come forward and work together to assemble the chair. Once that is done, you can write your longings for peace on the seat of the chair.

Prayers of the People

Holy God, we enter this place and suck in our breath in response to the mystery we feel within these walls. This sanctuary is prepared for the coming of something magnificent, something desperately needed, something life-changing. For the time of waiting has begun. The air is vibrating with anticipation. The stage is set for the holy drama to unfold. But not yet.

On this Sunday of Advent peace, we are all too aware of the absence of peace in our world. And so, God, we cry out to you to save us. Save us from a tradition, a history, a culture that has taught us that violence is the only way of redemption. Save us and show us a new way. For your heart breaks at the loss of any life and we know that revenge will not heal. Retaliation will not build bridges of compassion and understanding. Violent response only ensures that the cycle of violence will continue. You call instead for silence in the midst of devastation. Space to breathe, space to grieve.

God you call us to be greater than we are. But we cannot do it on our own. In this time of quiet prayer and meditation, we seek your strength. We summon your courageous spirit. We allow ourselves to be filled with your peace, the peace that can move us to reach out in love, the peace that can help us truly see the other, the peace that can enable us to forgive. We long for the coming of Emmanuel, God with us. Amen.

Images for Prayers of the People

- Peace
- Nonviolence
- Dove
- Joined hands
- Empty chairs

− ORDER OF WORSHIP −

✤ *Gathering* (see p. 188)

"Give Peace" #44 SPT

"Breath of God, Breath of Peace" #24 MV

✤ *Engaging* (see p. 189)

Welcome (see p. 189)

"Jesus Came Bringing Us Hope" #33 MV

"Awake! Awake, and Greet the New Morn" #107 NCH

Invocation (see p. 190)

God, the world outside is ramping up for the festivities of the season and we are at times overwhelmed by the hustle and bustle around us. And yet, even in the joy of the season, we live lives that are filled with conflict and violence and we long for another way. And so we come to this place seeking your wisdom, yearning for your guidance, striving for your peace. Give peace to every heart as we engage in this act of worship. Amen.

"Peace for the Children" #149 MV

Scripture Reading: Psalm 85:8–13 (see p. 190)

Let me hear what God the Lord will speak,
   for he will speak peace to his people,
to his faithful, to those who turn to him in their hearts.
Surely his salvation is at hand for those who fear him,
   that his glory may dwell in our land.

Steadfast love and faithfulness will meet;
righteousness and peace will kiss each other.
Faithfulness will spring up from the ground,
   and righteousness will look down from the sky.

The Lord will give what is good,
  and our land will yield its increase.
Righteousness will go before him,
  and will make a path for his steps.

Welcoming the Children (see p. 191)

Passing the Peace (see p. 191)

Building the Community (see p. 191)

Reflection (see p. 191)

✚ *Responding* (see p. 191)

"Make Me an Instrument of Your Peace" #92 CP

Prayers of the People (see pp. 191 and 227)

Outreach (see p. 193)

Communion (see p. 194)

"Put Peace into Each Other's Hands" #173 MV

✚ *Extending* (see p. 195)

Benediction (see p. 195)

"When God Is a Child" #132 CH

Going Forth (see p. 195)

Worship Service 7

BAPTISM OF THE LORD
(FIRST SUNDAY AFTER EPIPHANY), Year B

Prayer Station: The Waters of Life

Materials needed for this prayer station

A filled baptistery or a font of some sort (if you do not have either, you can use a basin filled with water), floating candles (tea lights work great and they are very inexpensive), a lit candle with which to light the tea lights.

Setup

If you want, you can hand the candles out to people as they enter the sanctuary. Or you can simply have them in a basket near the baptistery, font, or basin.

Presentation in Worship

The congregation sings the song that leads into the Prayers of the People and then one of the worship leaders introduces the prayer station for the week:

Water is a life-giving force on this planet. Without water, none of us would exist.

This is one of the reasons why water is such an important religious symbol. You received a candle at the beginning of worship. You are invited to light that candle at the front of the sanctuary and float it in the baptismal waters as a sign of the hope we receive as we reflect on Jesus' baptism. You can touch the baptismal waters and reflect on your own baptism. If you have not been baptized, you can come forward and light a candle and reflect on the life-giving power of water.

Prayers of the People

Loving Creator, the waters of baptism flow among us, giving us hope and reminding us of the new life you give us in every moment.

As we touch the waters and remember, we also lift up to you those in our midst, whether in this room or beyond, who are in need of your presence: those who are sick, those who are tired, those who are hurting, those who are struggling. Reach out through our prayers, through our hands, through our actions, that we may reflect your loving kindness, in times of need.

We are in need of the living waters, O God, for at times we shrivel away. We keep looking to some other source, to some other person, for the one who will come and make all things new. Open our eyes that we may see your presence among us, cleansing us, refreshing us, and making us new. Amen.

Images for Prayers of the People

- Water
- Baptism
- River chairs
- Candles

— ORDER OF WORSHIP —

✜ *Gathering* (see p. 188)

"Born in Human Likeness" #47 MV
"I Was There to Hear Your Borning Cry" #75 CH

✜ *Engaging* (see p. 189)

Welcome (see p. 189)

"Water Flowing from the Mountains" #87 MV
"Child of the Water" #120 CP

Invocation (see p. 190)

Holy God, your waters of life fill every molecule of our bodies and make our life possible. Move us this morning as we reflect on the baptism of Jesus, touch us with the waters of baptism, and remind us of what this water means in our lives. Amen.

"Like a Healing Stream" #144 MV

Scripture Reading: Mark 1:4–11 (see p. 190)

John the baptizer appeared in the wilderness, proclaiming a baptism of repentance for the forgiveness of sins. And people from the whole Judean countryside and all the people of Jerusalem were going out to him, and were baptized by him in the river Jordan, confessing their sins. Now John was clothed with camel's hair, with a leather belt around his waist, and he ate locusts and wild honey. He proclaimed, "The one who is more powerful than I is coming after me; I am not worthy to stoop down and untie the thong of his sandals. I have baptized you with water; but he will baptize you with the Holy Spirit."

In those days Jesus came from Nazareth of Galilee and was baptized by John in the Jordan. And just as he was coming up out of the water, he saw the heavens torn apart and the Spirit descending like a dove on him. And a voice came from heaven, "You are my Son, the Beloved; with you I am well pleased."

Welcoming the Children (see p. 191)

Passing the Peace (see p. 191)

Building the Community (see p. 191)

Reflection (see p. 191)

✝ *Responding* (see p. 191)

"Water, River, Spirit, Grace" #366 CH

Prayers of the People (see pp. 191 and 231)

Outreach (see p. 193)

Communion (see p. 194)

"When We Gather at the Table" #198 MV

✚ *Extending* (see p. 195)

Benediction (see p. 195)

"The Peace of the Earth" #189 CP

Going Forth (see p. 195)

Worship Service 8

EASTER SUNDAY, Year B

Prayer Station: Imagine a World

Materials needed for this prayer station

Index cards in a variety of colors that have the phrase "I imagine a world..." printed on them, writing utensils, a hollow globe (we use a globe that is a made of metal in a brassy color and has latitudinal and longitudinal lines like wires that hold the continents in place so that you can see whatever you put in the globe), a table for the globe set up at the front of the worship space, a microphone set up at the front of the worship space (for larger spaces), a screen and a projector (if your sanctuary has permanent screens and projectors, those will work just fine. It's just that one of the integral components of this prayer station is a PowerPoint presentation).

Setup

Before Easter Sunday, find an image that has a lot of color (colors that reflect the colors of the index cards would be ideal). I found an image of Strawberry Fields in Central Park, New York, with colorful paper cranes all over it. I then divided the picture up into twenty sections (five across and four down) and scrambled the sections so that the image was mixed up. I proceeded to unscramble the image over the course of twenty-three slides, with the final slide being the complete and clear image. I timed it so the image would automatically unscramble over seven minutes.

Presentation in Worship

The congregation sings the song that leads into the Prayers of the People, and then one of the worship leaders introduces the prayer station for the week:

The story of the resurrection inspires us to dream new dreams and to imagine the world anew. You are invited to reflect on how you imagine the world in light of the hope that resurrection brings. How do you see the world being different than it is? What are your biggest hopes and dreams for this world? You can either come up to the front and share your imaginings with the congregation or you can simply write your imaginings down on the index card, fold it up, and place it in the globe at the front of the sanctuary.

Note: Don't say anything that particularly draws their attention to the screens. Their eyes should naturally go there, but the PowerPoint presentation is meant to be a subtle undercurrent, not the main focus. It serves as a gentle reminder that all of the components are there for us to realize our imaginings, things are just often all mixed up. Because the screens are being utilized for this prayer station, the normal Prayers of the people PowerPoint presentation isn't used.

− ORDER OF WORSHIP −

✝ *Gathering* (see p. 188)

"Don't Be Afraid" #90 MV
"Woman In the Night" #188 CH

✝ *Engaging* (see p. 189)

Welcome (see p. 189)

"Alleluia, Praise to God" #59 MV
"Day and Night" #5 CP

Invocation (see p. 190)

We come to this place with hearts full of hope and hands open wide to the promises you have extended to us, Giver of New Life. Open our minds in this time of worship that we may dream new dreams with you. Speak through the story of resurrection that we may be not afraid of what the future holds. We pray in the name of the resurrected one. Amen.

"Never Ending Joy" #40 MV

Scripture Reading: Mark 16:1–8 (see p. 190)

When the sabbath was over, Mary Magdalene, and Mary the mother of James, and Salome bought spices, so that they might go and anoint him. And very early on the first day of the week, when the sun had risen, they went to the tomb. They had been saying to one another, "Who will roll away the stone for us from the entrance to the tomb?" When they looked up, they saw that the stone, which was very large, had already been rolled back. As they entered the tomb, they saw a young man, dressed in a white robe, sitting on the right side; and they were alarmed. But he said to them, "Do not be alarmed; you are looking for Jesus of Nazareth, who was crucified. He has been raised; he is not here. Look, there is the place they laid him. But go, tell his disciples and Peter that he is going ahead of you to Galilee; there you will see him, just as he told you." So they went out and fled from the tomb, for terror and amazement had seized them; and they said nothing to anyone, for they were afraid.

Welcoming the Children (see p. 191)

Passing the Peace (see p. 191)

Building the Community (see p. 191)

Reflection (see p. 191)

✝ *Responding* (see p. 191)

"To Love You" #145 CP

Prayers of the People (see p. 191)

Outreach (see p. 193)

Communion (see p. 194)

"Holy Light" #171 CP

✝ *Extending* (see p. 195)

Benediction (see p. 195)

"Hallelujah (Your Love Is Amazing)" #21 CP

Going Forth (see p. 195)

Worship Service 9
THIRD SUNDAY AFTER THE EPIPHANY, Year C
Prayer Station: Pieces of the Puzzle

Materials needed for the prayer station

An image of your choosing (at least sixteen inches by twenty inches and preferably an image that has a lot of components working together, lots of color, an image of diversity and unity), flexible magnetic tape with adhesive, a magnetic surface that can stand upright (or be propped against something in order to stand upright)

Setup

Laminate the image so that it is fairly sturdy. Then draw a puzzle pattern on the back of the image, write a number inside each of the sections (start with one in the upper right hand corner and number across and then continue numbering in ascending order on the next row until all the sections have a number. This will help orient people when they are trying to put the puzzle together) and cut along the lines to create pieces of the puzzle. Make enough puzzle pieces so that every person in your congregation will have a piece (this is definitely an activity meant for a small gathering of people. Our puzzle had between fifty and seventy-five pieces). Cut the magnetic tape into small pieces and adhere a strip of magnet to the back of each puzzle piece. Have the puzzle pieces ready to hand out as people come into the sanctuary for worship. It's a good idea to have a few people that you know will be starters for the puzzle when the time for prayer stations arrives (give them the corner pieces). If you have pieces left over, just give some people a second piece. The point is for the puzzle to be complete and whole by the end of the prayer time.

Presentation in Worship

The congregation sings the song that leads into the Prayers of the People, and then one of the worship leaders introduces the prayer station for the week:

> We are all individual members of the body of Christ. We are different and unique, but our differences brought together to form the whole makes us complete. During our time of prayer, you are invited to bring your puzzle piece up to the magnetic board at the front of sanctuary. Working together, we will complete the puzzle and reflect on the image of unity in diversity that is created from our joint endeavor.

Prayers of the People

> We are thankful, God, that you work through all of us in different ways to bring healing and wholeness to this fragmented world. It takes all kinds of people to make the world go round. Thank you for giving us each an important part to play.
>
> We pray for those who are still determining who they are called to be. We pray for those who feel used up. We pray for those who feel forgotten. We pray for those who are just waiting to be asked. Thank you for making a place for each one of them, for each one of us, in your puzzle of life.
>
> Open our minds to discern our part in the body of Christ. Empower us to play our part. Join us together to create unity in our diversity. Amen.

Images for Prayers of the People

- Diversity
- Unity
- Pieces making a whole
- People working together

− ORDER OF WORSHIP −

✢ *Gathering* (see p. 188)

"Santo, Santo, Santo" #111 CH
"Make Us One" #82 CP

✢ *Engaging* (see p. 189)

Welcome (see p. 189)

"Sing, Sing Out!" #180 MV
"One Spirit of Love" #151 CP

Invocation (see p. 190)

Divine presence, dwell richly in us. After a week of working long hours, a week of nothing to do, a week of mounds of homework, a week of silence in our homes, a week of chaos in our midst, a week of confusion, a week of joy, we seek solace in you, O God. From all of our different journeys, we gather in this place as your community, longing to renew our minds, our spirits, and our bodies for the week ahead. We gather together this morning as a diverse group of people. Weave us together, God, singers and speakers, dancers and teachers, contemplatives and doers, nurturers and builders, reminding us in this time of worship that we all together are the body of Christ. Amen.

"Like a River of Tears" #98 MV

Scripture Reading: 1 Corinthians 12:12–31a (see p. 190)

For just as the body is one and has many members, and all the members of the body, though many, are one body, so it is with Christ. For in the one Spirit we were all baptized into one body — Jews or Greeks, slaves or free — and we were all made to drink of one Spirit.

Indeed, the body does not consist of one member but of many. If the foot were to say, "Because I am not a hand, I do not belong to the body," that would not make it any less a part of the body. And if the ear were to say, "Because I am not an eye, I do not belong to the body," that would not make it any less a part of the body. If the whole body were an eye, where would the hearing be? If the whole body were hearing, where would the sense of smell be? But as it is, God arranged the members in the body, each one of them, as he chose. If all were a single member, where would the body be? As it is, there are many members, yet one body. The eye cannot say to the hand, "I have no need of you," nor again the head to the feet, "I have no need of you." On the contrary, the members of the body that seem to be weaker are indispensable, and those members of the body that we think less honorable we clothe with greater honor, and our less respectable members are treated with greater respect; whereas our more respectable members do not need this. But God has so arranged the body, giving the greater honor to the inferior member, that there may be no dissension within the body, but the members may have the same care for one another. If one member suffers, all suffer together with it; if one member is honored, all rejoice together with it.

Now you are the body of Christ and individually members of it. And God has appointed in the church first apostles, second prophets, third teachers; then deeds of power, then gifts of healing, forms of assistance, forms of leadership, various kinds of tongues. Are all apostles? Are all prophets? Are all teachers? Do all work miracles? Do all possess gifts of healing? Do all speak in tongues? Do all interpret? But strive for the greater gifts. And I will show you a still more excellent way.

Welcoming the Children (see p. 191)

Passing the Peace (see p. 191)

Building the Community (see p. 191)

Reflection (see p. 191)

✠ *Responding* (see p. 191)

"Restless Weaver" #658 CH

Prayers of the People (see pp. 191 and 239)

Outreach (see p. 193)

Communion (see p. 194)

"Christ Has No Body Now But Yours" #171 MV

✠ *Extending* (see p. 195)

Benediction (see p. 195)

"Glory to God" #36 MV

Going Forth (see p. 195)

Worship Service 10

FOURTH SUNDAY OF LENT, Year C

Prayer Station: Reflections on Forgiveness

Materials needed for this prayer station

A copy of the painting *The Prodigal Son* by Rembrandt, cut up into three different sections: the younger son, the parent, and the older son; reflection sheets for each image; three short tables and cushions or kneelers to place around the tables.

Setup

Here are questions to put with each image:

The Younger Son: Have you ever...

- felt lost?
- tried to find yourself in things that just made you lose yourself even more?
- squandered the gifts that have been given to you?
- had no choice but to "return home" and ask forgiveness?
- experienced forgiveness?
- felt extravagant hospitality?
- felt completely and totally loved by God, unconditionally?

The Parent: Have you ever...

- been hurt by a loved one?
- trusted someone only to have that trust betrayed?
- been disappointed in someone you love?
- felt great joy over a loved one's "return"?

243

- extended forgiveness?

- shared extravagant hospitality?

The Older Son : Have you ever...

- done what was expected of you?

- been the responsible one in your family?

- been jealous of someone?

- worked so hard only to have the one who didn't work at all get the reward?

- wished God would extend vengeance instead of mercy?

Have a different station for each of the people in the painting. Provide places for people to kneel or sit at each station.

Presentation in Worship

The congregation sings the song that leads into the Prayers of the People, and then one of the worship leaders introduces the prayer station for the week:

> There are three prayer stations set up near the front of the sanctuary, each featuring a different character from the painting *The Prodigal Son* by Rembrandt.
>
> You are invited to visit each station and reflect on each respective character in the painting. Do you identify with any of them? More than one of them? How has your life at times mirrored their lives?

Prayers of the People

> Forgiveness is a difficult thing. It is always there, like a blanket over our lives. There are times when each of us need it, and there

are times when each of us have the power to grant it. We can put ourselves in the shoes of the younger son, the father, and even the elder son. God, teach us again the richness of this story.

When we feel we have been wronged, keep us from retribution. When we have wronged another, we ask for forgiveness. God, out of our need for forgiveness, teach us to in turn forgive others.

Help us recognize your forgiveness by turning our hearts to forgive those who have wronged us. Show us your way of love, carrying us beyond the anger that binds us up in bitterness and poisons our ability to forgive. Loosen these chains and lift away the negativity, freeing us to healing action in our relationships. Amen.

Images for Prayers of the People

* Various artistic interpretations of the Parable of the Prodigal Son.

— ORDER OF WORSHIP —

✚ *Gathering* (see p. 188)

"Within Our Darkest Night" #37 SPT
"Tree of Life" #134 CP

✚ *Engaging* (see p. 189)

Welcome (see p. 189)

"A Wilderness Wandering People" #127 CP
"Come to the Table Again" #13 CP

Invocation (see p. 190)

Holy God, we come to you on this day bringing you all of our stuff. The stuff of life weighs us down and lifts us up. The stuff of life pulls us under and lights a fire beneath us. The stuff of life breaks us and teaches us. The stuff of life weighs heavy and so we come to this place wanting to release these burdens. All of this stuff brings us to you on our knees, praying for the wisdom to sift through it all, to discern some meaning from it all, and to grow closer to you and your will for us in it all. Move us to new ways of understanding your love that we may in turn love others as you love us. Amen.

"Love Us into Fullness" #81 MV

Scripture Reading: Luke 15:1–3, 11–32 (see p. 190)

Now all the tax-collectors and sinners were coming near to listen to him. And the Pharisees and the scribes were grumbling and saying, "This fellow welcomes sinners and eats with them." So he told them this parable...

There was a man who had two sons. The younger of them said to his father, "Father, give me the share of the property that will belong to me." So he divided his property between them. A few days later the younger son gathered all he had and traveled to a distant country, and there he squandered his property in dissolute living. When he had spent everything, a severe famine took place throughout that country, and he began to be in need. So he went and hired himself out to one of the citizens of that country, who sent him to his fields to feed the pigs. He would gladly have filled himself with the pods that the pigs were eating; and no one gave him anything. But when he came to himself he said, "How many of my father's hired hands have bread enough and to spare, but here I am dying of hunger! I will get up and go to my father, and I will say to him, 'Father, I have sinned against heaven and before you; I am no longer worthy to be called your son; treat me like one of your hired hands.'" So he set off and went to his father. But while he was still far off, his father saw him and was filled with compassion; he ran and put his arms around him and kissed him. Then the son said to him, "Father, I have sinned against heaven and before you; I am no longer worthy to be called your son." But the father said to his slaves, "Quickly, bring out a robe — the best one — and put it on him; put a ring on his finger and sandals on his feet. And get the fatted calf and kill it, and let us eat and celebrate; for this son of mine was dead and is alive again; he was lost and is found!" And they began to celebrate.

Now his elder son was in the field; and when he came and approached the house, he heard music and dancing. He called one of the slaves and asked what was going on. He replied, "Your brother has come, and your father has killed the fatted calf, because he has got him back safe and sound." Then he became angry and refused to go in. His father came out and began to plead with him. But he answered his father, "Listen! For all these years I have been working like a slave for you, and I have never disobeyed your command; yet you have never given me even a young goat so that I might celebrate with my friends. But when this son of yours came back, who has devoured your property with prostitutes, you killed the fatted calf for him!" Then the father said to him, "Son, you are always with me, and all that is mine is yours. But we had to celebrate and rejoice, because this brother of yours was dead and has come to life; he was lost and has been found."

Welcoming the Children (see p. 191)

Passing the Peace (see p. 191)

Building the Community (see p. 191)

Reflection (see p. 191)

✛ *Responding* (see p. 191)

"Because You Came" #64 MV

Prayers of the People (see pp. 191 and 244)

Outreach (see p. 193)

Communion (see p. 194)

"Bread of Life, Feed My Soul" #194 MV

✛ *Extending* (see p. 195)

Benediction (see p. 195)

"Go in Peace" #183 CP

Going Forth (see p. 195)

FOURTH SUNDAY AFTER PENTECOST, Year C

Prayer Station: Building and Tearing Down Walls

Materials needed for this prayer station

A lot of tissue boxes.

Setup

Have the tissue boxes where they are easily accessible for the preaching minister or speaker, but not out in the open for people to see. They are not meant to be a focal point until they are being used to build the wall during the reflection.

Reflection

The sermon for this service consisted of numerous little stories of people encountering walls on their way to worship. There were stories about:

- a woman becoming physically disabled and no longer able to worship in her home congregation because the building was not wheel-chair accessible;

- a little girl who was teased for being slow in school by one of her friends;

- a woman who got divorced and turned to her congregation for support only to discover they were more interested in supporting her husband since he had all the money;

- a U.S. Senator being for comprehensive immigration reform until he received numerous letters from constituents saying things like "Send them home!" and "Build a wall to keep them out!" and "We don't want their kind here!";

- a young man being beaten because a friendly smile at another man was misinterpreted;

- a young woman struggling to make ends meet and unable to continue contributing financially to her church receiving a phone call from the church, not to check on how she was doing, but to inquire about her lack of giving;

- an African American family moving into a small town in 1960s Ohio only to have their house dynamited shortly after they arrived;

- a man diagnosed with AIDS still physically able to work and yet unable to find a job;

- laws that are designed to curb illegal immigration, but instead end up targeting any person who has brown skin.

As each story is told, the tissue boxes are placed in such a way that a wall is built, blocking access to the communion table. The wall is built higher and wider as stories of ways in which people have been shut out and discriminated against are told. By the time the sermon is complete and the Prayers of the People are about to begin, the wall of tissue boxes (staggered in such a way that it looks like a brick wall), is an eyesore in the worship space.

Presentation in Worship

The congregation sings the song that leads into the Prayers of the People and then one of the worship leaders introduces the prayer station for the week:

> There is now a wall blocking access to the communion table. During this time of prayer, you are invited to dismantle the wall built during the reflection. As followers of Jesus, we are called to break down the walls society has built, walls that keep people in their place, walls that shut people out, walls that bar people from opportunities for wholeness. Even though Christianity has

too often been turned into something that places restrictions and conditions on people, we work to embody a faith that welcomes all people into our midst. We will start by turning this wall into a pathway that leads to the communion table, wide enough that all can gain access, showing that in this place, *all* are welcome at the table, "the poor, the crippled, the blind, and the lame."

Prayers of the People

Walls spring up in unlikely places. Walls separate the poor from the rich, the haves from the have-nots, the sick from the healthy. We keep one another at arm's length, afraid of the ways we might be called upon to change, fearful of the other in our midst.

But walls are not a part of your kin-dom.

And so we pray that we learn how to turn the walls we have built that keep people out into bridges that let people in. Help us to understand the awesome power of your love. The power of your love to bind together people of different creeds, races, and tongues. The power of your love to break down the barriers we have so skillfully erected. The power of your love to transform our means of exclusion into means of welcome. May the walls of separation crumble before our very eyes. Amen.

Images for Prayers of the People

- Walls
- Bridges
- Barriers
- Clear pathways

– ORDER OF WORSHIP –

✚ *Gathering* (see p. 188)

"Bless the Lord" #3 TSP
"Let Us Build a House" #1 MV

✚ *Engaging* (see p. 189)

Welcome (see p. 189)

"New Song" #9 CP
"Lord of Justice" #125 CP

Invocation (see p. 190)

God of incredible and beautiful diversity, the web of creation
is woven with a plethora of colors, and while we marvel at the
world around us, we sometimes forget to celebrate the differences of those in our midst. We pray your Spirit will infuse our
time of worship, tearing down the walls that keep out the very
ones we are called to serve. We open ourselves to you, inviting
you to transform us into the welcoming people you call us to
be. Amen.

"This Is Holy Ground" #55 CP

Scripture Reading: Luke 14:12–24 (see p. 190)

He said also to the one who had invited him, "When you give a
luncheon or a dinner, do not invite your friends or your brothers
or your relatives or rich neighbors, in case they may invite you in
return, and you would be repaid. But when you give a banquet,
invite the poor, the crippled, the lame, and the blind. And you
will be blessed, because they cannot repay you, for you will be
repaid at the resurrection of the righteous."

One of the dinner guests, on hearing this, said to him, "Blessed is anyone who will eat bread in the kingdom of God!" Then Jesus said to him, "Someone gave a great dinner and invited many. At the time for the dinner he sent his slave to say to those who had been invited, 'Come; for everything is ready now.' But they all alike began to make excuses. The first said to him, 'I have bought a piece of land, and I must go out and see it; please accept my apologies.' Another said, 'I have bought five yoke of oxen, and I am going to try them out; please accept my apologies.' Another said, 'I have just been married, and therefore I cannot come.' So the slave returned and reported this to his master. Then the owner of the house became angry and said to his slave, 'Go out at once into the streets and lanes of the town and bring in the poor, the crippled, the blind, and the lame.' And the slave said, 'Sir, what you ordered has been done, and there is still room.' Then the master said to the slave, 'Go out into the roads and lanes, and compel people to come in, so that my house may be filled. For I tell you, none of those who were invited will taste my dinner.' "

Welcoming the Children (see p. 191)

Passing the Peace (see p. 191)

Building the Community (see p. 191)

Reflection (see pp. 191 and 249)

✠ *Responding* (see p. 191)

"Kyrie" #96 CP

Prayers of the People (see pp. 191 and 251)

Outreach (see p. 193)

Communion (see p. 194)

"World Without Walls" #140 CP

✠ *Extending* (see p. 195)

Benediction (see p. 195)

"Thuma Mina" #447 CH

Going Forth (see p. 195)

TWENTIETH (OR TWENTY-FIRST) SUNDAY
AFTER PENTECOST, Year C

Prayer Station: The Persistent Widow

Materials needed for this prayer station

A blank image of the persistent widow (someone in our congregation drew an outline of the persistent widow with the details on her head covering visible. Other than that, the image was a blank slate), writing utensils.

Reflection

> The sermon that was preached on this Sunday at Brentwood pointed to the tendency many interpretations of the parable have to see God in the unjust judge. Instead, what if we considered God as the persistent widow, relentlessly pursuing justice on behalf of the least of these? God is then seen in the people rising up against the powers that be, demanding that the voices of the oppressed be heard. God is working tirelessly in this world, moving against forces that seek to thwart mutuality and compassion for all people. It's the refrain heard over and over in the Bible, stories of God coming to people through the least of these, in the least likely places, and this parable keeps that refrain going.

Presentation in Worship

The congregation sings the song that leads into the Prayers of the People, and then one of the worship leaders introduces the prayer station for the week:

This morning we heard a parable about humanity. For we are each both the widow and the unjust judge. We have cried out for justice and we have also turned away from the cries of others. We have worked and worked and worked to bring about good, and we have also done good only because it was easier than the alternative. There are voices crying out for justice. And in their voices we hear the very cry of God. What are some of the voices you hear crying out? Who are the persistent widows of our time? During our time of prayer, you are invited to come forward and name those who are crying out by writing their names on the persistent widow at the front of the sanctuary.

Note: One of the unexpected things that happened during this prayer station is that people wrote their words in such a way that they gave the persistent widow features. Even though we were essentially just using words on paper, there were still ways for people to be creative. This is one of the benefits of prayer stations.

Prayers of the People

Great nurturing Spirit, we open ourselves to you in this time of prayer. The paths we have traveled are varied, our experiences many, yet you turn your loving ear to each one of us, granting each of us your care and concern as our parent. For those who are crumpled under the weight of their own grief, offer your peace, wiping away their tears and lifting them up, that they may experience life after loss. For those who have built walls of protection to shield themselves from the dangers this life has so cruelly shown them, offer your tender guiding hand, drawing them gently from the haven they have built inside that they may experience the beauty and the kindness this world has to offer. For those who have met dissension at every turn, offer your spirit of reconciliation, giving hope and revealing possibilities that they may continue to strive for understanding.

Loving Creator, remind us of your presence in every moment. In the pale sunrise kissing the earth, in the winds that make the leaves dance, in the eagle that soars above the land, in a baby's cry during worship, in the uncontrollable giggles of children, in our lively conversations with one another, in our need for help when we wander from your way, in the tears we shed that melt the coldness we sometimes feel for others, in the passion to make the world a more just and compassionate place in the face of ignorance, bigotry, and hatred.

God, help us to realize that with you as our guide, we are capable of great things. This world does not need to be broken. You have entrusted it to us, charging us to be your hands and your feet in this world to bring compassion, healing, and peace. Push us to be more than we think we are, unlock your wealth of wisdom and love within us, give us a passion that will not quail in the face of adversity, but rather will rise up with renewed strength, for you are our God, and we can do all things through you who strengthen us. Amen.

Images for Prayers of the People

- Crying out
- People in need

− ORDER OF WORSHIP −

✚ *Gathering* (see p. 188)

"Holy Spirit Come to Us" #24 TSP
"God in the Darkness" #17 MV

✚ *Engaging* (see p. 189)

Welcome (see p. 189)

"Gather Us In" #284 CH
"My Soul Cries Out" #120 MV

Invocation (see p. 190)

O God of wonder, you come to us in unexpected ways. In a bush that is burning yet not consumed, in a still, small voice that we assume to be too insignificant for you, in a shabby barn, born to common people who knew not of the love preparing to envelop the world, in the voice of a woman, crying out for justice. We thank you for the many ways you meet us. Keep us ever on our toes, looking for you in the most unlikely of places. Amen.

"Spirit, Open My Heart" #79 MV

Scripture Reading: Luke 18:1–8 (see p. 190)

Then Jesus told them a parable about their need to pray always and not to lose heart. He said, "In a certain city there was a judge who neither feared God nor had respect for people. In that city there was a widow who kept coming to him and saying, 'Grant me justice against my opponent.' For a while he refused; but later he said to himself, 'Though I have no fear of God and no respect for anyone, yet because this widow keeps bothering me, I will grant her justice, so that she may not wear me out by continually coming.'" And the Lord said, "Listen to what the unjust judge says. And will not God grant justice to his chosen ones who cry to him day and night? Will he delay long in helping them? I tell you, he will quickly grant justice to them. And yet, when the Son of Man comes, will he find faith on earth?"

Welcoming the Children (see p. 191)

Passing the Peace (see p. 191)

Building the Community (see p. 191)

Reflection (see pp. 191 and 255)

✚ *Responding*

"God Weeps" #74 MV

Prayers of the People (see pp. 191 and 256 262)

Outreach (see p. 193)

Communion (see p. 194)

"God Bless to Us Our Bread" #193 MV

✚ *Extending* (see p. 195)

Benediction (see p. 195)

"Sent Out in Jesus' Name" #212 MV

Going Forth (see p. 195)

Bonus Worship Service

WORLD COMMUNION SUNDAY

One thing we noticed in planning worship for World Communion Sunday is that none of the lectionary readings for that Sunday in any of the three years of the cycle are explicitly helpful for that Sunday if the focus is in fact on World Communion Sunday. Sometimes we need to deviate from the lectionary in order to avoid cramming too many varied and sometimes conflicting themes and images into one worship service. So here we provide a bonus worship service, one that does not fit into the lectionary cycle, yet is an important Sunday in the life of the church ecumenical.

For this Sunday, we chose a reading from 1 Corinthians. The sermon was a collection of stories of bread being broken in different situations around the world and the ways in which that act of breaking bread tears down walls.

This Sunday does not have a prayer station. Instead, it has a great deal of preparation that goes into the service in order to make it a multisensory experience. The act of communion itself will serve as a prayer station in a way because it will be a different experience from other Sundays. The time with the children is a great moment to introduce the different kinds of bread, to let the children (and by extension, the rest of the congregation) see the different colors and textures of the bread.

Materials needed for this worship service

Bread from around the world, grapes, a bread machine with all of the ingredients to make bread. (I generally use a recipe for Argentine Chimichurri Bread because it has a lot of herbs and such in it, so the aroma while it is baking is delicious!)

Setup

The best way to do the bread is to have several people from the congregation bake it. Recipes for breads from around the world can be found on the Internet. Try baking breads that have a variety of textures, flavors, and colors. Some of the breads we've baked for this Sunday in the past are challah (it looks beautiful on the communion table), tortillas, Russian black bread, pita bread, noni afghani, Irish soda bread, and South African mealie bread. Place the bread and the grapes on the communion table so there is an abundance.

About an hour and a half or so before the worship service, set up the bread machine in the sanctuary with all the ingredients and plug it in. It's important to do this early so that the mixing and rising steps of the bread making will be done before worship (since the mixing will be noisy); the baking will occur during worship. This way the smell of baking bread will permeate the worship space.

Presentation in Worship

During the invitation to communion, a worship leader will lift up various places around the world, places where people are gathered together in worship breaking bread just like us, even in their varied circumstances. An example follows (this would obviously have to be amended to correspond with current events):

> We break bread with our brothers and sisters in Zimbabwe, whose lives are made increasingly more difficult due to alarming inflation rates and food shortages.

> We break bread with our brothers and sisters in Georgia, who are seeing the first real signs of Russian withdrawal from south Ossetia.

We break bread with our brothers and sisters in Haiti, who continue to plummet in the wake of four major storms in the Caribbean.

We break bread with our brothers and sisters in the war-torn countries of Iraq and Afghanistan.

We break bread with our brothers and sisters in Mexico who dream of a better life for their children.

We break bread with our brothers and sisters in this country and around the world as banks and stock markets continue to struggle in England, Germany, Japan, and elsewhere due to the stress and fear produced by the financial crisis.

As the worship leader lifts up each of these places, someone else stands at the communion table and breaks bread as each statement is made. Then varieties of bread are made available for people to choose from as they come forward for communion. This way there is a tangible connection to those in other parts of the world as we eat bread that is different from the bread we serve every other Sunday.

After the service, bring the bread out into the fellowship area so people can sample the different kinds of bread. This will further connect the theme of breaking bread together as an act of fellowship.

Prayers of the People

Here we are:

Lost	Searching
Aching	Wondering
Rejoicing	Questioning
Open	Waiting
Hoping	

On our varied walks of life, we meet here, at these crossroads, to join our hearts together in prayer and join our lives together in the act of communion.

All around the world, people are gathering at tables like this one, breaking bread together in an act of worship that reminds us of the extravagant hospitality you extend to us in this meal. In this act of breaking bread with the world, we envision the world as you long for it to be. We witness the inbreaking of your kingdom right here, right now. We embody the expansiveness of your love as we eat the bread of life and drink the cup of hope.

Join us together in this simplest of meals, reminding us that we are all members of the one body of Christ. Amen.

Images for Prayers of the People

- Bread
- Grapes
- Wine
- Chalices
- Multicultural gatherings
- People receiving communion in different countries

− ORDER OF WORSHIP −

✟ *Gathering* (see p. 188)

"There Is Room for All" #62 MV
"Bring Many Names" #10 CH

✟ *Engaging* (see p. 189)

Welcome (see p. 189)

"Joyful, Joyful, We Adore You" #4 NCH
"The Life You Want to Know" #12 CP

Invocation (see p. 190)

From many parts of the world, your people gather together this morning to break bread, God, in a powerful reminder of the global impact of your love walking and living and teaching and dying and being reborn among us. Nourish us with the bread that is you as we join our voices together in songs of praise, as we join our hearts together in moments of prayer, and as we break the bread together in the act of communion. Amen.

"In You There Is a Refuge" #84 MV

Scripture Reading: 1 Corinthians 11:23–26 (see p. 190)

For I received from the Lord what I also handed on to you, that the Lord Jesus on the night when he was betrayed took a loaf of bread, and when he had given thanks, he broke it and said, "This is my body that is for you. Do this in remembrance of me." In the same way he took the cup also, after supper, saying, "This cup is the new covenant in my blood. Do this, as often as you drink it, in remembrance of me." For as often as you eat this bread and drink the cup, you proclaim the Lord's death until he comes.

Welcoming the Children (see p. 191)

Passing the Peace (see p. 191)

Building the Community (see p. 191)

Reflection (see p. 191)

✝ *Responding* (see p. 191)

"You'll Find Love" #106 CP

Prayers of the People (see pp. 191 and 262)

Outreach (see p. 193)

Communion (see p. 194)

"One Bread, One Body" #393 CH

✝ *Extending* (see p. 195)

Benediction (see p. 195)

"Halleluya! We Sing Your Praises" #186 CP

Going Forth (see p. 195)

NOTES

Introduction

1. As related by Phyllis Tickle in Garrison, *Rising from the Ashes,* 2.

2. Carol Howard Merritt, "Yes, We Did," *Tribal Church,* January 22, 2009, *http://tribalchurch.org/* (accessed February 21, 2009).

3. So we'll talk about it in the endnotes. Robert Wuthnow, the director of the Center for the Study of Religion at Princeton University, notes that the declines that have taken place since the 1970s cannot easily be dismissed. Between the 1960s and 1980s, mainline Protestants lost between a quarter and a third of their memberships. Additionally, "the majority of younger adults either attend religious services rarely or, if they attend more than that, are hardly regular enough to be the core of any congregation." Since the 1970s, each congregation in the United States has lost on average twenty-one young adults. "I cannot think of a clergy person who would not like to have twenty-one more younger adults in his or her congregation," Wuthnow says. See especially Wuthnow, *After the Baby Boomers,* 18 and 76. See also Gibbs and Bolger, *Emerging Churches:* "We both believe the current situation is dire. If the church does not embody its message and life within postmodern culture, it will become increasingly marginalized" (8, see also 19).

4. Wallis, "Sojo Mail" (June 28, 2008). See also his *Great Awakening.*

5. Kimball, introduction to *Emerging Worship,* xii.

6. See especially ibid.

7. DeYoung and Kluck, *Why We're Not Emergent.*

8. In the most comprehensive analysis of emerging church culture, Eddie Gibbs and Ryan Bolger observe that generational issues often referenced in conversation with emerging churches are actually "imbedded in the much deeper cultural and philosophical shift from modernity to postmodernity." Karen Ward, one of the most prominent emergent church leaders in the United States, laments the ways that most established churches have assumed that the current crisis in church participation is rooted more in generational, rather than cultural, shifts. While working at the headquarters of the Evangelical Lutheran Church in America, she initially thought that generational analyses were most important, but later "realized that the changes were

much bigger than generational grouping." It just so happens that, in Ward's words, Gen-Xers are "the first marines on the beach" of postmodernity, and subsequent generations will inevitably be shaped and formed from a post-modern perspective. From this perspective, the shifts taking place within emergent culture have much more to do with the advent of postmodernism than with generational traits and tendencies.

9. See especially Gibbs and Bolger, *Emerging Churches,* 22–34.

10. This is the phrase Phyllis Tickle coined in her book by the same name.

Chapter 1: Becoming Conversant with the Emergent Church

1. Christian and Amy Piatt, *MySpace to Sacred Space,* 7.

2. As cited in Garrison, *Rising from the Ashes,* 11–12.

3. See Tomlinson, *The Post-Evangelical.*

4. Goodstein, "Obama Names Minister to Lead Prayer Service."

5. Or that the mainline church's institutionalism hadn't blocked the message so much.

6. "United Church of Christ Firsts."

7. To cite a simple example: on January 30, 2003, before the Iraq war started, leaders from eleven mainline traditions and four mainline organizations (including the National Council of Churches) sent a letter to the White House advocating a peaceful solution to the Iraq crisis (*www.ncccusa.org*).

8. Rollins, introduction to *How (Not) to Speak of God,* xv.

9. Ibid., xiv.

10. Ibid., xv.

11. Jones, *The New Christians,* 113.

12. Ibid., 109.

13. McLaren, *The Secret Message of Jesus,* 209.

14. McLaren, *Everything Must Change,* 242. McLaren's emphasis on the social gospel has led Leonard Sweet to criticize emergents as the new left (see Jones, *The New Christians,* 82).

15. Hall as cited in Gibbs and Bolger, *Emerging Churches,* 38–39; emphasis in the original.

16. See Baker and Gay, *Alternative Worship,* and also Gibbs and Bolger, *Emerging Churches.*

17. In her foreword for Kimball, *Emerging Worship,* vi.

18. Long, *Beyond the Worship Wars,* 10.

19. Byassee, "Emerging Model: A Visit to Jacob's Well."

20. Ibid.

21. Salmon, "Feeling Renewed by Ancient Traditions."

22. Ibid. See also Wuthnow, *After the Baby Boomers,* 223–25.

23. See especially Webber, *Ancient-Future Worship.*

24. "Church of the Apostles Community Worship," from Church of the Apostles.

25. Ibid. Church of the Apostle's website offers some great audio files that help others get a feel for their ancient-future style.

26. Available at *www.greenbelt.org.uk* (Greenbelt Festival Podcast).

27. McKnight, interview, *PBS: Religion and Ethics Newsweekly.*

28. See EmergentVillage.com. Also note that when we capitalize Emergent we are generally referring to those connected to Emergent Village.

29. Jones, interview, *PBS: Religion and Ethics Newsweekly.*

30. McKnight, interview.

31. McKnight, "Five Streams of the Emerging Church."

32. DeYoung and Kluck, *Why We're Not Emergent,* 17–18.

33. Gibbs and Bolger, *Emerging Churches,* 44–45. Critics have said this definition is so broad that it can encompass any group of Christians, emerging or not. However, Gibbs and Bolger are quite intentional in naming practices they view as distinctly postmodern.

34. As cited in Garrison, *Rising from the Ashes,* 5.

35. "The Search: A Worship Community," University Christian Church, *www.seekingthesacred.org/worship-values/* (accessed March 3, 2009).

36. Broaddus, "Further Musings on the Emergent Church and Race."

37. Gibbs and Bolger, *Emerging Churches,* 29.

38. Freeman, "On Being a Queer Queermergent."

39. Jones, *The New Christians,* 70. This leads Phyllis Tickle to quip, "Postmodern, post-Christian, post-Protestant, and post-denominational. What do all these posts mean? That we know where we have been but that we have no idea where we are going!" See Bass, *Christianity for the Rest of Us,* 22.

40. "About Emergent Village," *www.emergentvillage.com/about/* (accessed March 3, 2009).

Chapter 2: Different Types of the Emergent Church

1. Rollins, "Lessons in Evandalism Tour."

2. Jones, *The New Christians,* 70–71.

3. "Mark Driscoll on the Emerging Church."

4. Emerging authors like Dan Kimball (*The Emerging Church* and *Emerging Worship*) fall into this group.

5. Neil Cole has focused on this group in his books *Organic Church* and *Organic Leadership.* For more on the "New Monastics," see House, *School(s) for Conversion,* and also Heath and Kisker, *Longing for Spring,* or anything written by Shane Claiborne.

6. For a more formal look at Mark Driscoll's thought, see his *Confessions of a Reformission Rev.*

7. "Mark Driscoll on the Emerging Church."

8. Bell, *Velvet Elvis,* 182.

9. When it comes to writing about emerging approaches to worship, we retain the general usage of the phrase "emerging worship" simply because it is representative of approaches to worship that tend to be valued by those from both the "emerging" and "emergent" lanes. The primary difference has to do with theological appropriations of emerging worship, which is of course no small matter. While there are many "emerging" evangelicals from the first three lanes who participate in emerging worship gatherings that are friendly to evangelical theological approaches, very few "emergents" from lane four are able to find communities of faith that offer emerging styles of worship that resonate with their theological approach. This is much of the reason that we have written this book. We think that progressive communities of faith are good news to emergents every bit as much as emergents are good news to them.

10. See especially Bass and Tickle.

11. DeYoung and Kluck, *Why We're Not Emergent,* 22–23.

12. Phyllis Tickle, *The Great Emergence,* 164n.7.

13. As told in Gibbs and Bolger, *Emerging Churches,* 34.

14. The sequels to *A New Kind of Christian* are *The Story We Find Ourselves In: Further Adventures of A New Kind of Christian* and *The Last Word and the Word after That: A Tale of Faith, Doubt, and a New Kind of Christianity.*

15. See Jones, *The New Christians,* 51.

16. Robin M., "*A New Kind of Christian* — the Trilogy," *What Canst Thou Say,* January 19, 2009; *http://robinmsf.blogspot.com* (accessed on March 3, 2009).

Chapter 3: Listening to Ecclesiologies of the Emergent Church

1. Rollins, *The Fidelity of Betrayal*, 177.
2. As quoted in Jones, *The New Christians*, 201.
3. Gibbs and Bolger, *Emerging Churches*, 39.
4. Bass, *Christianity for the Rest of Us*, 42.
5. Ibid., 7.
6. King, "Letter from Birmingham City Jail," 300.
7. DeYoung and Kluck, *Why We're Not Emergent*, 19.
8. Gibbs and Bolger, *Emerging Churches*, 11.
9. Rollins, "Batman as the Ultimate Capitalist Superhero" (accessed June 18, 2009).
10. Gonzales, "A Hispanic Perspective: By the Rivers of Babylon," 92–93.
11. This can also be found in Pagitt and Jones, *An Emergent Manifesto of Hope*. For McLaren, see Garrison, *Rising from the Ashes*, 51.
12. We appreciate Doug Pagitt's permission to use this image. For an extended discussion of his quadrilateral, be sure to check out his forthcoming book, *Christianity Now: Faith in the Inventive Age*.
13. Ross Lockhart, telephone interview with Phil Snider and Emily Bowen, January 29, 2009.
14. Adam Walker Cleaveland, "Presbymergent: The Story of One Mainliner's Quest to Be a Loyal Radical," in Pagitt and Jones, *An Emergent Manifesto of Hope*, 125.
15. Lebacqz, *Word, Worship, World, and Wonder*, 60.
16. Bass, interview, *PBS: Religion and Ethics Newsweekly,* July 8, 2005, *www.pbs.org/wnet/religionandethics/week845/interview1.html* (accessed on March 3, 2009).
17. This isn't intended to draw attention away from the very stark reality facing mainline denominations and younger clergy. The average age of active mainline Protestant pastors in the United States is fifty-five. In the United Church of Canada, there are more ordained clergy over the age of one hundred than under the age of thirty. But those are just the statistics. Because very few seminarians enroll as first career pastors, it is difficult for pastors under the age of forty to be taken seriously by their colleagues and congregations. In Carol Howard Merritt's *Tribal Church*, one pastor, a doctoral student and father of two, reflects on an academic/professional society meeting he recently attended: "I was repeatedly addressed as 'young man,'

and asked by a stranger to 'run around' and set up the room for a seminar I was attending. Later, in line for a plenary session, I watched as the older people in front of me were greeted pleasantly by the usher; the same usher warned me sternly to take only one resource packet for the event. The next day I overheard someone lamenting the lack of younger people in the society. Go figure" (from Merritt, *Tribal Church,* 106, which we view as one of the best generational studies currently available). All of us have these stories, and we could fill several pages of footnotes with them (Phil is thirty-six; Emily is thirty-two). At most of the conferences we attend, several people look at Phil's badge marked "Brentwood Christian Church" and, invariably, assume that he is the youth pastor. Then they ask if he's considered going to seminary. Emily is usually asked if she is the youth leader or choir director, and, as a woman, she gets these questions at least twice as often. Perhaps our favorite story along these lines includes one of the world's most prominent mainline theologians (he's not mentioned in this book, by the way). He was set to speak at a conference, and one of our colleagues (who was in his early thirties at the time) was supposed to meet him and show him around — the usual hospitality sort of thing. This particular theologian got out of his car, saw this young minister standing on the sidewalk, opened the trunk, and said, "Here boy, carry my bags upstairs."

There is no doubt that young clergy face particular frustrations of their own. But in terms of the emergent church, we want to be clear in stating that a significant number of pastors in their forties, fifties, and even sixties are involved in the conversation. As much as prevailing assumptions in mainline circles might think otherwise, it's not just a "youth" movement.

18. This is true in evangelical circles as well, hence the emphasis that all four lanes of the emerging/emergent highway place on rethinking ecclesiology and worship.

19. Bass, *Christianity for the Rest of Us,* 6. One of the ironies of this dynamic is that several young leaders within mainline communities so frustrated with ecclesial structures still expect these very structures to ride in on a white horse and save the day.

20. Ibid., 10.

21. Jones, *The New Christians,* 137.

22. We're indebted to our friend and colleague Alex Ruth for first pointing this out to us.

23. Bass, *The Practicing Congregation,* 87–88.

24. Tickle, *The Great Emergence,* 142–43.

25. Gibbs and Bolger, *Emerging Churches,* 28–29.

26. Caputo, *What Would Jesus Deconstruct?* 137–38.

27. See Cleaveland, "Presbymergent," in Pagitt and Jones, *An Emergent Manifesto of Hope,* 119–28.

28. See Tickle's brilliant analysis.

29. Perkins School of Theology devoted its 2009 Ministers' Week to this topic.

30. "Mission of the Methomergent Lab," online at *http://methomergentlab .wordpress.com/mission-of-the-methomergent-lab/* (accessed February 17, 2009).

31. Barlow, "New Approaches to Worship Emerge."

32. Rollins, *Fidelity of Betrayal,* 177–78. This doesn't suggest that emergent movements can somehow avoid institutional trappings at every turn, no matter how hard they try. As Tickle has observed, "There is the church universal and the church intimate. And in between them is the church institutional. And it's the business of the church institutional to connect the intimate and the universal. So we can't have an emergent movement that doesn't become at some point the emergent church institutional" (Tickle, as cited in Garrison, *Rising from the Ashes,* 4). Emergent collectives will have institutional concerns, but not necessarily the same kind as established congregations.

33. Bolz-Weber as cited in Garrison, *Rising from the Ashes,* 16–17.

Chapter 4: A Passion for Justice

1. Bell and Golden, *Jesus Wants to Save Christians,* 179.

2. Wallis, "Come Let us Reason Together." Historically speaking, it's important to point out that many streams of evangelical thought have been deeply committed to social justice (one might wish to recall that altar calls were originally used in order to recruit participants to join in the struggle against slavery). Though emergents who are "evangelical expatriates" tend to be expatriates from the kind of Religious Right fundamentalism/evangelicalism that dominated the latter part of the twentieth century, this is hardly representative of evangelicalism as whole. In addition, progressives should certainly be "evangelical" in the sense of the good news they proclaim. From this perspective, we like the designation "evangelical" (we just recognize that such a term is associated with a lot of baggage in contemporary North American culture, especially in relationship to the Religious Right).

3. See Taylor, *After God*, 40.

4. Mullins, Concert.

5. As quoted in Claiborne, *The Irresistible Revolution*, 98.

6. As quoted in Borg, *The Heart of Christianity*, 133.

7. Ecclesia Church, Houston, *www.ecclesiahouston.org/* (accessed on March 4, 2009).

8. Jones, *The New Christians*, 72.

9. McLaren, "An Open Letter to Worship Songwriters."

10. Gibbs and Bolger, *Emerging Churches*, 54.

11. Ibid., 56.

12. Ibid., 54–55.

13. Sojourner Truth, as quoted in Griffith, *The War on Terrorism and the Terror of God*, 193.

14. See Wright, *Surprised by Hope*.

15. Rollins, *The Fidelity of Betrayal*, 97.

16. Tickle, *The Great Emergence*, 162.

17. "Why the Emerging Church Should Believe in Penal Substitution."

18. Chalke and Mann, *The Lost Message of Jesus*, 182–83. This passage met major resistance in evangelical communities, and Chalke has since suggested he doesn't deny penal substitutionary atonement. But the damage had already been done. See Piper, *The Future of Justification*, 47ff.

19. Hart, "Emerging Church and Atonement."

20. See Brock and Parker, *Proverbs of Ashes*.

21. Cited in Brock and Parker, *Saving Paradise*, 293.

22. Cited in ibid., 290–92.

23. It's important to point out that N. T. Wright (a household name in many emerging circles) happens to be one of the mainline scholars who does contend that Jesus viewed his own death through the lens of atonement theology. Scholars like Borg and Wright present variations on the meaning of the crucifixion — especially in relationship to the ways in which the historical Jesus understood the significance of his own death. Most pertinent for this conversation, however, is that while some tension exists between each of their perspectives, both Borg and Wright agree that none of the five interpretive approaches to Jesus' death in scripture come close to reflecting what is usually meant in today's most familiar appropriations of substitutionary atonement theology. See *Jesus and the Victory of God*, 579ff. and *The Meaning of Jesus: Two Visions*, as well as Joel Green, *The Scandal of the Cross*.

24. Borg, *The Heart of Christianity*, 94.

25. Ibid., 92.

26. Nelson-Pallmeyer and Hesla, *Worship in the Spirit of Jesus,* 85. Let us remember that in the teachings of Jesus, debts are for forgiving, not accumulating. As John Caputo puts it, "the only calculation forgiving allows is that one should forgive seven times a day, and seventy times seven, that is to say, innumerably, countlessly, incalculably" (Caputo and Scanlon, *God, the Gift, and Postmodernism,* 215).

27. Claiborne and Haw, *Jesus for President,* 1–8.

28. Mainstream evangelical scholars have long interpreted Revelation similarly; this just isn't what is seen in the popular landscape.

29. Claiborne and Haw, *Jesus for President,* 175.

30. Not affiliated with Mars Hill Seattle, where Driscoll is pastor.

31. Mars Hill, however, functions quite differently from most megachurches. For the record, Bell doesn't classify himself as emerging or emergent, though most people refer to him as one or the other.

32. *Publishers's Weekly* starred review, "Zondervan — Velvet Elvis," Zondervan, *www.zondervan.com/* (accessed March 4, 2009).

33. Bell and Golden, *Jesus Wants to Save Christians,* 44.

34. Ibid., 26.

35. Ibid., 87.

36. Ibid., 129.

37. Ibid., 121.

38. Ibid., 18 and 134.

39. Ibid., 18; cf. Crossan, *God and Empire,* 23–25.

40. Bell and Golden, *Jesus Wants to Save Christians,* 133–34.

41. Ibid., emphasis ours.

42. The *Harry Potter* series tops the list of bestselling book series, with sales of over 400 million copies. The *Left Behind* series has sold 65 million copies.

43. Rossing, *The Rapture Exposed,* 17.

44. Franke, *Barth,* 23–24.

45. Barth, *The Humanity of God,* 14.

46. Franke, *Barth,* 29.

47. Ibid., 31.

48. Ibid., 88.

49. Caputo, *What Would Jesus Deconstruct?* 87.

50. Bell and Golden, *Jesus Wants to Save Christians,* 18.

51. Ibid., 161.

52. Merritt, "Yes, We Did" (2009).

Chapter 5: Postmodern Paths

1. Caputo, *What Would Jesus Deconstruct?* 27–28.
2. Hall, *Bound and Free,* 24.
3. Taylor, *After God,* 304.
4. See Taylor, "What Derrida Really Meant." Recall here the way that cultural conservatives long to restore a mythic past, for example, through mandated prayers in public schools or making English the official language of the United States.
5. Taylor, *Erring,* 22.
6. See especially Raschke, *The Next Reformation.*
7. Pagitt, *A Christianity Worth Believing,* 23.
8. See especially Strobel, *A Case for Christ*; McDowell, *The New Evidence That Demands a Verdict*; and Geisler, *Christian Apologetics.*
9. See Caputo and Vattimo, *After the Death of God,* 43–44.
10. As quoted in Garrison, *Rising from the Ashes,* 51.
11. As cited in Gibbs and Bolger, *Emerging Churches,* 34.
12. One of the most formative voices in Rollins's early works is Jean-Luc Marion. For a brilliant essay that further captures this perspective, see Marion's "In the Name," in *God, the Gift and Postmodernism,* 20–42.
13. McKnight, "Five Streams of the Emerging Church."
14. Perhaps the primary difference is found in the way that Rollins appropriates the thought of Derrida and other postmodern theorists, for he's not afraid to enter into the desert of Derridean deconstruction.
15. Rollins, "My Confession."
16. Pagitt, *A Christianity Worth Believing,* viii.
17. Notice the way that Mars Hill (Grand Rapids, Mich.) structures their beliefs around narrative, as opposed to propositional perspectives: *www.marshill.org./believe/.*
18. Caputo, *What Would Jesus Deconstruct?* 38.
19. "Mark Driscoll on the Emerging Church."
20. Caputo, *What Would Jesus Deconstruct?* 39.
21. Taylor, *Erring,* 149–51.
22. See Caputo's comments on Derrida and the Step/Not Beyond, 39ff.
23. Caputo, *What Would Jesus Deconstruct?* 41–42.
24. Rollins, *How (Not) to Speak,* 6.
25. McLeod, "There's No Place to Go but Up."
26. Pagitt, *A Christianity Worth Believing,* 58.
27. Cathcart and Klein, *Plato and a Platypus Walk into a Bar,* 78.

28. For an excellent introductory essay to the interpretation that everything is an interpretation, see Caputo and Vattimo, *After the Death of God*, 27–39. Caputo also offers a good introduction in *What Would Jesus Deconstruct?* 40.

29. Caputo and Vattimo, *After the Death of God*, 28. Emphasis in the original.

30. Pagitt, *A Christianity Worth Believing*, 63–64.

31. Hall, *Thinking the Faith*, 260.

32. Caputo, *What Would Jesus Deconstruct?* 104.

33. See Derrida, *Archive Fever.*

34. See especially Caputo, *What Would Jesus Deconstruct?* 110–11.

35. See Borg, *The Heart of Christianity*, 13ff. This approach, Marcus Borg says, "sees the Bible as sacred scripture, but *not* because it is a divine product. It is sacred in its *status* and *function*, but not in its *origin*" (*archē*), 14.

36. Pagitt, *A Christianity Worth Believing*, 67.

37. As cited in Borg, *Heart of Christianity*, 4.

Chapter 6: Extravagant Hospitality

1. As quoted in Caputo, *What Would Jesus Deconstruct?* 111.

2. "What Is the Emerging Church?"

3. Misty, "Misty's Story."

4. Jones, *The New Christians*, 71.

5. The ads can be viewed online at *www.ucc.org/god-is-still-speaking/television-ads.html* (accessed December 30, 2009).

6. "Who We Are."

7. Adapted from Brown, "Communion Invitation," in *Shaping Sanctuary*, 224.

8. This practice, of course, abounds in Hebrew scripture as well.

9. "About Emergent Village," *www.emergentvillage.com/about/* (accessed March 3, 2009).

10. Kimball, *They Like Jesus but Not the Church*, 69.

11. Merritt, *Tribal Church*, 63 and 70.

12. Ibid., 69.

13. The primary texts are two verses from Leviticus, one from 1 Corinthians, one from 1 Timothy, and one from Romans. The other three references are from Genesis, Judges, and Jude. Jesus never mentioned homosexuality.

Often, critics point to the story of Sodom and Gomorrah in Genesis and the unnamed concubine in Judges, but mainline scholars have repeatedly argued that these stories are related to hospitality.

14. Rogers, *Jesus, the Bible, and Homosexuality,* see especially 71–73.

15. Placher, *Jesus the Savior,* 100–102.

16. Caputo, *What Would Jesus Deconstruct?* 110. Emphasis in the original.

17. Placher, *Jesus the Savior,* 100–102.

18. Caputo, *What Would Jesus Deconstruct?* 112.

19. A similar trope on Huck Finn has been adapted in Nanette Sawyer's essay "What Would Huckleberry Do?" in Pagitt and Jones, *An Emergent Manifesto of Hope,* 41–50.

20. McLaren, *A Generous Orthodoxy,* 250. Cf. Douglas John Hall's remarks in *Why Christian?:* "I know that my own 'natural' tendency, which has been reinforced by my familial, national, racial, class, and other backgrounds, is to look upon all or nearly all of these 'others' with a kind of half-conscious suspicion, or at least a certain caution. I may have learned to hide or soften or sublimate that 'gut' reaction, but I know all the same that it is deeply embedded in my psyche, part of my formation. The fact that I, by accident of birth, have belonged to a very 'successful' race and a very powerful civilization only accentuates whatever 'natural' tendency there may be in me to exclude others. But honesty compels me to admit that this tendency is still there in me, after all my humanistic education, and even after all my years of explicit Christian involvement. What continues to counteract and transform this aboriginal exclusivity of mine is chiefly... Jesus Christ! Far from sanctioning or encouraging the 'natural' habit of exclusion, the grace that comes from that Source constantly judges that habit, and strives to replace it with at least the beginnings of a far greater openness to others — greater, indeed, than I usually find comfortable! If I am not the chauvinist, the bigot, the sexist, the racist, and so on that I might otherwise have been (yes, I do not consider myself wholly superior to all that crowd!), it is chiefly because of the Nazarene.... I am saying that faith in Jesus as the one who makes God real and present to Christians, far from reinforcing and stimulating their sinful tendency to exclude others, positively drives them toward a greater — okay, a greater 'inclusivity.'" (145).

21. Ibid., 289–90.

22. McLaren, "An Open Letter to Worship Songwriters."

23. Hall, *Why Christian?* 148.

24. Caputo and Vattimo, *After the Death of God,* 41.

Chapter 7: Why Emerging Worship Is Good News for Progressive Communities of Faith

1. Jones, *The New Christians,* 96.
2. As quoted in Garrison, *Rising from the Ashes,* 13.
3. Again, emerging worship points to approaches in both emerging and emergent circles.
4. Bolz-Weber, as quoted in Garrison, *Rising from the Ashes,* 17.
5. Ibid.
6. Note the ways worship resource books often include "Contemporary and Traditional" resources in an either/or fashion that postmodern emergents grow tired of.
7. In several ways, as discussed above, it's a rebellion against contemporary approaches.
8. As quoted in Garrison, *Rising from the Ashes,* 14.
9. Ibid., 16. Capitalization as in the original.
10. Ibid., 60.
11. See especially Dawn, *Reaching Out without Dumbing Down.*
12. Rollins, *The Orthodox Heretic,* xi–xii. Emphasis original.
13. See Kimball, *Emerging Worship,* 3.
14. See especially Thomas Long, *Beyond the Worship Wars,* 31ff.
15. Elnes and the Studio, *Igniting Worship Series,* 33.

Chapter 8: Emerging Liturgy for Progressive Communities of Faith

1. Rollins, *The Fidelity of Betrayal,* 184.
2. Brock and Parker, *Saving Paradise,* 418–19.
3. "Faculty: Scott Haldeman," *Chicago Theological Seminary, www.ctschicago.edu/academic/facultyid4.php* (accessed March 1, 2009).
4. As quoted in Caputo and Scanlon, *God, the Gift, and Postmodernism,* 146.
5. See Driver, *Liberating Rites.*
6. Rollins, *The Fidelity of Betrayal,* 179.
7. We're indebted to Leonard Sweet for first presenting this to us.
8. "The Emerging Church."
9. Adapted from Brown, "Communion Invitation," 224.
10. Adapted from Elnes and the Studio, *Igniting Worship Series,* 48–49.

11. See Kimball, *Emerging Worship*, 78ff.

12. McKnight, "Five Streams of the Emerging Church."

13. For an example of the kind of PowerPoint presentation we have found helpful at the Awakening, see *www.brentwoodchristianchurch.com/multimedia.html*.

14. I attended an alt.worship conference recently that had several worship services woven throughout the course of the weekend. One of the things that distracted me in some of the services was the use of video loops under the lyrics for the songs we were singing. These presented flashes of light and color with constant and erratic movement, similar to what you might see on your Windows Media Player as you listen to music. Except it didn't go with the beat of the music. To me it was just visual noise that distracted from the flow of worship. While I can appreciate the thought that went into the presentation, we simply lean toward more contemplative forms of worship, recognizing that those in our context don't necessarily resonate with the MTV culture of flashing lights and images that change every nanosecond. In this respect, emerging communities exhibit a wide range of differences. The gatherings that are significantly influenced by the club culture of the U.K. feature more light and sound displays that lack a meditative feel that those from the Awakening are drawn to. It's not that we don't use technology, but we use it in a different way. Some emerging gatherings even wish to offer a counter-cultural experience in which no multimedia is present whatsoever. While Taizé gatherings aren't necessarily classified as emerging, the fact that several emerging collectives draw on Taizé-influenced meditation and silence in their liturgies points to this desire.

15. See Long, *Beyond the Worship Wars*, 53ff.

16. Bechtel, interview with Phil Snider and Emily Bowen, January 22, 2009.

17. Santa Margarita United Methodist Church.

18. *The One Campaign.*

19. Duck, *Finding Words for Worship*, 37.

20. Ibid.

21. Nelson-Pallmeyer and Hesla, *Worship in the Spirit of Jesus*, 66.

22. Cosgrove and Edgerton, *In Other Words.*

23. Northcutt, *Kindling Desire for God*, 6. Emphasis in the original.

24. Pagitt, *Preaching Re-Imagined.*

Appendix 1: A Guide to the Resources in This Book

1. See Long, *Beyond the Worship Wars,* 85ff.
2. Ibid., 86.
3. Adapted from Brown, "Communion Invitation," 224.
4. Adapted from Elnes and the Studio, *Igniting Worship Series,* 48–49.

Appendix 2: Worship Services

1. "Seasons of the Spirit," *Lent, Easter RCL Year C,* Kelowna, British Columbia: Woodlake Publishing, 2007.

BIBLIOGRAPHY

Baker, Jonny, and Doug Gay. *Alternative Worship*. Grand Rapids, Mich.: Baker Books, 2003.

Barlow, Rich, "New Approaches to Worship Emerge," *Boston Globe*, July 22, 2006, *www.boston.com/* (accessed on March 4, 2009).

Barth, Karl. *The Humanity of God*. Louisville: Westminster John Knox Press, 1960.

Bass, Diana Butler. *Christianity for the Rest of Us: How the Neighborhood Church Is Transforming the Faith*. New York: HarperCollins, 2007.

———. Interview. *PBS: Religion and Ethics Newsweekly*, July 8, 2005, see online, *www.pbs.org/wnet/religionandethics/week845/interview1.html* (accessed March 3, 2009).

———. *The Practicing Congregation: Imagining a New Old Church*. Herndon, Va.: Alban Institute, 2004.

Bechtel, Kim. Interview with Phil Snider and Emily Bowen. January 22, 2009.

Bell, Rob. *Velvet Elvis: Repainting the Christian Faith*. Grand Rapids, Mich.: Zondervan, 2005.

Bell, Rob, and Don Golden. *Jesus Wants to Save Christians: A Manifesto for the Church in Exile*. Grand Rapids, Mich.: Zondervan, 2008.

Borg, Marcus. *The Heart of Christianity: Rediscovering a Life of Faith*. San Francisco: HarperCollins, 2003.

Brewin, Kester. *Signs of Emergence: A Vision for Church That Is Organic/Networked/Decentralized/Bottom-up/Communal/Flexible/Always Evolving*. Grand Rapids, Mich.: Baker Books, 2007.

Broaddus, Maurice. "Further Musings on the Emergent Church and Race," *The Pontifications of the Sinister Minister*, July 6, 2005, see online at *www.mauricebroaddus.com/* (accessed January 21, 2009).

Brock, Rita Nakashima, and Rebecca Ann Parker. *Saving Paradise: How Christianity Traded Love of This World for Crucifixion and Empire*. Boston: Beacon Press, 2008.

———. *Proverbs of Ashes: Violence, Redemptive Suffering, and the Search for What Saves Us*. Boston: Beacon Press, 2001.

Brown, Gordon, W. "Communion Invitation." In *Shaping Sanctuary: Proclaiming God's Grace in an Inclusive Church*. Ed. Kelly Turney. Chicago: Reconciling Congregation Program, 2000.

Byassee, Jason. "Emerging Model: A Visit to Jacob's Well," *Christian Century,* September 19, 2006. *www.christiancentury.org/* (accessed on March 4, 2009).

Caputo, John D. *What Would Jesus Deconstruct? The Good News of Postmodernism for the Church*. Grand Rapids, Mich.: Baker Academic, 2007.

Caputo, John, and Michael J. Scanlon. *God, the Gift, and Postmodernism*. Bloomington: Indiana University Press, 1999.

Caputo, John D., and Gianni Vattimo. *After the Death of God*. New York: Columbia University Press, 2007.

Cathcart, Thomas, and Daniel Klein. *Plato and a Platypus Walk into a Bar: Understanding Philosophy Through Jokes*. New York: Abrams Image, 2007.

Chalke, Steve, and Alan Mann. *The Lost Message of Jesus*. Grand Rapids: Zondervan, 2003.

Church of the Apostles, *www.apostleschurch.org/* (accessed February 11, 2009).

Claiborne, Shane. *The Irresistible Revolution: Living as an Ordinary Radical*. Grand Rapids, Mich.: Zondervan, 2006.

Claiborne, Shane, and Chris Haw. *Jesus for President*. Grand Rapids, Mich.: Zondervan, 2008.

Cole, Neil. *Organic Church: Growing Faith Where Life Happens*. San Francisco: Jossey-Bass, 2005.

———. *Organic Leadership: Leading Naturally Right Where You Are*. Grand Rapids, Mich.: Baker Books, 2009.

Cosgrove, Charles H., and W. Dow Edgerton. *In Other Words: Incarnational Translation for Preaching*. Grand Rapids, Mich.: Wm. B. Eerdmans, 2007.

Crossan, John Dominic. *God and Empire: Jesus against Rome: Then and Now*. San Francisco: HarperOne, 2007.

Dawn, Marva J. *Reaching Out without Dumbing Down: A Theology of Worship for the Turn-of-the-Century Culture*. Grand Rapids, Mich.: Wm. B. Eerdmans, 1995.

Derrida, Jacques. *Archive Fever: A Freudian Impression*. Chicago: University of Chicago Press, 1996.

DeYoung, David, and Ted Kluck. *Why We're Not Emergent: By Two Guys Who Should Be.* Chicago: Moody Publishers, 2008.

Driscoll, Mark. *Confessions of a Reformission Rev.: Hard Lessons from an Emerging Missional Church.* Grand Rapids, Mich.: Zondervan, 2006.

Driver, Tom F. *Liberating Rites: Understanding the Transformative Power of Ritual.* Charleston, S.C.: Booksurge, 2006.

Duck, Ruth C. *Finding Words for Worship: A Guide for Leaders.* Louisville, Ky.: Westminster John Knox Press, 1995.

Ecclesia Church, Houston, *www.ecclesiahouston.org/* (accessed March 4, 2009).

Elnes, Eric, and the Studio. *Igniting Worship Series: The Seven Deadly Sins.* Nashville: Abingdon Press, 2004.

"Emerging Spirit: Living the Hope," *The United Church of Canada, www .emergingspirit.ca/living_the_hope* (accessed March 4, 2009).

Emergent Village, www.emergentvillage.com/ (accessed March 3, 2009).

"The Emerging Church," *PBS: Religion and Ethics* (July 8, 2005), *www.pbs .org/wnet/religionandethics/week845/cover.html* (accessed on March 5, 2009).

Franke, John R. *Barth: For Armchair Theologians.* Louisville: Westminster John Knox Press, 2005.

Freeman, Magenta. "On Being a Queer Queermergent," February 15, 2009, *queermergent.wordpress.com/* (accessed February 17, 2009).

Garrison, Becky. *Rising from the Ashes: Rethinking Church.* New York: Seabury Books, 2007.

Geisler, Norman. *Christian Apologetics.* Grand Rapids, Mich.: Baker Academic, 1988.

Gibbs, Eddie, and Ryan K. Bolger. *Emerging Churches: Creating Christian Community in Postmodern Cultures.* Grand Rapids, Mich.: Baker Academic, 2005.

Gonzales, Justo. "A Hispanic Perspective: By the Rivers of Babylon." In *Preaching Justice: Ethnic and Cultural Perspectives,* ed. Christine Marie Smith. Cleveland: United Church Press, 1998.

Goodstein, Laurie. "Obama Names Minister to Lead Prayer Service," *New York Times,* January 11, 2009. *www.nytimes.com/* (accessed January 11, 2009).

Green, Joel, and Mark D. Baker. *Recovering the Scandal of the Cross: Atonement in New Testament and Contemporary Contexts.* Downers Grove, Ill. InterVarsity Press, 2000.

Griffith, Lee. *The War on Terrorism and the Terror of God.* Grand Rapids, Mich.: Wm. B. Eerdmans, 2002.

Hall, Douglas J. *Bound and Free: A Theologian's Journey.* Minneapolis: Augsburg Fortress Press, 2005.

———. *Thinking the Faith: Christian Theology in a North American Context.* Minneapolis: Augsburg Fortress Press, 2001.

———. *Why Christian? For Those on the Edge of Faith.* Minneapolis: Augsburg Fortress Press, 1998.

Hart, Shane Vander. "Emerging Church and Atonement," *Caffeinated Thoughts,* November 6, 2008, *http://caffeinatedthoughts.com/?p=1724* (accessed January 30, 2009).

Heath, Elaine, and Scott Kisker. *Longing for Spring: A New Vision for Wesleyan Community.* Eugene, Ore.: Pickwick Publications, 2010.

Heyward, Carter. *Saving Jesus from Those Who Are Right.* Minneapolis: Augsburg Fortress Press, 1999.

Horner, Robyn. *Rethinking God as Gift: Marion, Derrida, and the Limits of Phenomenology.* Perspectives in Continental Philosophy. No. 19. New York: Fordham University Press, 2001.

House, Rutba. *School(s) for Conversion: 12 Marks of a New Monasticism.* Eugene, Ore.: Wipf and Stock Publishers, 2005.

Jones, Tony. *The New Christians: Dispatches from the Emergent Frontier.* San Francisco: Jossey-Bass Books, 2008.

———. Interview. *PBS: Religion and Ethics Newsweekly,* July 8, 2005, online at *www.pbs.org/wnet/religionandethics/week845/cover.html* (accessed March 3, 2009).

Joyce, Derek, and Mark Sorensen. *When Will Jesus Be Enough? Reclaiming the Power of Worship.* Nashville: Abingdon Press, 2008.

Kimball, Dan. *The Emerging Church: Vintage Christianity for New Generations.* Grand Rapids, Mich.: Zondervan, 2003.

———. *Emerging Worship: Creating Worship Gatherings for New Generations.* Grand Rapids, Mich.: Zondervan, 2004.

———. *They Like Jesus but Not the Church.* Grand Rapids, Mich.: Zondervan, 2007.

King Jr., Martin Luther, "Letter from Birmingham City Jail." In *A Testament of Hope: The Essential Writings and Speeches of Martin Luther King Jr.* Ed. James M. Washington. San Francisco: HarperCollins, 1986.

Labberton, Mark. *The Dangerous Act of Worship: Loving God's Call to Justice.* Downers Grove, Ill: Intervarsity Press, 2007.

Lebacqz, Karen. *Word, Worship, World, and Wonder: Reflections on Christian Living.* Nashville: Abingdon Press, 1997.

"List of Best Selling Books," *Wikipedia.com, http://en.wikipedia.org/wiki/ List_of_best-selling_books* (accessed March 4, 2009).

Lockhart, Ross. Telephone interview with Phil Snider and Emily Bowen. January 29, 2009.

Long, Thomas. *Beyond the Worship Wars: Building Vital and Faithful Worship.* Herndon, Va.: Alban Institute, 2001.

M., Robin. "A New Kind of Christian — the Trilogy," *What Canst Thou Say,* January 19, 2009, *http://robinmsf.blogspot.com* (accessed March 3, 2009).

"Mark Driscoll on the Emerging Church." February 26, 2008, *www.youtube .com/watch?v=58fgkfS6E-0* (accessed January 22, 2009).

McDowell, Josh. *The New Evidence That Demands a Verdict.* Nashville: Thomas Nelson, 1999.

McKnight, Scot. "Five Streams of the Emerging Church," *Christianity Today,* January 19, 2007, *www.christianitytoday.com/* (accessed February 15, 2009).

———. Interview. *PBS: Religion and Ethics Newsweekly,* aired on July 8, 2005, online *www.pbs.org/wnet/religionandethics/week845/cover.html* (accessed March 3, 2009).

McLaren, Brian. *Everything Must Change: Jesus, Global Crises and a Revolution of Hope.* Nashville: Thomas Nelson, 2007.

———. *A Generous Orthodoxy.* Grand Rapids, Mich.: Zondervan, 2004.

———. *The Last Word and the Word after That: A Tale of Faith, Doubt, and a New Kind of Christianity.* San Francisco: Jossey-Bass, 2005.

———. *A New Kind of Christian: A Tale of Two Friends on a Spiritual Journey.* San Francisco: Jossey-Bass, 2001.

———. "An Open Letter to Worship Songwriters," *New Wineskins: Desperate* (January–February 2001), see online at *www.brianmclaren.net/ archives/lettertosongwriters.pdf* (accessed January 26, 2009).

———. *The Secret Message of Jesus.* Nashville: Thomas Nelson, 2006.

McLaren, Brian, and Tony Campolo. *Adventures in Missing the Point: How the Culture-Controlled Church Neutered the Gospel.* Grand Rapids, Mich.: Zondervan, 2003.

McLeod, Melvin. "There's No Place to Go but Up: Maya Angelou in Conversation with bell hooks." *Shambhala Sun Online* (January 1998), *www.shambhalasun.com/* (accessed on January 26, 2009).

Merritt, Carol Howard. *Tribal Church: Ministering to the Missing Generation.* Herndon, Va.: Alban Institute, 2007.

———. "Yes, We Did," *Tribal Church,* January 22, 2009, *http://tribalchurch
.org/* (accessed February 21, 2009.)

Methomergent Lab, http://methomergentlab.wordpress.com/ (accessed February 17, 2009).

Miller, Donald. *Blue Like Jazz: Nonreligious Thoughts on Christian Spiri-
tuality.* Nashville: Thomas Nelson, 2003.

Misty, "Misty's Story," *Queermergent,* February 6, 2009, *http://queermergent
.wordpress.com/* (accessed February 17, 2009).

Nelson-Pallmeyer, Jack, and Bret Hesla. *Worship in the Spirit of Jesus: Theology, Liturgy, and Songs without Violence.* Cleveland: Pilgrim Press,
2005.

Northcutt, Kay L. *Kindling Desire for God: Preaching as Spiritual Direction.*
Minneapolis: Augsburg Fortress Press, 2009.

The One Campaign, www.one.org/ (accessed March 5, 2009).

Pagitt, Doug. *Christianity Now: Faith in the Inventive Age.* Minneapolis:
Sparkhouse, 2010 (forthcoming).

———. *A Christianity Worth Believing.* San Francisco: Jossey-Bass, 2008.

———. *Preaching Re-Imagined: The Role of the Sermon in Communities
of Faith.* Grand Rapids, Mich.: Zondervan, 2005.

Pagitt, Doug, and Tony Jones, eds. *An Emergent Manifesto of Hope.* Grand
Rapids, Mich.: Baker Books, 2007.

Piatt, Christian, and Amy. *MySpace to Sacred Space: God for a New
Generation.* St. Louis: Chalice Press, 2007.

Piper, John. *The Future of Justification: A Response to N. T. Wright.*
Wheaton, Ill.: Crossway Books, 2007.

Placher, William Carl. *Jesus the Savior: The Meaning of Jesus Christ for
Christian Faith.* Louisville: Westminster John Knox Press, 2001.

Publishers's Weekly Starred Review. "Zondervan — Velvet Elvis." See online
www.zondervan.com/ (accessed March 4, 2009).

Raschke, Carl. *The Next Reformation: Why Evangelicals Must Embrace
Postmodernism.* Grand Rapids, Mich.: Baker Academic, 2004.

Rogers, Jack. *Jesus, the Bible, and Homosexuality: Explode the Myths, Heal
the Church.* Louisville: Westminster John Knox Press, 2006.

Rollins, Peter. "Batman as the Ultimate Capitalist Superhero." *PeterRollins
.net,* June 16, 2008. *http://peterrollins.net/blog/* (accessed June 18, 2009).

———. *The Fidelity of Betrayal: Towards a Church beyond Belief.* Brewster,
Mass.: Paraclete Press, 2008.

———. *How (Not) to Speak of God*. Brewster, Mass.: Paraclete Press, 2006.

———. "Lessons in Evandalism Tour," *PeterRollins.net,* January 19, 2009, *http://peterrollins.net/blog/* (accessed February 15, 2009).

———. "My Confession: I Deny the Resurrection," *PeterRollins.net,* January 31, 2009, *http://peterrollins.net/blog/* (accessed February 20, 2009).

———. *The Orthodox Heretic: And Other Impossible Tales*. Brewster, Mass.: Paraclete Press, 2009.

Rossing, Barbara R. *The Rapture Exposed: The Message of Hope in the Book of Revelation*. Boulder, Colo.: Westview Press, 2004.

Salmon, Jacqueline L. "Feeling Renewed by Ancient Traditions: Evangelicals Putting New Twist on Lent, Confession, and Communion," *Washington Post,* March 8, 2008, *www.washingtonpost.com/* (accessed March 3, 2009).

Santa Margarita United Methodist Church. *http://smumc.com/* (accessed March 5, 2009).

Scifres, Mary J., and B. J. Beu, eds. *The Abingdon Worship Annual 2009*. Nashville: Abingdon Press, 2008.

Smith, James K. A. *Who's Afraid of Postmodernism? Taking Derrida, Lyotard, and Foucault to Church*. Grand Rapids, Mich.: Baker Academic, 2006.

Strobel, Lee. *A Case for Christ: A Journalist's Personal Investigation of the Evidence for Jesus*. Grand Rapids, Mich.: Zondervan, 1998).

Taylor, Mark C. *After God*. Chicago: University of Chicago Press, 2007.

———. *Erring: A Postmodern A/Theology*. Chicago: University of Chicago Press, 1984.

———. "What Derrida Really Meant," *New York Times,* October 14, 2004, *www.nytimes.com/* (accessed March 4, 2009).

Tickle, Phyllis. *The Great Emergence: How Christianity Is Changing and Why*. Grand Rapids, Mich.: Baker Books, 2008.

Tomlinson, David. *The Post-Evangelical*. Grand Rapids, Mich.: Zondervan, 2003.

"United Church of Christ Firsts," *United Church of Christ, www.ucc.org/50/ pdfs/firsts.pdf* (accessed March 3, 2009).

University Christian Church, *www.seekingthesacred.org/* (accessed March 3, 2009).

Wallis, Jim. "Come Let Us Reason Together," *Sojourners: Faith, Politics, Culture* (December 2007), *www.sojo.net/* (accessed March 4, 2009).

———. "Sojo Mail," June 28, 2008.

————. *The Great Awakening: Reviving Faith and Politics in a Post-Religious Right America*. San Francisco: HarperOne, 2008.

Webber, Robert. *Ancient-Future Worship: Proclaiming and Enacting God's Narrative*. Grand Rapids, Mich.: Baker Books, 2008.

"What Is the Emerging Church?" *Center for Action and Contemplation (CAC) Webcast,* November 8, 2008, *www.cacradicalgrace.org* (accessed March 4, 2009).

"Who We Are," House for All Sinners and Saints. *www.houseforall.org/* (accessed March 4, 2009).

"Why the Emerging Church Should Believe in Penal Substitution," *Open Source Theology,* September 26, 2006, *www.opensourcetheology.net/node/1026* (accessed January 30, 2009).

Wright, N. T. *Jesus and the Victory of God*. Minneapolis: Fortress, 1996.

Wright, N. T., and Marcus Borg. *The Meaning of Jesus: Two Visions*. San Francisco: HarperSanFrancisco, 1999.

————. *Surprised by Hope: Rethinking Heaven, Resurrection, and the Mission of the Church*. San Francisco: HarperOne, 2008.

Wuthnow, Robert. *After the Baby Boomers: How Twenty- and Thirty-Somethings Are Shaping the Future of American Religion*. Princeton, N.J.: Princeton University Press, 2007.